ADVANCE PRAISE
FOR BODY AND SOUL

Panthea Reid ... experienced "a loss that nearly destroyed my mind and life" when her husband, John Fischer, died after a four-month battle with a mysterious respiratory illness. She turned to writing about their marriage as a way of coping with her loss, and the result is worthy of comparison with classic memoirs of grief ... Throughout this book, Reid charts her spouse's rapid physical decline with agonizing clarity ...The author also points out that the best grief memoirs "provide both a powerful feel of the person lost and sharp insight into the writer herself." Her own book passes that test with flying colors.

— *Kirkus*, starred review

Like her biographies of Virginia Woolf/Vanessa Bell and Tillie Olsen, Panthea Reid's *Body and Soul* has many good things to offer. Above all, it gives us a vivid portrait of her husband, Swift scholar John Fischer: his magnetism, vitality, unbending intellect, sensibility, and sexuality; the impact of his heroic entry in her life at a time of crisis; and then the shock and pain of losing him to what seemed a preventable illness. Reid's book is also a deeply felt narrative of their relationship as lovers and soul mates sharing a passion for art, scholarship, and life.

— Stuart Mitchner
Columnist and author of *Rosamund's Vision*

This poignant memoir of love and loss tells a personal story with expansive implications. Narrating the physical decline and the death of a beloved husband, it records and confronts the physical, psychological, and spiritual pain of the process and its aftermath. Panthea Reid ponders her experience and its meanings, for herself and potentially for others. She has written an eloquent and forceful book.

— Patricia Meyers Spacks, PhD
Professor Emerita of English
and author of *On Rereading* and *Novel Beginnings*

An engrossing, beautifully written tale of a lifelong love that endures trials and sorrow and outlasts even death, Reid's story grips us from the start and never lets us go.

— William McKeen, PhD
Associate Dean, Boston University,
and author of *Mile Marker Zero* and *Outlaw Journalist*

This moving and candid memoir deals constructively with a widow's critical reaction to the medical diagnoses her husband received in his final illness, and with her own recovery of purpose. Panthea Reid celebrates her marriage to John Fischer, a union that shared passionate love, parental challenges, and scholarly adventure. Not surprisingly for an accomplished literary critic, help comes through writing her marital memoir and finishing Fischer's long-term project on Jonathan Swift. Both memoir and scholarly edition concern relationships between the sexes. She offers new insight into Swift's shortcomings in his much-discussed relationship to the real-life "Stella." But her work is also grounded in the everyday and will provide practical options for others in situations of loss and regret.

— Bonnie Kime Scott, PhD
Professor Emerita of Women's Studies
and author of *The Gender of Modernism*

Body and Soul is one of those rare memoirs that is more than a memoir. It is a searing account of watching a loved one die but also an inspired account of a loved one's life. John Fischer emerges from this book as a great human being whose loss becomes the reader's lament and also a cause for celebration of a life that enriched others' lives. Panthea Reid is unsparing in her account of her own failings as she details her daily efforts to live through her grief. She offers help to others experiencing similar losses, but she realizes there are no easy ways to just get on with your life. For those who put their trust in doctors, this memoir is a harrowing record of incompetence, even as Reid suggests ways of taking control not only of your life but also of the lives of those whom you are about to lose. Reid has read many celebrated memoirs on death and grieving and writes with an unusual grasp of literary precedents, noting both their strengths and limitations.

— Carl Rollyson, PhD
Author, *Confessions of a Serial Biographer*
and *Susan Sontag: The Making of an Icon*

This is a beautifully rendered memoir of shared lives, inspired love, sorrow-filled loss, and eventual healing through grief's journey. With grace and authenticity, it paints a picture elucidating how you can draw strength from your harshest, most devastating experience, proving that a storehouse of endurance can be built on a foundation of anguish and resilience. Although there is no blueprint for the journey of mourning, Reid's helpful references touch on many of the common denominators of grief. They add a valuable dimension while suggesting important stepping stones for healing for anyone who has lost a soul mate, spouse, or partner.

— Webb Brown, MLS, MDiv
Hospice chaplain and grief counselor for 24 years

With Best
wishes for
happiness and grace~
Panthea Reid

BODY
— AND —
SOUL

A MEMOIR OF
LOVE, LOSS, AND HEALING

Published by Wild River Books
PO Box 672
Lambertville, NJ 08530
www.wildriverconsultingandpublishing.com

Distributed by Wild River Consulting & Publishing, LLC.

Design and composition by:
Tim Ogline / Ogline Design for Wild River Consulting & Publishing, LLC.

Publisher's Cataloging-In-Publication Data
Reid, Panthea
    Body and Soul
ISBN: 978-1-941948-03-3

Printed in the United States of America

First Edition

BODY
— AND —
SOUL

A MEMOIR OF
LOVE, LOSS, AND HEALING

BY PANTHEA REID

**WILD
RIVER
LEGACY**

CONTENTS

For John

I don't think the soul leaves the body;

it has to be the other way around …

What if the body leaves the soul

to give the soul more room to wander?

What if the soul is thankful,

hovering, a dragonfly over water?

From "Revelation at Philpott Lake"

By Felicia Mitchell

Artemis Journal 2014 and

Waltzing with Horses (Press 53, 2014)

PREFACE

I've come to believe that to love truly means to risk loss, not to try to control or possess a loved one. Still the loss of my husband of forty years nearly destroyed me. After four months of struggling against a peculiar illness, he suddenly died. You might say, what else did you expect?

Certainly, John was not young anymore, nor am I. So why was I so devastated by his death? The answer begins with his exceptional character and our exceptional marriage. A friend wrote me about how "considerate John was—in the sense of fully considering and expressing all sides, eloquently and compassionately." That broad understanding, often peppered with irony, was part of John's uniqueness. Another aspect of his uniqueness was the greatness of his love for me and our daughter, Hannah. Losing John broke my heart, shattered my composure, and nearly destroyed my mind. I was infuriated that medical incompetence or disinterest hastened his decline. It dawned on me, too late, that I did not assert myself and insist on alternate medical care. Those recognitions added fury and guilt to my grief. The combination was almost unbearable.

I have gotten beyond outrage and guilt—though not grief—by writing about my terrible loss. Hesitantly, I have tried to replace pain with peace, numbness with curiosity. Hannah too has gotten through her grief by writing and by making similarly healing explorations.

I said "beyond" and "through," not "over." Neither of us will ever get over the loss of John Fischer.

Some readers are not inveterate scribblers, as Hannah and I are. The act of writing about grief has helped us get through our loss, so I hope that reading this book will also help you get beyond grief. I have added an appendix of references to websites and books that can help you change doctors, find counseling services, and discover consolation. Ideally, this memoir will engage you and help you heal too.

– Panthea Reid

IMPROBABLE BEGINNINGS
OF LOVE AND DEATH

It's no easier to decide when John Fischer and I began our marriage than when he began his dying. I do have dates, but even the official wedding date is confused. It took place the Saturday after Thanksgiving 1976 at the Baton Rouge Hilton, much to the distress of my mother, who even though I was marrying a Jew expected a church wedding. I wore a beige suede suit, John a blue velvet jacket. Someone took a snapshot of us on the Hilton's patio. We are looking into each other's eyes with great intensity. Looking at the photo forty years later, I think not only how happy we were but how thin. After the birth of our daughter in 1978, I could never get that suede skirt zipped up again. After a year or so of trying, I regretfully gave it away, as John did his outfit, lacking further occasions to wear a velvet jacket.

After eggs Benedict, fruit, and champagne, we surprised everyone by our vows: to be married only "so long as love shall last." Raising his champagne glass, John's Uncle Jerry Fischer toasted: "May your troubles last no longer than that ceremony." Our guests cheered and emptied their glasses. John and I were hosting the event, so we ordered more bottles as people lingered on. Belatedly we realized that they expected the bride and groom to exit first. After John made sure the bill was paid, we newlyweds made a rather tipsy exit, followed immediately, we later learned, by even tipsier guests.

Most people thought we were an unlikely couple: a granddaughter of a Southern Methodist preacher marrying a grandson of Russian Jewish immigrants; a former Junior Miss Alabama and a former dirt bike racer; a person who largely missed the Civil Rights struggle and an activist in it. But however odd a match we seemed to others, we were meant for each other. Soul mates, we shared a deep devotion to literature and a capacity for adventure. We also each had a tendency, for better or worse, to live near the edge.

Despite our pride in our unconventional wedding ceremony, neither John nor I could recall its date, Thanksgiving being a Moveable Feast. I often maintained that we married on 29 November. John argued that it was on 30 November. Or vice versa. When we checked our files and consulted the marriage license, we found that the true date was 27 November 1976. But we kept forgetting, probably because John liked to say that our real marriage was the first time we made love, in early May of 1975.

John's death, or its beginning, is even more complicated to date than our marriage. A lung therapist might argue that his death really began sixty years before when he smoked his first cigarette and liked it. John gave up cigarettes in his early fifties and his pipe in his late fifties (1998, to be exact). Or perhaps John began dying not because of his first cigarette, but because of our primary care doctor's nonchalance. Or maybe his death really began with two specialists, a gastroenterologist and a pulmonologist, who concluded that John's mysterious ailment was just COPD aggravated by a clogged esophagus. Each was so sure of those hypotheses that neither saw that John had pneumonia. Compounding those doctors' failure was our naïve trust in them.

I do know the official date of John's death—15 May 2015—just before his seventy-fifth birthday. From his hospital bed a week before he died, he announced to me that it was our fortieth anniversary—not of our official 1976 ceremony, but of the first time our happy bodies had coupled together, forty years before his body wasted away and 2015 turned fatal.

ESCAPES

After emigrating from Scotland, my father's father built a handsome Victorian home on land just outside Owensboro, Kentucky, in 1873. In the 1940s, my parents and I lived in a rented house in Owensboro, but I felt that my true home was the Victorian establishment. To me it seemed a mansion, with its alternating dark and light floorboards and wainscoting, brass doorknobs and chandeliers, a two-story curving staircase, and the first indoor bathroom in Daviess County. Grandpapa planted the land around the house with fine fruit trees, and the tradition continues today on the "Reid Orchards."

No one consulted me before my parents decided to move when I was eight to join my mother's family in Tuscaloosa, Alabama, a place I disliked intensely. I longed for time back on the Reid Farm, where I spent all school holidays, sometimes with both parents, but always with my father at what had been his birthplace. I was twelve when the beautiful Reid home burnt to the ground and my happy holidays there ended.

Perhaps that early dislocation and longing explains why I have a history of trying to escape places I've come to dislike or resent. I calculate that after my parents moved into my grandmother's Alabama house—which seemed like an old folks' home to me—it took me nearly twelve years to escape it. My escape hatch was a foolish marriage. Twelve or thirteen years became the timeframe that shaped much of my adult life. It was how long I stayed in my first marriage; how many years passed between marrying John and my purchase of a transformative new house; and how many years passed before I insisted we leave Baton Rouge, Louisiana, for Princeton, New Jersey.

By 2014, after thirteen years in Princeton, I'd begun to argue that we should leave the North for a warmer place. John maintained that the South was too imbued with old hatreds and prejudices to move there. I reminded him that he'd survived thirty-five years in Baton Rouge. "Not happily, until you came," he reminded me, blowing a kiss across our kitchen table and fixing those still-sexy eyes on me.

John and I had met back in 1974, when I made my most decisive escape. Here William Faulkner played a small part. I had written my dissertation at Chapel Hill on Faulkner, finishing in 1971. Revising my dissertation into a book in 1972, I read with fresh attention Faulkner's most experimental novel (and my favorite), *The Wild Palms* (a title eventually changed to *If I Forget Thee, Jerusalem*, the title Faulkner originally wanted for the book that his publisher had rejected). It juxtaposes two narratives: "Old Man" is about a convict who surmounts the challenges of the Mississippi flood of 1927 but returns to prison rather than live with a woman; while "Wild Palms" is about two lovers who choose to give up everything to live together. I liked the unconventional device of alternating the stories and loved the romance in "Wild Palms." I had no intention of dying, as Charlotte does at the end, but "Wild Palms" reinforced my sense that romance and passion were completely missing in my poor stunted life.

I wanted to escape that life and my increasingly crazy first husband, Claude. When I first mentioned divorce, he torpedoed himself off the second-story deck of our house, landing in the bushes and suffering only a few scratches. I was traumatized, since even the word "divorce" brought from him threats of violence, to himself or to me. So he pretended to shift gears by arranging, through an acquaintance, for me to have five days alone in a grand mountain house so I could finish revising my dissertation on Faulkner into a book. But like a stalker, Claude intruded my privacy. He brought our four-year-old son, Reid, and told him to go play on the deck. (I had given my son my maiden name as a middle name, but he was always called "Reid.") With Reid outside, Claude pushed me backwards into my room, locked the door, and unzipped his pants. Perhaps "rape" is not the right word, since I didn't resist. How could I? He was nine inches taller than I and weighed at least twice as much. In other such instances, I seemed to have no choice about sex, being his wife and hence, he thought, his property. When I said I wasn't going to remain his property, Claude tried another strategy, promising to build me a study in a tower, where I could write and be mostly, he claimed, free of him. I knew better.

I felt like the mouse in Robert Burns's poem, a "cow'rin, tim'rous beastie / O, what a panic's in thy breastie!" Burns apologized to the mouse: "I'm truly sorry man's dominion / Has broken Nature's social union." Claude assumed that man's dominion was Nature's social union, his dominion over me. Despite the feminist movement, I remained a timorous beastie, afraid to start divorce proceedings against Claude. Instead, I plotted escape.

After LSU Press accepted my book on Faulkner, a visiting teaching post at Louisiana State University seemed a possibility. Walker Percy, author of *The Moviegoer*, was scheduled to teach one class a week in LSU's English Department. An appointment there would enable me to edit a book of essays on Percy's fiction and nonfiction. Under those circumstances, Virginia Tech, where I taught, was willing to grant me a leave of absence. I had an interview at LSU in June of 1974.

Back in Blacksburg after the interview, my good friend, who knew some of the craziness of my life with Claude, asked if I'd met any attractive men. "Only one," I said. "He's magnetically handsome, slightly taller than I, with thick black curls and penetrating eyes that looked right into me. Unfortunately, he's married." I meant John Fischer.

During my two-day interview in Baton Rouge, the head of the department had escorted me down Allen Hall's main corridor to introduce me to John Fischer, the department's eminent eighteenth-century scholar and an authority on the works of Jonathan Swift. The head asked John if he could entertain me while I waited to see the dean. Outside Allen Hall, in a Louisiana sprinkle, John asked, "Hey, lady, can you run in the rain?" I could, and we did. He jogged along slowly, kindly checking to see if I could keep up. I could. At the entrance to the student union, we paused to shake raindrops out of our hair and off our shoulders, giggling together.

While John went for coffees, I'd sat alone, feeling a rush of happy relief and a quiver of excitement. I was surprised to find that a handsome, sexy-looking man could also be a brilliant and apparently very good man. I had not known that that magical combination existed. I just hoped I didn't seem dull to this exciting guy. In later years, John liked to retell the story about the department head bringing a beautiful woman into his office and asking him if he could entertain her. John would laugh and say that he'd been entertaining me ever since, but on that June day in 1974, I had no way of knowing that he would one day become my lifelong entertainer and lover.

That fall, LSU gave me a visiting post. Claude reluctantly acquiesced, since I was accepting only a temporary appointment. I moved with Reid, then five, to Baton Rouge, grateful to my mother for shipping me an ugly sofa from her den and better furniture from her Alabama attic. I enrolled Reid in the public kindergarten near my rented house.

Settled and secure, I thought, I phoned Claude to tell him that I was not returning to Blacksburg. Before long, he came down to Baton Rouge, entered the elementary school, grabbed Reid, and ran.

I've called Claude crazy. But as I look back over those fraught times, my behavior is suspect too. Before I left Virginia, I had secretly, stealthily, stashed the good china, silver, my valuables, and clothes for me and Reid in my friend's house until I drove away with it all, planning never to return, all the while assuring Claude that I had only a temporary post at LSU.

I fear I was too distracted to be much of a teacher. (I remember rereading Emerson's "Nature" in preparation for teaching it the next day but falling asleep. I don't suppose I made it very accessible to students; perhaps they fell asleep too.) My book on Faulkner was published quickly and was on display at the Modern Language Association's convention after Christmas 1974 in New York City. At the book display, John Fischer began reading my book. The elderly man who had headed LSU's English department for thirty years saw John at the book display and asked what he was reading. John showed him my book and apparently expressed surprise that it was so good. That night, John asked me out for a simple omelet dinner, affordable for an assistant professor. When my pockets produced only one of my new leather gloves, John insisted on going back to find the other one, which he did. I was as entranced as I'd been the previous summer, but despite how exciting I found John, my life was too torn up to get involved with another man, especially a married one.

That next semester, Walker Percy often stopped by my little Baton Rouge house after his Thursday class, bringing a bottle of Wild Turkey or Early Times. I gather that the English Department was rife with rumors that he and I were having an affair, but two events squashed those rumors. First, Walker publicly entertained me and his wife, Bunt, and daughter, Ann, in the Union's Plantation Room. I recall Bunt talking about a monastery where monks bound books in leather with gold tooling, as their predecessors had done for centuries. She planned to have all of Walker's books so bound, as she said to Ann, "to remember your father by." Ann, whose eardrums had burst on a flight when she was a baby, quacked, "How could I forget him?" Walker smiled wryly, seeing that the Percy women and I had made friends. The second event ending that rumor was another rumor—that I was having an affair with John Fischer. The first rumor was false, the second premature.

With Reid snatched from me, I got a Virginia lawyer, who advised me to come to Virginia and retrieve my son. I can't recall all the details, but I was certainly less timorous now, even adventurous. A former student of mine knew that Reid spent afternoons with a young woman, perhaps a girlfriend of Claude's. After considerable plotting, I secretly returned to Blacksburg, and my student drove me to the woman's trailer. "Mommy," Reid called as he ran to me when I walked in.

"We're going back to our house," I said, grabbing his coat off a couch and slipping it on him. My student drove us by back ways to the Roanoke airport. I can't explain his devotion to helping me see my plan through. I don't think it was desire; though he was an older student, not much my junior, he never made a pass at me. Maybe he had some reason to detest Claude. Maybe he was just loyal to his favorite teacher. Now, I'm sorry to say, I don't even recall his name.

Back in Baton Rouge, John Fischer picked us up, and Reid and I spent a couple of nights with him and his wife. I remember three things about that stay with them. One, I thought John's wife kept a terribly messy refrigerator. Two, I disagreed when John said that Reid carried a lot of suppressed anger, but then I had to admit that Reid did look troubled while playing with John's knife. And third, I felt a thrill of future intimacy when John smiled at my bare feet on his kitchen floor.

Back in my cozy little house, I felt settled and happy to have my child with me. Before long, however, his father once again snatched him from his school. My courage had accomplished nothing. I felt utterly defeated. Permanently reclaiming my child seemed simply hopeless. I felt broken, defeated.

I hated losing my son and feared that Claude would next come for me. All I could do was to muster the courage to go to court. In Louisiana, I was granted custody of Reid, but a Louisiana court order was a worthless piece of paper in Virginia. I was not going to snatch Reid back and continue the kidnapping cycle. My distress was so obvious that Walker sent me a note regretting my troubles and offering to help. Of course there was nothing he could do. There was not much that I could do either, except teach my classes (poorly, no doubt) and argue with lawyers. John Fischer listened to my troubles and advised me to pursue a custody hearing in Virginia. My lawyer agreed and began the procedure.

Between teaching my classes, grading student papers, and trying to reclaim my son, I was exhausted. I knew that LSU colleagues thought the department had hired me as John Fischer's competition, in hopes that he'd publish books and articles more quickly if he had to compete with a woman who already had a book out and was planning to edit another. LSU tenured and promoted us both in the spring of 1975. John's Jewish parents and grandparents would have been shocked to know that a female colleague now earned more than he did. John was shocked too, but his manhood was not challenged by a few hundred dollars. Still, he was pleased when his salary later topped mine.

By then, John and his wife were breaking up, and he and I began courting. On Thursday afternoons, he joined Walker at my house. Then John began returning on other days on his BMW sidecar, looking like a World War II warrior. He and I would sit on Mother's old sofa in my little house or he'd drive us to the university lakes, where we'd walk and talk together. Though I was terrified of motorcycles, I naïvely thought the sidecar was safe and in no danger of flipping. Thankfully John's arms were strong enough to anchor it to the road, and I always thrilled to see the muscles in his arms tense as he took curves, sinews in his right arm rippling with strength.

Our meetings were ever more tender and intimate. John began kissing, licking, and fondling me, not aggressively, but gently. I was already entranced by the combination of excitement, brilliance, and decency John embodied. He lit up my life. We had yet to undress each other. When he asked me, "Any scars?" at first I didn't even understand him, but when I did I said, "Only from chicken pox and a bee sting. How about you?"

"Just one." He opened his shirt a few buttons to reveal some dark chest hairs and a hardened blister-like scar.

"May I touch it?"

"Of course."

Fingering that smooth pinkish skin, I felt an electric shock course through my body. "What happened?"

"It was in London in 1971. I picked up my new Triumph motorcycle to clean it before crating to ship it home. A bleb in the lining of my lung burst. It's called a spontaneous pneumothorax."

The little pink spot looked rather like a burn just below his clavicle. I touched it again. "How did you survive a hole in your chest?"

"The wonders of the National Health Service."

"The Brits saved you?"

"Handily, I fell just a block from the University of London hospital."

I felt something like Charlotte's passion in "Wild Palms" from the Faulkner novel I so loved and longed for further intimacy with John.

Instead of avoiding sex, as I'd tried to do with Claude, John's romancing and teasing made me, for the first time in my life, long for it. It's a cliché, but I really felt like a sleeping princess awakened by her Prince Charming. I fell deeply in love with John, and he with me. In early May 1975, we disrobed each other and became lovers. His body was taunt and strong and even more exciting than it had seemed under clothes. "Thank you for being you," I said. He said the same to me.

John not only awakened me, he rescued me from the mess I'd made of my life. With him, I must have seemed a combination of the two women Jonathan Swift called Stella and Vanessa. In his dissertation, John had written of them as opposites, like reason and love. By then I seemed both passionate and sophisticated, like Vanessa, and docile, like Stella. (Swift defined docility as "an aptness to learn.") Really, I was neither Stella nor Vanessa. As I've said, John and I made an improbable couple. I was sheltered and Southern, the granddaughter of a Methodist minister from the South Alabama Conference as well as a Scottish Presbyterian patriarch, married to a Scotswoman who had been, it was said, a formidable horsewoman. John was the grandchild of two sets of Russian Jewish immigrants, who each settled in Chicago. His maternal grandparents were forceful characters; not so his Fischer grandparents. John was most like his maternal grandfather, who, after he retired to Surfside, Florida, regularly took John for early morning walks on the beach trying to instill in his brilliant studious grandson the notion that he was meant to be a rabbi.

I was told that I was like my maternal grandmother, whose name I bear. She was a talented painter in oils, until she decided that a preacher's wife shouldn't paint. Then she took up "fancy work," embroidering tea towels, crocheting doilies, carding wool for extra-warm comforts, stitching exquisite lace tablecloths—all, she felt, more proper expressions of her Methodist talents than oil painting. People who said I was like her did not mean in artistry but in strong-headedness. The more snobbish objections she voiced about Claude, for example, the more determined

I became to marry him anyway. (Back in the early 1970s, trying to figure out how to leave him, I was glad Grandmother wasn't around to say, "I told you so." In the later '70s, I was sorry she didn't know John, whose theological seriousness would have pleased her mightily.)

When John and I announced to a few friends, including Herb Rothschild and Walker Percy, our plans to marry, Walker invited us into his office, opened a file drawer that held only some paper Dixie cups and a bottle of Early Times, poured us hefty doses of bourbon, and toasted us. John said that was the only time he ever taught a class tipsy, but his students didn't even notice. Walker sent me a card with a Miro painting on one side and his congratulations on my "new happy life" on the other. When word spread around the English Department, the elderly gent who'd found John reading my book at the MLA convention dropped by his office to congratulate him. He also warned John not to read any more books by female authors when he was next at a convention.

I was not yet rid of Claude, who was threatening to kill us both. John borrowed a shotgun and stashed it by the front window of my rented house and enrolled in a police gun-training program. I gather that he became quite a legend among Baton Rouge law enforcement circles for refusing to be passive before such threats and for turning out to be a deadly accurate shot—oddly enough with his left hand, despite being right-handed.

I think Claude lost his job, which gave him freedom to harass John and me while we maintained heavy professional responsibilities. I knew that Claude told Reid that John had stolen his mother from him—despite the fact that I had never heard of John when I first told Claude I wanted a divorce. Claude's mother lived near Mobile, Alabama, so I suppose he used her house as a staging ground for ongoing intrusions into my life. Once he got into my house and stole my birth-control pills as evidence that I was an adulteress. He also read John's letters, including one in which John described our relationship in Jungian terms, then called me to tell me how silly such ideas were. I was furious, but my anger was as ineffective as the little mouse's protest against Burns's plough. I was sure Claude wouldn't physically hurt Reid, but I worried that his emotional manipulation could psychologically damage my son. I felt panicked for Reid's sake but also stymied in this as in everything having to do with Claude. I so despaired over losing my child, and even John's calming presence did not help much.

During the appalling child-snatching saga, I had sought another escape by applying for a teaching fellowship abroad. Despite my then-chaotic life, I won a Fulbright to teach American literature in Porto, Portugal, in the spring of 1976. I arranged for Reid to join me, but his father would not allow it. Claude was mounting a manic claim that I could not divorce him because I was still a resident of Virginia. He claimed that Louisiana law did not apply to me, much less to him or to Reid.

John returned the shotgun to its rightful owner before leaving to join me in Portugal on his sabbatical in February 1976, a month after I had arrived there and had begun teaching a weekly class in American literature. My first class in a big room was filled with about seventy students. I passed out a syllabus of reading assignments and told them (with some trepidation) that I expected each of them to write a short paper in English before the term's end. At the next class, I had only twelve students, all female, all with the first name Maria, all trained by nuns. They were eager to write in English and to benefit from my teaching.

John and I were so deeply in love, even bombs celebrating the anniversary of the Carnation Revolution did not faze us. After I taught my class, we read and wrote and enjoyed exciting sex. We drove a rented Mini into Paris with little guidance other than the map in my high school French book. We even invited my mother to visit. While she was with us, one of my students invited us to her home in Viseu. Her father spoke to John exclusively in Spanish, which John knew from a semester in Mexico as a twenty-year-old. The father shocked John with his support for the deposed dictator, Salazar. (Ever afterwards, when I copied the marinated mushrooms dish we were served that day, John called them "mushrooms fascisti.") The mother took us into the town of Viseu to see lace-makers, all dressed in black sewing in a darkened cave-like room and, it seemed to me, going blind. We toured an ancient church, and John and I actually crawled out of a window and balanced on the roof beam. I was not paralyzed by fear of falling because, as in so many ways, John gave me confidence.

We also took Mother on an excursion to Spain. On an overnight train, we had to suppress giggles when we heard her in the next compartment tell the Spanish customs inspector at the border, in a Blanche Dubois voice right out of Tennessee Williams, "You know I don't speak a word of Portuguese." Still, we gave her a good time, and she conveniently forgot that we were living "in sin," as her Methodist parents might have called it. John and I did not think of sin. We felt joined, body and soul, our union ordained by our love. Our behavior further scandalized the English Department at LSU and ended expectations of competition between us.

Reid was with us part of the summer of 1976, thanks to arrangements my Virginia lawyer made. At the end of the summer, when I took Reid to the airport, John went to the police academy to practice his marksmanship. At the airport, I found that Claude had not paid for a return ticket to Virginia. "That's great, Reid," I said, victoriously. "You can stay on with John and me and go back to your Baton Rouge school."

When we got home, John had taped up on the kitchen window a large paper with a man's frame outlined in it. There was a hole right in the center of the man's chest. Reid noticed it immediately and asked, "What's that?" I rolled my eyes at John, tempted to say, "Your father with a bullet in the chest, well placed by John." Instead John tore it down, and I offered Reid ice cream and he forgot about it. Neither John nor I did.

Claude eventually paid for Reid's return ticket to Virginia, and so I lost my child again. After a Virginia judge finally dismissed Claude's claim that I was a resident of Virginia, I got a divorce in both states in time for John and me officially to marry two days after Thanksgiving 1976. Shortly thereafter, my Virginia lawyer finally got a court procedure scheduled to determine custody. Claude's behavior was still aberrant, while mine as a settled married woman and associate professor at LSU was stable. I flew to Roanoke and my lawyer and I drove to Pearisburg, Virginia, for the final determination. There the judge granted me custody of Reid, with only supervised visiting rights for his father. After the hearing, Claude asked my lawyer if we could stop by the road to his house so he could hand over Reid's suitcase. I should have known better, but I had no clothes for my now almost eight-year-old boy, and it seemed reasonable to get at least a suitcase of his things. Instead, Claude leaned into the backseat of the lawyer's car, pulled Reid out, ran to his car, and took off with my son.

"The best laid schemes o' mice an' men / Gang aft agley," I remarked.

"What's that?" my lawyer asked, chasing down Route 460 after Claude.

"My father's favorite poem by Robert Burns: Our best laid plans often go awry."

The lawyer soon gave up the chase. "He's burnt his bridges now," he exclaimed. Then, when he took me to the airport motel in Roanoke, he offered to come up to my room. I can't recall exactly what he said, but it became clear he'd reduce his fees if I'd have sex with him. I refused.

After I flew to Baton Rouge the next morning and told John about the lawyer's propositioning me, John was outraged. "You mean the guy who's supposed to be protecting you from a sexual predator was one himself?"

"Well, at least he didn't force himself on me," was my weak reply. It seemed these men all just wanted to "get in my pants," as the phrase went, and it had been happening to me for years. When I'd been twenty or so, I worked as a secretary at the country club. If I arrived early, I'd sit on a bench waiting for the office to open. Then the president of that august organization would sit beside me and try to feel my breasts. I didn't know how to stop such harassment. (More recent cases including Clarence Thomas, Bill Cosby, Roger Ailes, and Donald Trump suggest that the problem has not evaporated.) I suppose one reason for marrying Claude had been that he was big enough to protect me from such behavior. I wanted to escape from such men, who John knew all about. In terms of sex, he waited until I invited him to be intimate with me and he promised never to force himself on me.

Meanwhile, Claude kept Reid hidden for nearly a year. My lawyer claimed to be pursuing some kind of a compromise. I didn't see much of a compromise, but I did see more legal fees, which John paid from his savings. Maybe he'd planned to buy a sports car with the money, but he gave it up to help me get back my child—to no avail.

I began beseeching sheriffs and law enforcement officers in places I suspected Claude might hide. Something cowardly kept me from hiring a private detective. Maybe I was just being frugal. Maybe I didn't want any more trauma. Or maybe I didn't want my good life with John ruined. I went to a counselor on the university staff who suggested that if Claude wanted Reid so much, maybe he should keep him during school years. That idea shocked me, but it did also open the possibility of simplifying my harried life, at least for the immediate future. John and I proposed it to my lawyer. Frustrated by the lack of coordination between states, I wrote a brief op-ed piece on "The Nightmare of Child-Custody Laws." It began:

> Joyce Carol Oates's novel *Do With Me What You Will* begins with a scene in which a very nervous man waits outside a school playground for the chance to kidnap his daughter. Actually, given the condition of family law in this country, he need not be apprehensive. Our legal system is almost impotent against a divorced parent dissatisfied with a custody decision. In fact, it virtually invites such a parent to "snatch" his or her child across state lines.

After the *Washington Post* printed my piece, I received calls from two California congressmen, both wondering if I would testify before a House committee. I put them off, and neither congressman called back. Still, I am glad to note that states have modified their child custody laws to consider other states' rulings too. Perhaps I played a very small role in that change.

The Virginia lawyers finally reached a custody truce between Claude and me in time for the Christmas holiday of 1977. Before we drove north to pick up Reid, John took the pistol he bought for target practice, beat it with a hammer, then trashed it. This was not beating swords into ploughshares but it was much the same idea. On our way, we stopped in Tuscaloosa to visit my mother and see my dying father, a World War I veteran. Then we headed north to Blacksburg. I recall hearing Whitney Houston singing "You Light Up My Life" on the car radio. We sang along, I poorly, but John really did light up my life. I was alive with passion and tenderness and a new sense of strength and responsibility.

I recall getting out of our car in near-blizzard conditions outside the home of Ann Goette and her first husband. Dating from the eighteenth century, the house was drafty and uninsulated. "Geez! It's cold," John remarked. "No wonder you wanted to get the hell out of Blacksburg."

Ann had left out a bottle of bourbon, but it didn't warm us until we could curl up together on the sofa bed in her front room. The next day, we picked up Reid at a neutral shopping center and headed to Columbus, Ohio, to see John's parents. On the trip, Reid was mostly quiet, except to ask why the window panes fogged up or why they were wet inside or why glasses left wet circles on tables. "Explaining condensation must be the trick to teaching elementary science," John remarked.

We spent the next summer of 1978, when I was pregnant, in Newark, Delaware, where John was working with a coeditor on a collection of essays on Swift's poetry. The Delaware countryside reminded John of the landscape around York, Pennsylvania, where he'd spent the happiest years of his childhood, mostly, I gathered, roaming the fields collecting butterflies after school. Then his parents took him to a seminar about becoming an Eagle Scout. (I doubt they cared about scouting, much less nature, but they did care to have their elder son win acclaim.) John told me that, though a manly young preteen, after the seminar he'd gone home to cry by himself. He realized that he'd soon be forced into jumping hurdles and overcoming obstacles. Quitting was not an option, so he'd have to accumulate badge after badge, which his mother could sew on the resplendent chest of his scout uniform, to transform him into an Eagle Scout. There would be no more happy-go-lucky butterfly chasings. Nor, I think, would John ever again have much appetite for fierce competition in search of acclaim. He'd had enough of that.

On the way to Delaware, we picked up Reid at some Virginia designation, where he informed us his father had left us a present. The cardboard box did not contain a bomb, as I'd feared, but a blue-gray Siamese kitten. Over the summer, the cat, whom Reid named Aslan after the great lion in C. S. Lewis's Chronicles of Narnia, became devoted to Reid.

We rented a cozy furnished Cape Cod house on the edge of campus. John spent the days working on Swift in an office the English Department loaned him. I spent mornings at home working on a review of the past year's writings on Faulkner while Reid went to day camp. In the afternoons, I often took Reid swimming. Sitting by the pool, I felt like a balloon in my borrowed maternity swimsuit. John thought my swollen belly was lovely. "You're rosy all over," he remarked, patting me gently. When a tick at camp embedded itself near Reid's private parts, I asked him if he'd rather have me or John remove it. He chose me, I suppose as a mark of our restored closeness. At the end of the summer, Claude wouldn't take Aslan, so John and I inherited him.

Back in Baton Rouge that fall, despite my advanced pregnancy and my already overdue Faulkner review, I opted to teach one course. I timed it so the class could get to the section of Restoration drama just about the time I'd be having a baby. John's parents booked a three-week trip to Baton Rouge, also timed for the baby's birth. Our baby was expected in September but she did not arrive. I kept writing my Faulkner review and teaching my class, with major help from John when I had to teach a Congreve play. John's parents were increasingly impatient. They didn't like seeing Aslan playing with the mobiles above the baby crib, and John's mother told me that it wasn't natural for a pregnant woman to work so hard. She suggested that I should induce labor. Infuriated, I complained to John. Always my protector, he told them to leave me alone. When he told me what he'd said to them, I thanked him again for being himself; then I collapsed into an easy, comforted sleep beside him.

On the night of 4 October, while the Fischers watched the World Series, I finished my review of the year's work on Faulkner for *American Literary Scholarship*. At dawn the next morning, my labor began. (John's parents were convinced that I kept the baby from coming until I met my deadline; maybe they were right.) We were the first Lamaze couple to have a baby at the Baton Rouge hospital, and several nurses and doctors asked to observe. John coached me through the entire natural childbirth.

Some nurses cried. One of them later told me how wonderful John had been during labor. "Can I borrow him when I have a baby?" she asked. "NO," I said, loud and clear. My mother drove over from Tuscaloosa when John's parents had only a few days left before their flight home.

Soon they all left, and we were delighted to escape all the grandparenting "help" and be alone with our adorable baby: Hannah Cornelia Reid Fischer. Our only problem was lack of sleep. "You didn't tell me how tough it would be," John remarked. "I forgot," I said, truthfully. When she woke in the night, I would nurse her, and then John would sing to her or recite poems. He even read her the poems of Theocritus, so it is no wonder she became a poet. John was such a devoted father that he gave up his BMW sidecar outfit knowing it was not a fit mode of transportation for a baby.

HOMES FAR AND NEAR

Over the next years, my yen for escapes was more than satisfied by travel to England with John. We spent our first summer abroad together in Cambridge, England, in 1981. (Our vet took in Aslan, making him the office cat, where he charmed clients for years.) We rented a modern house with a back lawn stretching down to the River Cam. It came with an electric lawnmower, which John frequently cursed, and with a Sheltie, in whom he delighted. Named Soda, Hannah called her Soda-de-dog. After Reid joined us, he spent many late afternoons playing catch with Soda and Hannah while John and I relaxed on lawn chairs.

Once after leaving a bathroom light on all night, we found in the morning that the white walls were covered with little insects called midges. After John scrubbed them off the walls, he said, "We could make a fortune selling window and door screens in England!" He suggested this plan to several English people, who uniformly dismissed it saying, "Certainly not. There are no flying insects in England." John said to me, "Yeah, and they don't need dentists either because they all have perfect teeth."

That summer, John and I each won research grants, and we went on to win more that took us back to England again and again. John always wrote about Jonathan Swift, whose "savage indignation" (Yeats's phrase) at human foibles reified John's own. I switched my loyalties from Faulkner to Roger Fry. John and I spent most days doing research in the Cambridge University Library, a monolithic 1930s building whose tower reminded us of Huey Long's capitol building in Baton Rouge. We allotted some babysitting duties to Reid, then twelve, but we also hired a young woman named Celia as Hannah's nanny. While Celia pushed a rickety rented stroller along cobblestone lanes and over arched bridges, little Hannah recited countless nursery rhymes, so delighting Celia she devoted her Montessori thesis to Hannah. (Celia's confidence was justified eleven years later when Hannah published her first poem.)

We were so pleased with Soda-de-Dog and so enamored by pictures and stories of the Queen's Corgis that back in Baton Rouge for Hannah's third birthday, we bought her a Corgi. I fetched the puppy and came home to ring the doorbell. John brought Hannah to the door saying something like, "Maybe it's Mom. She might have a surprise for you." Indeed I did. When they opened the door to find a puppy in my arms, Hannah reached out to clasp the little dog close, saying, "She's just my size." She named her Lucy-de-Dog. Lucy could irritate John and me by chewing on our shoes or books or draperies, but we always forgave the precious puppy.

In 1983, we escaped the Louisiana mugginess (though sadly missing the beauteous spring flowers) and spent the entire calendar year in England, thanks to John's having a National Endowment for the Humanities Fellowship and my having a summer NEH and a year's Fulbright research grant. We rented our Baton Rouge house to graduate students, who cared for Lucy and deducted the costs of her food and their chewed-up shoes from their rent.

In London, we rented a "maisonette," the top two floors of what was once a tall town house. A bright red door with a fan of windows above testified to some former elegance. Our place was just a tight little staircase up onto a floor with a living room and small kitchen, then another flight of stairs to a bedroom for us with a tiny one for Hannah, and then a third set of stairs up to a tight little bathroom. We went away during August, renting a spacious house in Cambridge. On our return, though, we were appalled that the landlord and his mother had stayed in the bottom two floors, and he'd "decorated" all four floors with "trophies" from his father's long-ago excursions out to the colonies. He nailed a crocodile skin to the wall on our first flight of stairs, and a leopard skin, antlers, and some guns and swords to our living room wall. An elephant's foot served as a doorstop. Sometimes we could joke about such horrors.

Hannah went to nursery school in the mornings and spent the afternoons in the care of a woman whose younger son was Hannah's age. John would walk from the British Library to get Hannah and hoist her on his shoulders for the walk home to our maisonette in Islington. He experimented with different routes, but often they passed the Sadler's Wells ballet theatre. Once, a huge crowd blocked the streets. Four-year-old Hannah asked her dad why all the people were there. He didn't know, but someone beside them said, "Didna ya hear, child, the Prince and Princess are coming to the ballet." Hannah of course wanted to stay and see Princess Diana. Not wanting to stand in the cold and wet with a heavy child on his shoulders much longer, John told her they must get home to me and to dinner. She was resistant until he suggested that Hannah could invite the princess to visit us. Hannah was full of fantasies about Princess Diana coming to tea. I ended up typing a letter, dictated by Hannah, to the Princess. Much to our surprise, a lady-in-waiting answered. She said that Princess Diana was delighted that Hannah liked living in London. She thanked Hannah for the invitation, but said the Princess's busy schedule kept her from taking tea with Hannah.

Hannah understood my days fairly well. I wrote mostly at home from my books and from notes I'd taken in Cambridge. I told her I was writing about a man named Roger Fry who was a writer and painter. He thought painting wasn't just a picture of something else but its own composition, an arrangement of lines, shapes, and colors. I showed her some Cubist prints, which helped make my point, maybe. What John did when he trekked off to the British Library or the Public Record Office, though, mystified her. He explained that he read through very, very old papers, letters, hand-copied poems, early books, and even government documents. When she asked why, he said he was looking for clues about what Jonathan Swift actually wrote but that he had to kiss a lot of frogs before one turned into a princess.

In late afternoons after John and Hannah got home, I'd pour milk for her and scotch for him and me, and she would settle on her kitchen chair, nibbling peanuts with us. Then she'd look up at John and ask, "Daddy, did a frog turn into a princess today?" He usually responded that he'd just turned over lots of really old yellowed and crinkly papers, none of them adding much to what he already knew, saying, "Just frogs, no princesses today, sweetie."

John did actually have some days of research that were really fulfilling. He once figured out that the British Library must own a copy of a Sotheby's auction catalogue not on its shelf list. After he presented his case, two librarians took him into the hallowed stacks, where no mere reader normally goes. There John discovered the Sotheby's volume that the Library had said it did not own. John was vindicated for researching with unblinking curiosity.

Another time, John was investigating the price put on the heads of Swift and his publisher for his anonymous comments on King George II and Prime Minister Robert Walpole. In the unheated old Public Records Office, John's feet were once so cold he took off his shoes and socks and sat cross-legged, tucking his bare feet under his thighs for warmth. When he was ready to leave the PRO, however, he found that his socks had frozen to the stone floor. "And our colleagues envy us a posh life in elegant London," John remarked later with a touch of bitterness. Despite the discomfort, John made many real finds in those dusty, centuries-old records. On the day of the frozen socks, he found the evidence that government lawyers had mounted against Swift, which John wrote up in a prize-winning essay, "The Government's Response to 'An Epistle to a Lady.'" Though John's research was often inconvenient, his socks only froze once, and he enjoyed the occasional payout of discovering a document no other scholar had noted—but he had to kiss a lot of frogs to find such treasures.

That summer, Reid joined us in our cramped maisonette, sleeping on a sofa in the living room. He soon became an expert on the London Tube system and the films shown in theatres all over the city. He also spent a week hiking in central Scotland, trying to make it to the top of Ben Nevis, the highest peak in the UK. It was too cold and wet for him to reach the peak, but Reid returned with a new sense of self-sufficiency, as well as an enhanced appreciation of the security we offered him. When he was with us, John asked Reid, then fourteen, if his dad had ever talked to him about sex. Reid said Claude hadn't, so John and I set out to tell him the basics. John did most of the talking, while I shyly sat by and mostly nodded and said things like, "That's right." I do recall that John told him never to do anything the girl didn't want to do. I spoke up then to agree wholeheartedly.

If a dog can be ecstatic, Lucy was when we returned to the States. She was a grown dog now and rather heavy, but Hannah could still pick her up and hold her on her lap. We had a fenced-in backyard in which Lucy wore a path running from the back patio, where we let her out, to the side entrance, where she could see our car return. Once we had kids over for a party, and Lucy herded them along that path, as her ancestors had herded cattle on hillsides in Wales. The kids took it as a game of chase, outwitting Lucy by splitting into groups of twos or threes, more than she could corral. Exhausted, Lucy stretched her short little legs out, fore and aft, her tummy flat on the cool concrete patio, and took a nap. During our later escapes, Lucy boarded with a dog-loving friend, who kept Collies outside, while Lucy became her privileged inside dog.

During our later stays in London, John's job was dropping off and picking up Hannah from her different schools. At a tea shop after school, they'd stop for a Kit Kat bar or a cup of cocoa. A favorite shop featured little ceramic animals that Hannah treasured. John saw that she got an allowance just large enough to buy one little animal, if she saved for two and a half weeks. She understood the discipline and slowly gathered quite a collection of little animals, which she still displays. John had a great knack for entertaining her. When he heard the phrase "seal of approval," he would clap his wrists together and croak "arf arf" like a seal, sending Hannah into peals of laughter. He sang silly songs, remembering all the verses in "There was an old woman who swallowed a fly" and "There's a hole in the bucket," to Hannah's complete delight. As they walked past a shop labeled "Family Butcher," he sang, "Oh, please, dear family butcher, don't butcher my fam-a-lee." John spent the time with Hannah after he left the British Library so that I would be free to write about Roger Fry and additionally Virginia Woolf. My part was doing the shopping and cooking. As I look back, his job took more time but was more joyful.

Hannah attended so many public and private English schools that, when we returned to Baton Rouge, her classmates called her the "little English girl." On one flight back we bought a bottle of Irish whiskey at the duty-free shop. It came with a small Irish crystal shot glass. John was so impressed by its pretty cut-glass prisms that I ordered a box of six such glasses. When John unpacked the first one, he held it so carefully and tightly that he shattered it. Afterwards, he refused to touch the other five glasses. Given that he had such strength in his hands, I think he was also afraid of breaking Hannah or me, one reason behind his astonishing gentleness with us.

While I have written much about our happy sex life, I admit that sometime in my late forties, I did become a less sexual creature. It seemed natural to lose interest in sex, as other women my age seemed to. After I told John so, he set about proving me wrong. He played with me and teased me sexually, but teasing was all he did. At first I found it a rather pointless waste of time, but then I began to long for sex again. The more he teased me, the more aroused I became. Finally, I told him I could not delay coming any longer. Then he took me in his arms and we made love as of old. I'd learned my lesson, thanks to his patience, and became again a sexual creature, though no doubt a less energetic one than when I was first John's Sleeping Beauty.

Thirteen years had passed since I'd met John and moved to Baton Rouge. Before going to London in the summer of 1987, John joined fellow Swift scholars Arch Elias and James Woolley in Philadelphia to work on determining the texts of Swift's poems. While he was away, I entertained my visiting mother by house hunting. I found the perfect abode, a dazzling house designed by a Czech architect, and immediately offered to buy it. We sent a flurry of faxes, photos, and documents back and forth to John before he approved and the purchase became official. Then Hannah and I embarked for London, where John and then Reid joined us a few days later. John said, "If a man leaves his wife for three weeks, he's lucky if she falls in love only with a house." I had to thank him again for being himself. We were extraordinarily happy in ourselves and in that dramatic house. It had a vaulted living-room ceiling, over two stories high, with a balcony above leading to our bedroom on one side and three others on the opposite side of the second story. Outside we had a back deck and a spacious yard that grew magnificent but no-longer-productive pecan trees. John and I gave many a party there, especially when, in the 1990s, John chaired the English Department and then served as director of graduate studies.

Once John and I were flying from Baton Rouge to Nashville, where Vanderbilt held an eighteenth-century conference at which John was to speak. I was going along to keep him company, free of the pressures of LSU. Our plane had just taken off when we heard a loud explosion. The pilot announced that an engine had blown out and we'd have to return to Baton Rouge. Flight attendants were rushing up and down the aisles calling, "Brace!"

"What does that mean?" John called out. There was no time for dictionary definitions. We watched others across the aisle, then also knelt, ducked our faces, and put our hands behind our heads. In what we feared were our last few minutes together, we said how much we loved each other and thanked the other for our great life together. Suddenly we felt a huge shattering bounce and looked up to find that we were back on the runaway in Baton Rouge, now surrounded by ambulances and fire trucks. They weren't needed, but the passengers needed food and drink, courtesy of Delta. In the airport bar, everyone talked about their fears and hopes, loved ones, and beliefs, as a remarkable camaraderie developed among passengers who'd never seen each other before almost dying together.

When the bar got quiet, John whispered, "I'm sorry you couldn't say you loved me too."

"What?" I said. "Of course I love you, as I said clearly! First thing after this conference, you see an ear doctor."

"Okay," he said, "if you go too."

John's presentation at Vanderbilt was dynamic, as always. Perhaps our recent near-death experience, however, heightened our awareness of how much he coughed while delivering his talk. I'd agreed when we married that cigarettes were part of John's personality, and a rather seductive part at that. Now John admitted how destructive they were. In the Nashville airport, John took his last pack of cigarettes and, without comment, threw them in a trash bin. Back in Baton Rouge, he bought pipes with pipe-smoking paraphernalia. At home, as he puffed on a new pipe, I said, "What a lovely musty fragrance. It's mystical."

"And you won't have to guess about birthday presents," he replied. I soon learned what a meerschaum pipe was and how handy were the tobacco pouches, stands, filters, and pipe tampers for gifts.

I also reminded John of our promises to see an audiologist. It turned out that we each had hearing loss, but in different ranges. He couldn't hear the trebles, I couldn't hear the bass sounds. In this, as in so much else, we complemented each other. Maybe he had to ask his female students to speak up in class. Certainly, I asked both male and female students to repeat their questions. But the most embarrassing aspect was in intimate moments when John whispered sweet nothings into my ear. I could hardly say, "Pardon?" or "What's that you said?" and break the mood. So I learned to turn my head to the side, and he learned to whisper into my left, better ear. Still, the audiologist's tests suggested that neither of us was yet quite in need of a hearing aid.

My father died in 1980, a remarkably long life for a man born in 1895 and who'd been shot in the head in the Argonne Forest just before the Armistice in 1918, receiving a Bronze Star for "gallantry," as it was called. In the fall of 1989, around Thanksgiving, my mother had a serious stroke; John, Hannah, and I rushed to be with her. It was soon clear that she would not live for long and that I would inherit her house and furniture. Belatedly, I asked Mother about the history of her antiques. She told me they were shipped from France about 1835 into

Mobile, Alabama, then boated up the Alabama River to Demopolis and taken by mule and wagon to the old plantation home in Greene County, Alabama.

"Mother," I said, as she lay flat on a hospital bed, "did you ever read *Absalom, Absalom!*?" Of course she hadn't, Faulkner being known to her generation as a dirty old man trying to besmirch the glorious image of the Ole South. Still, her story of the shipment of love seats, fragile chairs, an inlaid secretary, and a marble-topped table almost replicated the tale in *Absalom, Absalom!* of Thomas Sutpen's importing French furniture to prove himself a Southern gentleman.

Mother died in March of 1990. She was buried in Demopolis beside my father in her family's plot. John and I redecorated our house with her furnishings, creating an eclectic mix of modern architecture and historical rugs and furniture.

"Just tell me none of these things was made by 'slave labor,'" John said when the furniture arrived.

"Definitely not," I replied. "They were made in France during the reign of Louis-Philippe. I think he was the king who conquered Algeria."

"Some comfort," John remarked. He'd once walked out of a plantation tour when docents bragged that a table or bed had been made by slave labor. "I'm no Southern gentleman," John said, then he admitted, "But I do like that secretary." The secretary is nine feet tall with shelves above, a cabinet below, and a rolltop desk between. When the desk cover rolls back, it reveals little drawers and a writing platform with glass ink bottles and even a stand for holding a quill pen!

Among other treasures we inherited from Mother was the piano she'd had as a girl. Hannah began piano lessons, and Lucy, who followed her everywhere, would sit under the piano stool as she practiced. Lucy's foxlike ears were so sound-sensitive John once said, "Hannah, just as an experiment actually try to hit bad notes." When she did, Lucy abandoned her post behind Hannah's feet. "Hannah, your dog is a music critic!" John announced.

A few months after Mother's death, we disembarked for London. A friend said to me, "Your mother dies, you redecorate the house, you rent it out, you pack up for London. Any one of those could give you each a nervous breakdown." Not us. We found a renter, our dog-loving friend offered to board Lucy again, and Hannah was accepted at the City of London School for Girls.

In London, we rented a tiny apartment up four flights of steps, with another flight going up to two small bedrooms. (All those steps could set up agonizing back pains, making us grimace again about folks envying our stay in elegant London.) We'd hardly arrived when John got a phone call saying that his father had had a heart attack in the San Francisco airport. John, ever the paterfamilias, flew from London to San Francisco, too late to see his father alive. Then he spent ten or so days back in Columbus helping his mother learn some basics, like balancing a checkbook. When he returned, we dined at a nearby Thai restaurant whose staff loved John. He actually got in a tipping war with them. He'd overtip to show gratitude, then next time they'd add an appetizer to our order. Again, he'd overtip, and next they'd add an appetizer and a dessert. The take-home bags jammed our little apartment fridge, until John found a tactful way to suggest that they could give us a going-away dinner but in the meantime should just serve what we ordered, no matter how generous his tip.

My work on Fry and British art had morphed into a study of Fry's influence on Virginia Woolf, a subject easily researched in London at the British Library and the Tate Museum. Hannah rode city buses to the City of London School, and she and her best friend Miranda spent many a Saturday on scavenger hunts that I designed, taking them all over London in search of a certain statue at the Tate or information about the kinds of ducks in St. James's Park. In all their excursions, John and I had no qualms or worries for Hannah's safety. Baton Rouge High, where we returned after that year, was scarier.

John had long held a reputation at LSU for being a rebel, something of a wild man. Even when I first arrived in 1974, stories still circulated about how he'd shocked the administration by driving up on a motorcycle on his first day there. On their first meeting, the then-dean said, "I know how to treat assistant professors." John had innocently asked, "How?" The dean replied, "Keep them in the dark and feed them plenty of shit." John had stormed out of the office.

In Louisiana, the gubernatorial runoff the fall of 1991 pitched Democrat Edwin Edwards, running for his fourth term as governor despite his reputation as a crooked politician, against David Duke, former Grand Wizard of the Ku Klux Klan, a white supremacist and neo-Nazi. That such a racist anti-Semite might become governor provoked thoughtful citizens begrudgingly to put bumper stickers on their cars: "Vote for the Crook. It's Important." John and I called Republican voters, saying that we didn't approve of Edwards but Louisiana must not be governed by a Nazi. Once when Duke's plane flew over Baton Rouge's Episcopal High, the kids outside cheered. When John heard about that, he was outraged. "What kind of readings do they assign? What kind of values do they teach at that elite school?"

At LSU, John challenged administrators for their misuse of power, and he questioned the dean's policy of appointing heads of departments. He argued publicly that the English Department was bigger than most colleges and so its faculty should have the right to choose its leaders, who should be chairs, not "heads." Reluctantly, the upper administration agreed that the English Department might hold an election. They were in shock when John won, and for several weeks the dean actually avoided speaking to him. (Maybe he was conferring with John's opponent in the hopes that, should John turn out to be too revolutionary, his election would be revoked.) Finally, the dean and the upper administrators named John chair of the department.

One of his first acts as chair was to call the head of human resources management and say, "English faculty members are not human resources to be managed. They are human beings of talent and integrity." The head of HRM must have thought, "Uh oh, this guy really is a troublemaker."

To initiate his new administration and the new academic year, John and I decided to give a huge party on the last Saturday in August 1992. In hopes of healing rifts between ranks, we invited the entire English Department faculty. On Friday, I asked John to pick up bottles of wine and other beverages too heavy for me to carry, so he left the closing of the front office to the secretaries. That Saturday was wonderfully cool for a Louisiana August backyard party. We had everyone put on name tags, and it seemed that people got to know each other better and that this convivial atmosphere helped vanquish old rivalries, despite ominous heavy gray clouds and a wind that picked up as guests were leaving. That night we heard that Hurricane Andrew had crossed Florida and was headed for the Gulf Coast. On Sunday, we talked a tree expert into lopping off branches from our old pecan trees. While the tree guys were swinging near treetops, like monkeys with chainsaws, John and I worked below cleaning up party debris.

That Monday, as Andrew hit us, electricity went out, and John went to check damage in the English Department at LSU. He found that windows in the front office had been left open, and papers had blown off desks and mail out of faculty mailboxes. He spent the rest of the day mopping and sweeping and trying to dry out papers and mail. With no school, Hannah mostly stayed in her room. I tried to work on my Woolf book, despite having a Welsh Corgi underfoot. With winds howling about us at ninety miles an hour, Lucy did not feel our tall brick house was as impervious to danger as Hannah and I did. Usually a Hannah follower, that day Lucy stuck with me, even in the bathroom, as if my grown-up powers could shield us from Andrew's howling. For her own bathroom breaks, John must have taken her outside before he left and, when he got home in those still-fierce winds, let her use the garage and then cleaned up after her, as he'd been cleaning up for the faculty the entire day.

After he scrubbed up and settled at our breakfast-room table, with Lucy now under his feet, John drank his bourbon, without ice, and complained about the mess he'd inherited in the English Department, both literally and figuratively. Hannah appeared and kissed her dad's forehead, saying she was glad the storm hadn't hurt him. When John asked about her day, she said she'd spent the day memorizing Puck's speech at the end of *A Midsummer Night's Dream* and playing the Red Hot Chili Peppers endlessly on her new Walkman. She had studied *A Midsummer Night's Dream* at the City of London School for Girls, so I supposed that nostalgia had returned her to the play during the storm—though how it fit with the Red Hot Chili Peppers, I could not imagine. John too recalled Shakespeare's lines and remarked that he'd just mopped and would try to further "mend" or make amends for what had been mishandled in LSU's English Department.

While he was chair, restoring amends meant very hard work for John as he restructured the organization of the English Department. I was involved in renovating seminar rooms. Most importantly, we founded a "town and gown" speaking series in which townspeople made modest contributions to support a series of lectures and readings. Together, we named the organization Readers And Writers, which became a great success. John and I also gave more big parties and many dinners. I meant to have every single faculty member, with a spouse or partner, over for dinner. My plan often included using a fallback Louisiana dish. Frozen crawfish tails were inexpensive, as was a good, quick étouffée mix. I bought a large supply and made many, many crawfish étouffée dinners, though I did not get around to cooking for every member of the English faculty. Still I made étouffée often enough never to want to eat or even see it again.

Baton Rouge High School, where Hannah was assigned as a freshman, was in a rundown neighborhood, and the school was as rundown and neglected as its environs. Educating the students seemed such a low priority that we worried about Hannah's education. She did too, especially after she heard about the publicly supported Louisiana School for Math, Science, and the Arts (LSMSA). When we attended an orientation there, it seemed as if this school was meant for Hannah and her many talents. On our return, Lucy-de-dog seemed disconsolate, as if she knew Hannah would be leaving her.

LSU regularly brought in foreign teachers and scholars to study with faculty in our library. John was distressed that too often these people arrived with no one to befriend them. When he heard that an English professor from India was coming to study Southern literature, John was determined to do better by him, part of restoring amends at LSU. He drove to the airport to greet the man, brought him some of our sheets and towels, gave him an introductory tour of the campus, and invited him to supper. We were rather weary from our trip to northwest Louisiana for Hannah's LSMSA orientation. I was thawing out crawfish tails when Hannah came into the kitchen to say to John and me, "Something's wrong with Lucy." We found her eleven-year-old dog dead before the off-limits living room fireplace. She had ventured there in a formal gesture, a farewell wake for herself. Her short legs, front and back, were stretched out flat, and she left a puddle behind her rear end. Hannah was bereft and too upset to talk much for the rest of the evening. John cleaned up, but didn't have time to dig a hole and bury Lucy, so we did as a neighbor suggested and put Lucy in a plastic bag into the garage fridge, which we used for beer, wine, party food, or the occasional watermelon.

Then John fetched the Indian scholar, who seemed glad to sit on the deck and talk about Flannery O'Connor while having a beer. He said his main interest was in the Southern Gothic. I said Southern literature wasn't necessarily gothic or macabre, but he thought it was. Lest we argue, John asked if the man would like another beer. The man volunteered to get it himself, saying he'd seen John go to the garage for the first one. The specter of an Indian scholar reaching over a dead dog to get a beer was almost too much for John and me. We went inside and did a crazy little dance as John sang, "Lucy in the fridge with beer" to the Beatles tune. I stayed in the kitchen, stirring crawfish tails into mushrooms and onions and getting our meal together, leaving John to change the subject out on the deck.

After dinner, John took the man back to his dorm. While he was gone, I tried to make up a rhyme, as I put dishes in the washer. Not many words rhyme with "gothic." (I thought of "soffit," "caught it," "taught it," and "how doth it," but couldn't do better.) On John's return, he laughed, "Perhaps you and I are 'Southern Gothic.'"

"We doth it," I said, and the two of us nearly collapsed in giggles. "At least he didn't open the fridge. Otherwise he would have written a scholarly paper on a late instance of Southern Gothic in Louisiana with a six-pack of fresh beer stuck beside a dead dog!"

The next day, after his afternoon seminar, John dug a big hole in the side yard. Hannah wore a black cape and read a poem she'd written for Lucy. Then we buried the clever dog who had played such a vital part in Hannah's growing up.

As chair, John reformed the workings of the English Department. He computerized the administrative calendar, so all chairs since then have known what is expected of them and when. John so democratized the department that the associate professors resented the powers he saw were granted to instructors, while instructors resented that they were now expected to acquaint themselves with literary theory like the professors. After three years of reform, John lost the next election to the man he'd initially beaten. One colleague compared John's fate to Khrushchev's, given that reforms most alienate those threatened by them.

After all his work to restore and reform the department, John was deeply hurt by that election. I was furious and ready to leave. I couldn't sleep at night, waking up silently cursing all those who'd benefited from John's wise direction but turned on him when his opponent made promises for things that he could not keep, like bigger salaries. It may have been then that I began knitting a sort of emotional cocoon around the two of us. I had already thrown John's parents out of that nest. I recall John's taking them out to dinner on one visit, when they began retelling stories of his brother Jeff's high school triumphs. I told them I was tired of hearing praise for Jeff and never John. Maybe they were chastened, but at least they no longer bragged about Jeff's high school math awards.

John was a born administrator, and he next served as director of graduate studies, a post he enjoyed because he worked closely with graduate students, freed from most academic politicking. Still, losing the chairmanship after he had worked so conscientiously, putting in ten-hour days even on many weekends, made John question his capacities. I think it also weakened him. Those long hours, with inadequate rest and endless worries, certainly tore up his internal organs. After so much effort went unappreciated, I suggested we look for other jobs. But neither of us could imagine being separated or enduring a commute between us. Since those Eagle Scout days, John had no desire to enter the competitive job market anyway and just wanted to edit Swift. Since he'd rescued me, I had no wish to be apart from him. I think he prayed a lot over it, but he was furious with our minister, who preached a sermon on academic politics, saying something like, "The best man won and the best man lost." John refused to return to that church, saying, "I will not be the object lesson of a sermon when the whole congregation knows what has happened to me!"

My study of Woolf's debt to Roger Fry and the visual arts evolved into a biography of Woolf, published in 1997 under the name Panthea Reid. (I'd previously used Claude's last name and occasionally hyphenated the surnames of my two husbands. When I thought about what name should be on my tombstone, however, I wanted my true name, the one I was born with. I'm happy to have reverted to it, though I won't have a tombstone.) I belatedly discovered that writing biography—combining research, literary criticism, and storytelling—was what I'd been meant to do all along.

Next I wanted to write the biography of an American woman writer. I was teaching a collection of American novellas that included *Tell Me a Riddle* by Tillie Olsen, which I hadn't read in a couple of decades. In the 1990s, this story of an old woman's approach to death, with allusions to all the hopes and disappointments and horrors of the twentieth century, seemed even more profound than I'd remembered it. Olsen was then in her eighties, no biography of her existed, and she was a great feminist hero. I read more, visited her, and got her cautious permission to write her biography. While John had been skeptical of Woolf, Olsen's advocacy for working people pleased him. Here was a project of mine he could endorse wholeheartedly.

I remained furious with the English Department and was also weary of academic chores like paper grading and committee service. John was more than a bit tired of all the burdens that fell on his shoulders. We hoped someday to retire so we could get our real work done: John's studies of Swift's poetry and my biography of Olsen. When we visited archives at other universities, we would ask ourselves if we could live in places like Stanford, Austin, New Haven, Philadelphia, or New York City. The answer was mostly "no." Stanford and Austin were too far from family, friends, and libraries on the East Coast; New Haven was too cold; Philadelphia and New York were too metropolitan. We wanted a small college town with access to big cities but without the hassles of city living. Chapel Hill was tempting, but its library would not support John's eighteenth-century studies, and it seemed too far from city resources and diversions.

In 1998, we visited John's Swift colleague James Woolley and his wife, Susan, in Easton, Pennsylvania. They had suggested that Princeton, New Jersey, might be just the place for our retirement. John researched Princeton University's Firestone Library and found that its collection of eighteenth-century volumes was very good. It was one of the least used great libraries in the country and also was close to metropolitan centers. I drove over from Easton one day and found myself enchanted. When John and I left the Woolleys, we drove together to Princeton, where a realtor showed us a few houses. John loved one, which he saw as a proper New England professor's cottage with built-in bookshelves in almost every room. I loved it too, though its eight-foot ceilings were too low for antiques like our secretary. As we began the drive back toward Louisiana, we could talk about nothing but the charming Princeton house. We were somewhere near John's favorite old town of York, Pennsylvania, when we decided to buy the house. We made an offer, which was accepted after a bit of negotiation. Our Princeton house rented immediately to a young couple, and we became landlords, with vague plans to move to Princeton someday ourselves. As an indicator of new beginnings, John gave all his pipe paraphernalia to the local pipe shop and gave up smoking for good, soon finding that he was coughing less.

After the death of Swift biographer Irvin Ehrenpreis, Hermann Real and other Swift scholars founded the Ehrenpreis Centre for Swift Studies in Münster, Germany. Since the 1980s, the Centre held international symposia on Swift's work every five or six years. In the summer of 2000, at the fourth symposium on Swift, John and Arch Elias presented significant papers. Afterwards John and I took trains through Germany, Switzerland, and as far south as Rome. There I conducted exhaustive interviews with Tillie Olsen's brother, Gene Lerner, who had been a film agent in post–World War II Italy when films like *Roman Holiday* were enormously popular. Gene and I relaxed in the lobby of the Hotel Nazionale, where Anna Magnani and Anita Ekberg had given a lavish eightieth birthday party for him. Gene vented, rather loudly for an elegant Roman hotel, his anger over what he saw as Tillie's scheming falsities. I was shocked and intrigued. Gene's stories belied her image as "Saint Tillie" but promised a great tale, though John wisely suggested that the story must be more complicated.

John and I knew that the idyllic academic town of Princeton would be our haven and inspiration, but we kept secret the fact that we'd purchased a house there. Twenty-seven years after my arrival at LSU and about thirteen after buying our Czech-designed house, I convinced John that it was time to take early retirement and make the move to Princeton. Our announced departure shocked our colleagues and the administration, which might have had something grander in mind for us. Instead, we received cut-glass bowls and other tributes, including a gold watch for John with a Louisiana pelican spreading its wings across the watch's round face. Our tenants vacated the Princeton house, and we moved into our Northern center-hall colonial home in May of 2001. We took apart the antique secretary, putting the rolltop desk part with its under-cabinet on one side of the fireplace and the bookshelves on the other. John filled them with rare books from his Swift collection. I spread one of Grandmother's embroidered cloths over the desk, to hide its toplessness.

Princeton turned out to be the perfect haven for us. We had, for a while, temporary appointments at Princeton University, with library and parking privileges. Later when some administrator realized that we weren't actually on the faculty, we lost the parking sticker and had to pay to check out books from the Firestone Library. We made many new friends through an organization called Community Without Walls (CWW). We took the train into the city to see exhibits, like one of Leonardo drawings at the Met, and to hear talks, like one on political biography. From Princeton, we took frequent drives to Columbus, Ohio, to see John's aged mother. Sometimes we'd circle down from Ohio to see my Kentucky relatives on the Reid Orchards. Sometimes we'd get to southwest Virginia to see Reid and my friend Ann Goette.

We adopted a gray-blue cat. A foundling left with a cat rescuer, she had no pedigree, but she was clearly either a British or a French Blue. "She's a beautiful aristocrat, like you," John sweetly said to me. We named her MagnifiCat, Maggie for short. At first she shyly slunk around the edges of rooms, but then she started devotedly trailing John. When he was out, she'd listen for the grind of the automatic garage door's opening, then she'd leave me in my study to race downstairs to greet the "Daddy-Cat," as I called him to her. I made up a poem, "The Maggie Rap," with lines like, "Up the stairs, rat-a-tat-tat / Two at a time goes Maggie-the-Cat!" She actually went faster when I chanted the poem.

Once we hired workmen to paint and fix the house's interior while we were visiting John's mother. We left Maggie at home and hired the cat rescuer to care for her. She knew Maggie was okay, given evidence in the food dish, water bowl, and litter box, but the workmen's hammering and sawing must have terrified Maggie, who wouldn't appear even for her rescuer. When we returned, I called, but no Maggie showed up. Then I began walking about, chanting "The Maggie Rap." "Engines running?

What is that? / Just the purring of our Maggie cat." Then she crawled out from behind a stack of old journals and let me hug her close.

When John spread his working papers on the dining room table, Maggie hopped up under the armchair's arms and sat there observing him. After watching for a while, she'd hop onto the table and settle on his papers. Maggie was not allowed near our food, but when only books and papers covered the dining room table, she was free to join John at his work. At some point, John would gently lift her off, saying, "I ordered a cat, not a paperweight." When Hannah first met Maggie, she said, "She grins like the Cheshire cat in *Alice's Adventures in Wonderland*."

"Well, not quite," my English teacher's voice put in. "As I recall, Alice says she's seen a cat without a grin, but never before a grin without a cat. That's when the Cheshire cat has faded away, leaving its grin hovering behind." Since John had read everything, it seemed, and remembered it all, it was nice to know one book he didn't. Perhaps Alice had never seemed serious enough for him. Anyway, with or without a grin, Maggie grew fond enough of Hannah to sometimes sleep with her when she came up from DC to visit.

After John's eighty-nine-year-old mother fell on the ice in Columbus, we moved her in 2003 into assisted living about thirty minutes from us, and John began a wearying routine of visits to her. I accompanied him on maybe half of these visits. When I came for lunch, I tried to cheer up conversations at her dining table, to no avail. After a while, even her fellow residents did not want to have her at their table because her regurgitating habits were unpleasant to watch. She no longer would or could talk. After such lunches, on the way home, I would hope to get John to laugh over some of the absurdities we'd seen. He'd laugh too, but he still felt an obligation to visit his mother, no matter what she was like now, or how poor a mother she'd been to him. Once he remarked that

I was lucky: my parents had died relatively quickly while his mother was going through a drawn-out decline.

In Princeton, we could walk to our doctors' offices next to the hospital (before it moved), and John walked occasionally all the way to the Firestone Library. We could easily visit Philadelphia and New York. Always accessible was Washington Crossing, from which George Washington crossed the Delaware on that fateful December night in 1776. Nearby we could visit the remarkable Princeton University Art Museum, the Princeton Battlefield, and Nassau Hall, into which Washington had fired a cannon ball routing British interlopers. We took guests to such historical and cultural spots so frequently that I knew every statue at Grounds for Sculpture and could have narrated my own tour of Washington's Crossing.

John's brother had contracted a rare blood disease, and John visited him in a Manhattan hospital faithfully until he died. Those sad visits rubbed off the glamorous patina of trips into the city for shows or gallery visits. John did make a few trips to examine manuscripts at the Pierpont Morgan Library or the New York Public Library. And once we both enjoyed attending an auction of a Swift manuscript at Christie's. The glamour of that occasion was heightened by John's involvement with the manuscript and by his interest in Trinity College Dublin's purchase of it.

Still, I began to fear that we were going to use up Princeton, and I'd begun to talk of leaving for a different and warmer climate.

4

INVINCIBILITY

The night of 21 December 2014 was cool and cloudy but warm for a Princeton winter. John and I had hung a holly wreath on the front door and had decorated a small tree in front of the fireplace. We piled Chanukah and Christmas presents around it. We had made elaborate preparations and were ready for the arrival of my son Reid Broughton. By then forty-five years old, Reid had decided to visit us while we were still near New York City. He lived not far from Blacksburg, Virginia, with his girlfriend, whom I call Louise, and their ten-year-old son, Reid Jr. John and I had often visited them at their house and taken them on various holidays, most often to a lovely beach on the Chesapeake, near Mathews, Virginia. But Reid Jr. had only been to Princeton once before, at Christmas in 2009, a visit cut short by his mother's desire to leave as soon as presents were opened and his father's hope of avoiding an approaching snowstorm. So little Reid had almost no sense of us in our own home.

I can't explain Reid's relationship with Louise. Certainly, he was attracted to her beauty, and her vulnerability stirred his caretaking instincts. When he first brought her to see us in Baton Rouge, they were about five hours late because she'd insisting on stopping at the Biloxi casinos. She stayed in the bathroom on that visit for hours at a time, apparently not because she was sick but because she washed and rewashed her hair and put on and took off makeup all day long. (Fortunately we had two and a half baths.). Reid had turned out to be as tall as his father, Claude, but with my Reid family eyes and a more generous mouth than his father had. He also was much smarter and kinder. He had previously brought two interesting, attractive young women to meet us, and the second had clearly loved him, but he'd let her go.

Louise was not just attractive; she was a stunner, tall with eye-popping, elegant Snow White features. I had once cattily remarked to John that almost any woman who spent that much time putting on layers of makeup could be a stunner too, but of course I knew that wasn't true. "You know," John had said, "once at their place, when I was getting out stuff for lunch and making coffee, she appeared without makeup. She looked just fine."

At Christmastime in 2003, Hannah took a train up from DC, where she then lived, to be with us in Princeton, and Reid brought Louise to visit. After hearing Louise repeatedly curse Reid, however, Hannah warned him, "Do not marry that woman."

"Where'd he find her?" Hannah asked us after they'd left.

"I think Claude introduced them," I replied. Reid had told me his father had met her in a checkout line at Walmart and had somehow taken her to meet Reid.

"It figures," John said.

Louise got pregnant, perhaps on that visit, and their baby boy was born on 24 August 2004. I spent time with them afterwards down in Virginia trying to help, washing clothes, cooking and laying in supplies, feeding and bathing the baby. After about ten days of what seemed like exile, I could hear Louise regressing from a sweet early-mothering stage into her former complaining-at-Reid stage. I wanted to go home.

When Reid put me on the early morning train out of Lynchburg, I asked him how he thought he could manage. "I just have to hang in for another eighteen years," he replied. As the train clicked along through beautiful Virginia woodlands, I dozed off but woke to recall Reid's last heartbreaking words. It seemed that Louise was incapable of doing much except primping or complaining and cursing. My dear son had survived so much childhood trauma, it seemed unfair for him to be subjected to adult trauma. Still, the baby was precious and seemed precocious and, as a characteristic gap between his big toe and his other toes proved, he was clearly Reid's child. He became Reid Jr.

When I got off the Amtrak in Trenton, I fell into John's arms. "Just please hold me tight." After he started the drive back to Princeton, I said, once again, "Thank you for being you!"

After the birth of Reid Jr., John and I made more frequent trips to southwest Virginia. Ann Goette and her second husband, Rick Claus, built a spectacular house over a bend in the New River. I loved to relax there behind glass windows that replicated the curve of the bluff on the opposite side of the river. Once, when little Reid was about four, John and I had a good visit with him and then left to spend a night at Ann and Rick's. Then we came back for another night or two at Reid's house, but the little one was no longer glad to sit on my lap for a story. He seemed mad at us. I concluded that he could understand our leaving for a faraway home, but leaving him to stay with nearby friends seemed like a betrayal. Or maybe I'd just wanted to believe that he cared.

For several years, John and I took our extended (albeit small) family to a beautiful beach house near Mathews, Virginia. In the mornings, little Reid wouldn't speak to me or anyone else except his dad for hours. Once when Barbara and Weldon Thornton joined us for a few days at the beach, Barbara observed the little one's behavior and hugged me, saying, "I'm so sorry." On one of our visits down to Blacksburg, Reid took John and me and Reid Jr. to look at some river property. Driving back, the small one began singing about hanging granny from a tree, seeming to think it was funny. I was horrified. He must have gotten such nasty ideas from his mother, whose idea of humor seemed still to date from middle school. "Okay, we're out of here." John said, but the backseat of Reid's SUV was hardly a place to make an exit. John and I spent the night in Reid's office/guest room and left the next morning.

I think that was the beginning of a turnaround in Reid's relationship with his son. He of course had made the little boy apologize to me, but he realized that Louise's meanness and negative feelings could transfer to their son if he didn't intervene. Reid began counseling kindness. His gentleness became a transformative, positive influence on little Reid, to my great relief and pleasure, for I did not want to see my grandson grow into a bitter, negative adult.

John and I planned to make Christmas 2014, with Reid's cooperation, a special time. Like tour guides, we energetically threw ourselves into arranging trips, buying tickets, gathering information, and cooking. Reid and his family arrived sometime in the early hours of Monday, 22 December. We had left the door unlocked and had tried to sleep, but I woke with every creaking floorboard or rustling branch above our roof. Reid chose to drive through the night, getting to Princeton as the sun was rising. When we woke I found my son his usual affectionate but laconic self, his well-trimmed beard almost half gray. Little Reid had grown several inches since we'd seen him last. "I bet you're almost as tall as our neighbor C. J., who's three years older than you," I told him. We went across the street to meet C. J. and his little brother, but Reid Jr. would not stay with them, so I entertained him while his parents slept. I couldn't nap because I had to prepare the evening dinner, featuring boeuf en daube (which I'd started long ahead of time) and ending with fruitcake and lemon squares. As usual, John set the table and helped in the kitchen.

We tried to engage everyone in conversation at cocktail time, an endeavor that worked well enough with the guys while Louise sat like a mannequin before retreating to bed again. At dinner, while John and I ate sparingly, all three of them ate ravenously then vanished while John and I cleaned up. By then exhausted and irritated, I went upstairs to change from my tight new jeans into comfortable pajamas and a robe. I hoisted myself up onto our antique bed but the force that should have wiggled me out of the jeans instead propelled me off the bed. My cheekbone hit the corner of the stool that gave Maggie a step up onto the bed. It wasn't a big blow, but soon I had a very big black eye.

The next day, John and I drove Reid and his family to the "Dinky," the Princeton train that connects with trains into New York City. We'd bought their tickets and given them maps, schedules, and tips on what to do in the city. Then John and I went to the grocery, where we ran into our friend Mary, who asked what happened to my eye. I said, with minimal truthfulness, that I'd lost my balance and hit my cheek on the corner of a piece of furniture. When we went to the liquor store and John was gathering wine bottles, the female clerk told me, "I hope you gave him as good as you got"—a statement I could not reconcile with my dear and always gentle husband. Other people made similar remarks, making me wonder what their lives are like, if they assumed that men and women, husbands and wives, have fist fights or regularly knock each other about on the face.

After the grocery and liquor stores, John and I found solace in bed, where we pleasured each other as we'd been doing for forty years. After our sexual respite from our houseguests, we both slept soundly and contentedly. On waking, John called Walmart's photo operation. Weeks earlier, his cousin Mary Jane, whom he hadn't seen in sixty years, had resurfaced with film of their families taken in the 1940s. Getting old celluloid film digitized for modern machines is no easy matter. Photography studios don't do it, our local computer guru doesn't do it, the university doesn't do it, but Walmart does. John had taken the film there in November. When he called on 23 December, he was told that there had been further delays in the customarily slow process and resigned himself to a continued wait.

We also took a scholarly respite from our guests, getting back to our computers and books. John had devoted his scholarly life to the poetry of Jonathan Swift, that great defender of human liberty and of the Church of Ireland, and that work continued into our retirement. When his revised 1968 dissertation was published as *On Swift's Poetry* in 1978, John had created controversy by demonstrating that Swift, Dean of St. Patrick's Cathedral, really intended the Christian implications in his poems. In December 2014, I was trying to write an historical novel set in post-Revolutionary War Virginia. John and I spent half a day writing in the independent but mutually supportive manner we'd perfected over forty years. When I came down from my study, he looked up from the dining room table where Maggie-the-Cat was sitting on his notes. I listened as he read a passage he'd just finished. John wrote that Swift made Esther Johnson into "a moral exemplar; thus, he placed the woman herself beyond our ken. Centrally, he occludes the most important relationship of her life, her attachment to him."

"That sounds perfect," I responded. "Can I heat your coffee?"

"I'm fine, but how about your novel?" John had remarked earlier that I couldn't set my novel in the early South and skirt the issue of slavery. I had taken my plantation owner's family from historical records, including some from my family. And I had invented a slave protagonist, an "octoroon," only one-eighth black, who could "pass" for white. Her mixed-race heritage was part of my story, but I had largely failed to put the horrors of slavery on center stage. I needed to invent new characters and a new plot—not that I had much of one as it was. At any rate, I had nothing to read to John.

"I'm sure you'll invent something wise and telling," he said encouragingly. "Let me read it whenever you want."

Our sweet day of love and writing fortified us for the return of Reid's family on Christmas Eve, when Hannah, with her husband Michael Pinck, also joined us. In 2009, Hannah had converted to Judaism and married Michael. For their wedding, during the Cherry Blossom and kite festivals in DC, Fischer relatives, Reid relatives, Hannah's college friends, our Princeton and Virginia friends, and Reid, little Reid, and Louise all traveled to DC, where the wedding was held in the Arts Club. During the ceremony, four-year-old Reid dangled upside down from the back of his chair, almost upsetting the chair and shedding the jacket of his little seersucker suit. Later, we were nearly as disruptive as he, dancing on and on to an assortment of songs, from Cajun and Jewish folk tunes to classics like "Dance Me to the End of Love." Hannah and Michael were radiant, as was John, especially as he danced with Hannah.

As I've suggested, John and I had such a complicated religious history that Hannah's conversion seemed unsurprising. In 1981, when Hannah was three, John had converted to Christianity. With our friend Herb Rothschild (himself a convert from Judaism to Christianity) as godfather to them both, John and Hannah were baptized together, to the distress of his parents and the gratification of my widowed mother. I felt I grew up over-churched, and Michael's family seemed at first to Hannah to be over-synagogued. They have large family gatherings for all the Jewish holidays and attend, it seems, every family Bat or Bar Mitzvah and wedding, even those in the far West. At first Hannah was fairly skeptical, describing the activities in the Pinck house during the High Holy Days as cooking, eating, praying, and cleaning up, then beginning the cycle of cooking, eating, praying, and cleaning up all over again, but soon she came to cherish these rituals, as did John and I.

We first met Michael's parents, Ed and Linda Pinck, one day in New York City for brunch and an afternoon in the Museum of Arts and Design, an outing engineered by Hannah. John was abashed to realize that, when he ordered eggs Benedict, he hadn't thought about the ham. He was relieved to find that though the Pincks keep Kosher, they couldn't care less about a slice of ham under an egg at their table. Soon we began going each year to their home on Long Island for Seder, which Linda made into an elaborate feast for twenty or so. Michael usually presided at the services, sometimes with the help of his sister Marleen and also of John. I recall that at the first Seder we attended, Linda gave a prayer of thanks for Hannah. We expressed similar gratitude for Michael and for their happiness together.

Michael's Aunt Phyllis, Linda's older sister, whom we met at several Seders, assumed that because John knew the Jewish rituals so well he was still a practicing Jew. When she learned that he had converted to Christianity, she concluded that I was responsible. Actually, John's deeply felt faith had brought *me* back to the church. John and I drove into the city for Phyllis's funeral, glad to see the synagogue packed with mourners and to hear testimony about Aunt Phyllis's work with educating the city's underprivileged. Going to Seders and to the Bat or Bar Mitzvahs for Michael's nieces and nephew deepened my understanding and appreciation of Judaism, so our family melded two religious traditions.

On Christmas Eve 2014, with Reid's family and Hannah and Michael, we attended the candlelight service at Princeton University Chapel. There a spotlight illuminated a many-pointed star above us. As people passed flames from candle to candle at the close of the service, they sang "Silent Night" and "Joy to the World" while the Chapel's massive organ sent booming reverberations throughout the Gothic building. John and I fled from the Chapel's back door to walk briskly to the car in the darkness and get home in time to heat the dinner of leftover beef, plus fish for Michael, who, unlike Hannah, keeps kosher. Even Michael agreed that the Princeton Christian service was literally awesome, especially the music.

Late the next morning, we opened terrific Chanukah and Christmas presents, which had been supplemented by gifts from Reid and Louise. We gave a chess set in its own wooden case to little Reid. I'd bought walking sticks for me from "Santa." In the early afternoon, we enjoyed another holiday feast, this one from our grocery's catering department. As John started to dismantle the McCaffery's cardboard box, big enough for two dinners, I stopped him. "We might need it for packing," I explained.

He knitted his brow and smiled at me quizzically. "Are you really scheming to move South?" I just smiled back.

As Hannah and I were putting food in the fridge and plates in the dishwasher and cleaning kitchen counters, we giggled to hear John in the brightly lit dining room singing under his breath the Tom Lehrer song about a maid who killed her entire family but doesn't lie about it to the police because "lying she knew was a sin, a sin." The song covertly expressed John's irritation with guests who spilled food on the floor and then left the cleanup for us. Later that afternoon, John and I took the others to the Princeton University boathouse. John guided us up and down the boathouse stairs and out onto the sunny launching platform, telling stories about his brother's career as an MIT coxswain. Reid Jr. was entranced by the elongated racing shells until a coach told him if he wanted to be a coxswain, he'd better stop growing.

On the day after Christmas, we took two cars into North Jersey, where we caught ferries to Ellis Island and then the Statue of Liberty. On the walk back, Reid and his mother started pinching each other. "Hey, cut it out," John growled.

"She started it," complained Reid.

"No, he did," whined Louise, sounding more like his teenage sister than his mother. In the car, John and I tried to enlist little Reid in civil conversations.

Back in Princeton, Hannah confided in me, "I can't bear to see Dad sweeping that floor again," so we all dined at a nearby Indian restaurant.

The next day we took all three cars to Grounds for Sculpture, where peacocks left warming huts to bask in the sun. John had to rescue me from tripping over my new walking sticks, which we returned to the car. Reid Jr. giggled at the enormous statues, including a giant version of Matisse's *Dance* depicting nudes dancing on a hilltop. We waved good-bye to the "chillun," as I call my son and daughter, as they left the sculpture park for I-95 and their drives home, an especially long one for Reid. I stroked John's short salt-and-pepper beard, thanking him for his kindness to the chillun.

Despite how nice it had been to be with family, it was lovely to be healthy and now alone together in the bright December sunshine! For New Year's Eve, we simply walked next door where our neighbors provided a feast for ten or so seventy-somethings, who seemed to think that we were younger than they. In the early New Year, John and I walked around our neighborhood and once by the fast-flowing Delaware River. Chilly gusts of wind blew up from the river caressing us like ocean breezes—not so warm, but not cold either. Lawn furniture still sat in gazebos on the riverbank. People walking dogs wore only light jackets. I tucked my hair into my knit cap as we walked in the middle of Titusville's River Road, opposite the Pennsylvania base for Washington's river-crossing. "Let's walk as far as Miss Emily's house," I suggested. It had been in serious disrepair when we first saw it, peeling paint, shutters hanging off, a fallen-in porch, a broken window upstairs. Since then the owners had redone it. We knew they did it themselves, because we'd seen them at it and complimented them over the years as we'd walked along. By the beginning of 2015, it was a charming frame house of three stories in shades of cream and mauve with a handsome mansard roof and a lovely little cupola on top.

"When we first came here, it seemed like Miss Emily Grierson's house in 'A Rose for Emily.' Creepy to imagine her sleeping with the remains of her lover in a top room, maybe like that little cupola," I said.

"Good thing you didn't tell the owners that story when we first saw them with their sandpaper and paint brushes. Very pretty now. Let's get some lunch."

I was not ready to move on. "John," I'd said, touching his arm, "we've been here long enough to see this old house totally revitalized."

He put his hand over mine and smiled. "True. But I'm not ready to leave yet."

"I guess I just get restless. But if you're not leaving, neither am I. Still, you should put on your gloves."

Over lunch, as we watched cars and a few larger vehicles navigate the narrow bridge over the Delaware, we talked about politics, the chillun, and our writing. The balmy close of 2014 and start of 2015 seemed an emblem of the extraordinary health and happiness that we had enjoyed together since 1975 and in New Jersey since 2001. Other than Louise's meanness to my son and curious mothering of my grandson, John and I had nothing to worry about. We too had been revitalized. We were happy. We felt invincible.

We were not.

5

WARNINGS

On 10 January 2015, in suddenly frigid weather (the temperature was around 7 degrees Fahrenheit), John drove out Route 1 to the giant Walmart there. Even on that blustery cold day, the store was full of shoppers returning gifts and looking for further bargains. John was not shopping. The reproduction department had finally called in the late morning to say that John's disk, remade from Mary Jane's film, was ready. John was eager to again see his grandparents, parents, brother, cousins, and of course the little boy that he'd been in the 1940s, so he'd rushed out, braving cold and traffic. He picked up the old film and the new DVD and put them safe in a Walmart bag—but unbeknownst to him, he wasn't safe.

At home, I was wondering why, though the big box stores are outside central Princeton, John took so very long getting home. Then, just when I was getting worried, I heard the garage door crank itself open. John stumbled into the kitchen, rasping. He collapsed at the kitchen table, still bundled in his barn coat and muffler. John had hardly any eyebrows, one reason his eyes always looked so penetrating. That day, his eyes darted back and forth, as if threatened. He did not talk until a cup of hot tea with honey thawed out his throat.

"What happened?" I asked, putting a piece of chocolate beside his teacup.

"Cold stabbed me like a dagger. Oh, Panthea, I feared I'd faint in the freezing wind."

I reached to touch his hand across the table. "That sounds dreadful, dear."

"Felt spasms in my chest. Couldn't even think where I'd parked the car. Had to hold onto one of those cage things where you leave shopping carts till I could think what to do. Took me a minute to remember the red button on my key. You know what it's called?"

I didn't.

"It's a panic button, just what I needed then. Heard the horn tooting, over a few lanes and at least halfway out from the store on what looked like frozen tundra. I must have looked a drunkard holding onto car after car until I could get to ours. Practically fell into it. Turned up the heat to 85 degrees. Sat there until my lungs quit quivering."

"You poor dear. Is it warm enough in here?"

"Sure. Remember Swift's 'Verses on the Death of Dr. Swift'? Once I could breathe again, I had a giggle thinking there are plenty of people who'd rather I didn't make it."

"People I suppose whom you've criticized in those reviews that everybody reads. And by everybody I mean every Swift scholar. What are those lines about wishing rivals to hell?"

He recited from memory:

"I've had them by heart most of my life.
'What poet would not grieve to see,
His Brethren write as well as he?
But rather than they should excel,
He'd wish his Rivals all in Hell.'"

"Well, you're not going to hell, whatever your rivals want. Just please stay out of this horrid cold," I said.

Our post-fifty-five friends' group, CWW (Community Without Walls), encourages aging at home and fosters informative meetings and friendly subgroups. Our friends Lynn and Mary had started a new one called a Get-Away Club for excursions to interesting out-of-town restaurants. January was too cold to get away, so Mary invited the club for dinner at her gracious town house that evening. Lynn brought appetizers, while Mary cooked coq au vin. John and I brought wine and jars of the cranberry-orange-date relish I used to make each holiday season. Over dinner, everyone complained about the cold, ice-coated tree branches breaking, tanks of heating oil perilously close to empty. I said that on returning from the grocery, I actually stuck my hands in the toaster oven along with our sandwich to thaw out my nearly frozen fingers. One friend told of a neighbor who walked to her mailbox and fell on the ice. Floundering on her back, unable to right herself, she had used an almost forgotten backstroke to paddle herself up the icy driveway until she could grab a porch railing, pull herself up, get inside, and call 911.

"Didn't somebody see her and come to help?" Lynn asked.

"Apparently not. Everyone else was inside, scared of the cold."

"That's quite a shiner you have," Bill remarked, looking at my eye.

Hoping to explain my black eye truthfully and to amuse the others around the table, I told about Reid and his family's recent visit. I said the lemon squares I made from Mary's recipe were so delicious Louise ate about a dozen, leaving only two or three for all the rest of us. No doubt my irritation, combined with too much wine, had later caused me to slip off the edge of the bed and hit my cheek on the stool beside it. I confessed that when we'd seen Mary at the grocery store the next day, we'd bought, among other things, more lemon squares. Later

Hannah said she'd heard Louise complaining to Reid that I'd hidden my homemade lemon squares from her and substituted mere store-bought ones. Hannah had also heard Louise complaining that at Grounds for Sculpture I'd exposed Reid Jr. to statues of nude women. I remarked to our friends that those nudes were too huge to hide. We'd also learned that, despite the many suggestions John and I had carefully set out of places and activities young Reid would enjoy in Manhattan, they'd only gotten to the top of the Empire State Building. The Reids had sat outside Rockefeller Center for ages while Louise shopped for perfume.

"Does he ever think about finding a more considerate partner?" someone asked.

"I doubt it." I took a swig of chardonnay before explaining. "He suffered through some pretty traumatic custody battles when I left his dad. He wouldn't want to put the little guy through anything like what we put him through."

As we moved from the table, someone mentioned the recent Paris massacre of the *Charlie Hebdo* staff, an attack on free speech that especially resonated with John. He remarked, "Swift's publishers could get prison sentences or lose their ears for printing his political satires. Three hundred years later, a whole staff got massacred for printing satiric cartoons."

"Running a kosher grocery store seems pretty risky too," Bill remarked.

With everyone settled in Mary's living room, our discussion of risks and of terrorism continued. As we drank coffee or wine, the discussion somehow turned to *Antony and Cleopatra*, a production of which most of us had seen in the fall at McCarter Theatre.

John said that that play once had saved his life.

That silenced everyone until Ilse asked, "How could a play save your life?"

John explained that over twenty years before, in Baton Rouge, he had suffered a spell of terrible fatigue. Though he looked gray, he didn't want to see a doctor.

I admitted that I'd been too preoccupied over meeting some writing deadline to take John's sallow skin seriously, too willing to believe his testimony that he was fine.

Then one day, seeing his ashen face in a mirror as he shaved, John explained how he actually heard Shakespeare's words echoing in his brain. He paraphrased them as: "'How dost my lord?' 'Dying, Egypt, dying.'" That echo, welling up from his subconscious, had compelled him to go to a doctor.

I recalled that he'd stopped on the way to call and ask how to get on I-10 and find the office. I'd thought it strange that he didn't remember.

"Well, I did get to the clinic door, but I collapsed there," John explained. "Fortunately the hospital was next door. Medics wheeled me over. Found I had little blood pressure at all."

"My Lord," someone said. "Yet you were carrying on, almost literally bloodless?"

"Almost. Had a bleed in the lining of my stomach. The doctors were at a loss to explain it. Then I told them about having a bleb bursting in my lungs years before. That provided them with the theory that I had a similar bursting bleb in my stomach lining."

As I sipped my wine, I told our friends that when I'd gotten a call from a nurse, I'd sped there, pausing only to call the parents of a friend Hannah was visiting. They rushed Hannah immediately to the hospital. "It's hard to imagine a chubby thirteen-year-old, as she was then, actually shaking with fear over seeing her dad at risk, but she was."

John told how the still-mystified doctors at last found a textbook explanation. They'd declared that John had Dieulafoy's syndrome, a condition where lesions form on different parts of the digestive tract and can hemorrhage at any time. Then they'd told him there was no cure.

I explained that John's near-death experience had hit Hannah especially hard. She was shocked to see her dad in a hospital bed. As he recovered, he told us, "The docs said I should never leave first-world medicine in case I have another bad bleed."

"What is first-world medicine?"

John had explained and then said to Hannah, "Sorry, sweetie, but I guess we'll have to cancel our African safari."

She was one of few childhood contributors to the World Wildlife Fund and had always longed to go on an African safari. It would have been very expensive, but John and I had promised to take her someday.

I remarked that probably third-world doctors could do as well pumping in blood as first-world docs did. Still, it had been too big a chance to take, so we'd reneged on that major promise to Hannah.

"Hannah, God bless her, understood, and never complained," John told our friends with pride.

He'd never experienced another flare-up of Dieulafoy's syndrome, and we'd almost forgotten about it, along with the spontaneous pneumothorax implosion of nearly a half a century before.

Our friends shuddered over John's strangely literary death warning. But John did not mention his trauma in the Walmart parking lot that very afternoon. It too had offered a warning, but he had seemed to ignore the message, which might have echoed, "Dying, Panthea, dying."

I had many fond memories of sledding during my childhood in Kentucky. During my young adulthood in North Carolina and Virginia and then in our first years in New Jersey, I had relished beautiful fresh snow and its crunch beneath my boots. This snow was different. It first had indeed been beauteous, blanketing the landscape in dazzling white, looking like a giant meringue sprinkled with sugar. But it would not quit falling. Winter seemed to be taking retribution on the gods who had treated us to that balmy late December and early January. Princeton declared a state of emergency. In one day, we had sixteen inches of snow with winds at thirty-five miles an hour. Trash pick-up and other basic services were postponed, though oil delivery trucks somehow got through to desperate households. John fretted about not being able to shovel snow in such weather. I said to wait until it melted, if it ever did. John hired a man to shovel the snow into tracks our car tires could follow. But more snow fell, covering the cleared paths and making the drive even more treacherous, with icy belts, like flattened trolls under a bridge, hiding beneath powdery fresh snow to sabotage our car.

Then three children knocked on our door offering to reshovel the driveway. (That was the first time in our nearly fourteen years in privileged Princeton that neighborhood children sought to earn money by working.) We hired the teens and their little sister of eight or so. All wore caps, mittens, and layers of clothes and worked very hard. I served them cups of hot tea with honey, which they downed gratefully with cookies before their father appeared with a snow blower to finish the job for them. Their mother sent us a homemade breakfast cake as a thank-you.

Unable to go outside, John and I made the best of confinement, reading, writing, listening to music, making love slowly, gently. John sometimes played our favorite songs, which he'd downloaded on our sound system from iTunes: Duke Ellington at the Newport Jazz Festival, Peggy Lee singing "You give me fever," or Johnny and June Carter Cash singing, "If I Were a Carpenter," with her lines "If I were a lady," rhyming with "have your baby." Formerly, we'd both danced to such songs, until John would sit and watch with those sexy penetrating eyes as I threw my arms above my head like someone at a gospel sing. In January John no longer danced. Soon bad coughs got both of us down. I too quit dancing.

On 19 January, I drove us to see our primary care physician. Out on Route 1, blocks of snow were flying off tops of trucks, making explosive noises as they hit the asphalt. "It's just snow, which is just harmless flaked water," I remarked.

"Yeah," John said. "Remember the *Titanic*."

While we waited to see our doctor, John began singing in a whisper the children's song: "Here we sit like birds in the wilderness." In Virginia, we'd often extemporized on it after picking up little Reid from kindergarten when stuck in traffic. Instead of "Waiting for our food," we'd sing "waiting for ice cream," or "to be fed," or "for a green light," or "to be loved." In the clinic, as John subsided in coughs, I finished the song quietly, "waiting to be seen."

When she finally saw him, our doctor told John that his lungs were in decent condition, with only mild emphysema. Oddly, she prescribed Azithromycin to help clear my lung congestion, but nothing except a pocket inhaler for him. Later, he told me he'd asked her how long he might live and of what he'd die. She said he'd probably die in five or more years of heart disease. He had no heart problems then, but his father and aunts and uncles on both sides of his family had died of heart troubles. She figured such troubles would take him down too, if his gut problems didn't get him first. I was shocked when he told me that he'd asked her about death. My cough sounded as bad as his, but I wasn't thinking about dying. He was such a healthy man, except for acid reflux, which could ruin his pleasure in food, and irritable bowel disease (IBD), which kept him too long in the bathroom—neither condition terribly grave.

Still, that John asked about dying suggests that he had taken that Walmart parking lot warning more seriously than I had realized.

On 3 February, the troublesome gut problems sent John, after a weekend of fasting and clearing his bowels, to ambulatory surgery for a colonoscopy and endoscopy. Afterwards, in the waiting room, the gastroenterologist told me John's colon was fine but his esophagus was "a mess." When I asked what that meant, he said, "All clogged up." By that time, John's cough was much worse than mine. Sometimes it stole his breath away, inside the house as well as outside in the cold. The GI doc was convinced that food particles were escaping his clogged esophagus and infiltrating his lungs. Perhaps feeling simpatico, Maggie-the-Cat stopped eating.

Writing now of these painful developments reminds me of how much the doctors stuck to their theories, willy-nilly. I became the driver, next taking John back to our primary care doctor. Though she'd only seen mild emphysema three weeks before, by 9 February she referred him to her medical group's pulmonologist. Then John fasted again, this time to take a swallowing test. When he did, on 11 February, the barium he swallowed began slipping into his lungs, until the radiologist yelled, "Stop!" That doctor concluded that John had pneumonia. John called me, and I left my weekly Pilates class in a rush to pick him up. "You needn't have done that," he insisted, "you need the exercises for your back." I thought I needed to get him to the clinic right away, but our doctors thought he could wait to see the GI doctor the next day, as scheduled. That doctor dismissed the pneumonia hypothesis, being ever more convinced that aspirating food from his esophagus into his lungs was all that made John cough.

Our Get-Away Club next met on Valentine's Day, this time at Lynn's. As we settled in the living room, Mary mentioned that she'd just seen *The Winter's Tale* at the Pearl Theatre in New York.

"'Tis the season," Bill remarked.

Another member of the group said, "That's the play with so many switching names, I never could keep straight who is really who."

"But," John said, "it's so moving when the statue of Hermione comes to life …"

"I still don't think it's a very good play."

John disagreed. "That ending offers a lovely story of redemption and forgiveness."

Mary told us that she first had seen *The Winter's Tale* at the Brooklyn Academy of Music, shortly after her husband's death. The play had left her and her daughter convulsed in sobs.

"Yes," John said. "It's really about the power of love." John asked Mary about her husband, whom he'd never met. Mary worried about John's cough, but he laughed it off, saying a cough in his seventies was just what he got for smoking in his teens.

We'd both had bad coughs before. John's didn't seem much different from his previous coughs. I laughed as we carefully skirted the ice on Lynn's back patio and around her fence. Safely in our car, I patted his thigh. "Maybe the power of love can cure your cough!"

John smiled and started the engine. "I wouldn't bet on it."

There apparently was a more scientific cure. If he was aspirating into his lungs, a clogged esophagus was easy to fix by just opening, stretching, and cleaning the passageway. It was true that John had felt a severe lung palpitation in the Walmart parking lot, but he'd told the doctors about that and they hadn't seemed especially worried. Their lack of concern should have signaled to John and me that it was time to look for new doctors and second opinions, but we were not heeding warnings.

We were, I later realized, in denial.

6

UNTIL MY HUSBAND RECOVERS

Driving to the clinic, I remarked how the transportation department had sliced the embankments of snow along the edges of Route 1, leaving it looking as if a giant knife had simply lopped off the side of a snow cake. The sliced-off banks of snow now looked less like a cake and more like the concrete boulders imported for road construction, except these snow boulders were filthy, yellowed with early age, gray with soot and fumes.

"Where do they take the snow they cut away?" John asked. "They can't dump it in Carnegie Lake or the Delaware River."

"It would just sit on top of the ice, since it's too cold for anything to melt."

I could name any number of literary heroes who'd left for Italy, Aix-en-Provence, or Taos to escape the chill clammy air of England. I felt that we likewise must escape the frozen, clammy air of Princeton. Hot sunshine on our chests should cure our coughs if we decamped— the sooner the better. For us, Charleston, Savannah, or St. Augustine would do. I had contacted a former student who invited us to visit and advised us about hotels and B&Bs near Charleston. I'd also made hotel reservations as far south as Savannah. When we told the GI doctor that we were going South, however, he advised against leaving Princeton, as if his care were essential to John's recovery or as if Charleston were in a third-world country. He ordered another breathing and swallowing test, which prevented our leaving. It showed little aspiration; still that doc did not revise his diagnosis. Driving home, I thought that the snow boulders looked like miniature Cliffs of Dover, only dirtier.

Months later, I found a note John had written to our primary care doctor and the GI doctor on 16 February. He said he gathered that they both thought his shortness of breath and acid reflux were "structurally related." He went on: "I may be losing ground against my ailments. Just two minutes out of doors yesterday left me gasping for air, and I continue to lose weight. Nevertheless, with your help, I mean to learn what is wrong with me and to overcome it." Then he added, "Are there other tests that I should undergo?"

I found it because John did not send it.

Maybe he didn't send it because on 17 February, for the first time, John saw Dr. G., the pulmonologist associated with the practice. In cahoots with the GI guy, Dr. G. said that John coughed because he was aspirating food into his lungs. He prescribed a new inhaler. I suppose John took Dr. G.'s word as authoritative and so dropped the idea of having more tests. In retrospect, I think certainly by then we should have found new doctors who would diagnose John's shortness of breath as a lung problem, not acid reflux or a stopped-up esophagus.

After the first appointment with Dr. G., as I was driving us home, John said he wanted to gas up the car and have it washed and waxed. Our Honda has a strong heater, so I agreed that he might drive for a change, if he stayed inside and forgot his usual routine of getting out and paying for the gas, pumped in New Jersey by a service attendant.

John always got out to thank the attendant for pumping the gas, but on this day, he promised to stay inside and just pass his credit card through the window.

When we got home, I buzzed open the automatic garage door and left the car to John. Once inside, I watched him circle the car, holding on to it lest he slip on ice, then lower himself into the driver's seat. I saw him drive off. After some time, John called to say something dreadful had happened. I nearly panicked thinking he'd been taken to the hospital. Instead, he said his wallet had been stolen, but he couldn't talk and hung up. His next call telling me not to worry only made things worse, but I didn't know what to do. When he finally got back to the house and recovered his breath, he told a remarkable story about picking up a hitchhiker who rewarded him by stealing his wallet. John said he offered $100 to get the wallet back to which the guy offered him a blow job.

"He what?" I exclaimed. "That's a story I couldn't have invented."

"Well, it happened." It was already dark on that gloomy February afternoon. John changed the subject. "Isn't it cocktail time? I'll have a bourbon with a square of dark chocolate."

I poured drinks for us both and then called, "Maggie, cocktail time." She appeared quickly in the kitchen, anxious for treats too.

I asked John if he minded if I wrote up his hitchhiker story. "It's all yours," he replied, so I wrote up and then fiddled with the narrative as John had told it to me.

On 23 and 24 February John saw both specialists, who still insisted that John's problem was aspiration. Dr. G. shook his head again and again, saying that people with COPD usually have a steady decline over the course of years. He used his hand to illustrate a slow downward decline. Then his hand dropped suddenly as he said that John had "fallen off a cliff," which he didn't understand. Though our primary care doctor had only seen mild emphysema in January, Dr. G. saw COPD as the one and only instigator of John's fall off some cliff. Dr. G. had a daughter studying English in graduate school, and he and John had chatted several times about English studies. As a result, John grew rather fond of Dr. G.

On the first day of March, John gave up chocolate and bourbon and everything else to fast for yet another procedure, back in ambulatory surgery, this time to stretch his esophagus, a procedure that the GI doctor believed would solve the aspiration problem and hence ensure John's recovery. We tried to be as hopeful as the gastroenterologist. Three days later, Dr. G. put John on Prednisone, a powerful steroid for treating a variety of diseases, especially those involving inflammation. In John's case, the swelling could have been in the esophagus or the bronchial tubes or the lungs. Thanks to the surgical procedure, his esophagus was no longer clogged up, so he should have stopped coughing, but he didn't. Thus the swelling must have been in the bronchial tubes or lungs, or both. He was to take 60 milligrams of Prednisone a day at first and rapidly decrease the dosage. On 4 March, I saw a new doctor, in the same group, who listened to my cough and ordered a chest X-ray for me.

The sky remained mostly gray. The ground was frozen. No birds chirped. It was too cold to go outside, except for trips to doctors and the grocery. The snow was ever more filthy and gray, but still it wouldn't melt. My friend Leslie drove over, though she lives only a block away, on some late afternoons. Owner of two cats, she knew how to talk to Maggie, curled by the front door on a pallet beside the furnace register. If I turned on the gas fire in the living room and called Maggie, she actually joined us a few times, curling up on the fireplace pallet. After Leslie and I had discussed Rutgers University Press, where she was senior literary editor, and various literary magazines, John would sometimes join us as Leslie speculated about the next year's presidential election. John mostly listened, but he did remark how he'd never before seen

Maggie not intimidated by a stranger.

"I think she puts up with me, as I'm harmless enough," Leslie commented. "She just wants to sit on that pallet in its green pillowcase by that nice warm fire."

John was not working on Swift. Detailed scholarly work tired him, so he'd begun reading Sir Walter Scott's *Waverley*. When John recorded schedules for doctors' visits or pill regiments in our Smithsonian appointment book, he did so with a shaky hand. Mine is wobbly too, as the result of arthritis, so I drew no conclusions. I later realized, though, that John's shaky handwriting must have signified a somewhat depleted oxygen supply.

I had completed my version of the hitchhiker story and gave it to John. He thought it was good enough, but he still treated it like his story.

"I never threatened him with the police."

"But it's my story now. It's fiction," I retorted.

"Still it was mine first," he reminded me. "I wouldn't have threatened him."

I realized that for John this experience had been a morality play, in which not a fear of arrest but rather an awakened soul prompts the guy to regret the theft. The short story form allowed me to adopt John's perspective, but fiction could hardly improve on what really happened, so I cut out most of my additions to his story. While I worked away in my upstairs study, John sat below me at the dining room table reading Scott, who long ago had himself edited Swift.

I now wonder if my absorption in writing up the hitchhiker story paralleled my absorption twenty-plus years earlier when I hadn't taken John's ashen color seriously, the only thing prompting him to get to the doctor the lines from *Antony and Cleopatra* that warned him he was in real danger.

Like his doctors, I downplayed or overlooked the warnings of 2015.

Icy snow and sleet continued to plague us. We asked a computer fix-it man to make a house call, as it was too cold and our equipment was too heavy for John to haul it to the shop. At dinner a short drive away with another couple one evening, the other guy complained about expensive haircuts, and our hostess said hers cost nothing since she cut her own hair, as she'd done for her kids. "It's easy," she said, "when something sticks out, I just chop it off."

In a deadpan voice, John remarked, "I'm sorry to hear that," sending me and the other guy into peals of laughter. Such quick, vaguely naughty wit was typical of John, even that winter. To another friend he seemed "ebullient."

Sometimes he fooled me. He did seem in dire straits in the mornings. He made an elaborate chart, wheezing all the while, with medications listed across the top of the page, the days of the week down the side. He'd line up his pills in regimental order and manfully swallow them, slowly. He wouldn't eat or drink anything but water until he'd gotten them down. He explained acid reflux: "when cold water comes down, acid comes up." In his increasingly shaky hand, he'd mark each time he took each pill each day. Occasionally he'd say something like, "This is the end." Or, "I'm doomed." Or, "I can't go on like this." The implication was, "I am dying." I reminded him that he always took the pessimistic side of issues. My optimism seemed vindicated in the evenings, when John's vital self reappeared. When Hannah called, he would put the phone on speaker so we both could hear. If it squawked he'd say, "This is the squeaker of the house." He'd argue with newscasters, amusing me with his take on worldly matters. When he heard that Brian Williams had invented personal involvement in a military raid and Hillary Clinton had suppressed her email accounts, John invented a name for them both: "Cliniams."

Back on 15 February 2003, we'd taken the train into New York to participate in an international protest against the expected invasion of Iraq. After hours of walking in the cold, John and I retreated to the Oyster Bar beneath Grand Central Station, where other protesters also ended up. Too exhausted for formalities, we complained between tables about being kept from the UN by the police and about our helplessness to prevent the invasion.

John paused between sips of hot clam chowder to comment, "It's Bill Clinton's fault."

"What?" the people at the next table responded.

"Sure. If Clinton had just resigned after the impeachment, Al Gore would have become president. As an incumbent, he would have easily won re-election in 2000. Then we wouldn't have George W. Bush or this Iraq war." In this, as with so much else, John was astonishingly prescient. Even in the troubled spring of 2015, John retained his foresight and wit. I told him I'd heard that Donald Trump was considering running for president as a Republican, to which John replied, "That blowhard. He only wants publicity for the Trump brand. He'll run not as a Republican but as a joke." My witty guy could extemporize so readily, I couldn't imagine he was truly sick. Probably I suffered from a failure of the imagination.

We had tickets to see a farce called *Baskerville*, a Sherlock Holmes spinoff, at the McCarter Theatre. But John said breathing in the cold was too difficult for us to go out. We had been told that stretching his esophagus would solve his problem, and we had waited, but nothing had improved. Still Dr. G. seemed confident that Prednisone would cure John, so maybe, we thought, his current breathing difficulties were just a temporary setback. Instead, we should have packed up John's records, sent Dr. G. packing, and found another doctor.

Our resilience, however, was being worn down by procedures and promises. I did not know then that John had written, "I mean to learn what is wrong with me and to overcome it" in a note intended for our doctors. I've suggested that he didn't send that note at first because he hoped having his esophagus stretched and taking Prednisone would cure him. By the first week in March, he knew otherwise. Maybe he gave up but didn't tell me. I hadn't quite given up, but after my strategy of escaping to a warm climate had been discredited, I'd probably just gotten too numb to think of a better course of action. I did think to call the theatre and explain that my husband was too sick to see the play on schedule. The receptionist kindly postponed our tickets until, as I told her in a Pollyanna voice, "my husband recovers." For I still fully believed that, in time, he would.

7

THE BEAUTIFUL OLD MAN
AND THE HITCHHIKER

As the temperature finally began to warm, all that dirty snow began melting. Gutters filled up with water cascading down the streets. Drains were clogged with leaves and other debris. Sometimes the sky was blue again. I revised what was now my hitchhiker story. Thinking that no one by then wanted to read about dirty snow, I retitled it "After the Cold." Here it is:

Banks of filthy snow have long since melted, but potholes aren't fixed. Forsythias and tulips bloom, but people are weary. Many are still sick, including my husband.

Back when the temperature was barely above zero, I left him checking out of the pulmonologist's office while I got the car. I was grateful for sea-green crystals, which stuck in my shoe treads but kept me from slipping. I climbed precariously over piled ice, snow, and soot at the end of the parking lot before I could wriggle into the car. When I pulled up at the clinic's front door, John shuffled out, wheezing in the cold. On our way home, after he caught his breath, he produced an inhaler. "If new meds don't fix me, I'm done for."

I suppressed a brief vision of widowhood to ask, "Does this doc know what's wrong?"

"He says COPD. I've had a flare-up, thanks to the cold."

Before long, as I steered around the dirty snow on either side of our driveway, John said he wanted to get the salt washed off the car and gas it up, in case we ever drive South. I suspected he hated being chauffeured and just wanted to drive again. I figured there'd be no harm if he stayed inside the warm car at the gas station. I used the garage opener to get inside, leaving the car's motor and heater running.

From our dining room window, I watched John hold the car to round it before he eased himself inside. He did not drive off. I imagined him adjusting mirrors and arranging, as usual, his cell and wallet, also a tip for the car washers. Or maybe he just paused to catch his breath.

The news was all about snow: over 100 inches in Boston, roofs collapsing, trucks jackknifing, cars stranded, passengers with only snow to eat, people dying of hypothermia, a baby calling for help—some tales of meanness, others of generous, even miraculous, rescues. Cold beyond imagination all over the country, making it easier, I thought, for folks to deny global warming.

Our phone's piercing ring interrupted the news. A mechanical voice announced the familiar numbers of John's cell. He was rasping. "Something dreadful has happened."

I imagined him in an ambulance on the way to the hospital.

"It's not me," he croaked. "My wallet's been stolen. Bye."

I keep my credit cards in my key case, which John had, so I was at a loss to call the card companies. Unsure what to do, I anxiously started a load of laundry, collected trash and recyclables.

Though I'd hoped for it, the next ring with that voice announcing the cell's numbers startled me. "Don't worry," John whispered, "I'm with a very nice young man."

That sounded worse than an ambulance. Did this nice young man have a knife at John's throat? Or a gun to his back? Was John talking as much to him as to me? Perhaps the nice young man would order John to drive to an ATM and withdraw all the money he could, then make him drive to some isolated place, like Trap Rock Quarry, shoot him, bury him in the snow, take our car, keys, and money, and head for Miami or Santa Fe. That was a B-movie scenario, but I couldn't imagine what else John might be doing with a "very nice young man."

Outside the landscape was black and white, dimpled where clean snow had sunk into deer tracks. I wondered what I could tell the police: that my husband was kidnapped in a late model Honda, gray, like millions of others. I dumped the trash in one bin, the recyclables in another. I considered paying bills and doing more chores but decided to call John's cell and try to get him to hint at his assailant's appearance, their location, something to tell the police. When John answered, I said, "First, please do tell me where you all are now."

"Just me. I'm in the kitchen."

I rushed downstairs and there he was, leaning against the counter, where he'd placed my keys. When he'd stopped coughing, he sat and told a remarkable story.

Because the kid wore only sweats against the cold, John picked him up and gave him a lift.

As they drove along, the guy kept looking at John's wedding ring. "You married?"

"Yes."

"You and your wife go to church?"

"Sometimes. How about you?"

"Sure. I pray too."

"Good. Where can I drop you off?" John left him at a shabby office complex on Princeton's oddly named Wall Street.

The guy thanked him and said, "You have a blessed day."

At the Clean Car Wash, John discovered that, though his cell and the singles he'd left out for a tip were still on the console, his wallet was not. He sped back to the complex in time to see the kid just leaving a building. John pulled up right in front of him.

He opened the door and leaned on it. "You!" he cried out. "You stole my wallet." The guy froze, and John advanced a step to the sidewalk's edge. "You betrayed your blessing."

The guy tried to brush past him. "Just words."

John grabbed the fellow by the shoulder of his sweatshirt. "We need to talk."

The guy twisted away. "Musta been somebody else."

John stumbled. This time the guy caught and balanced him. John struggled back toward the car, mindful of treacherous ice. "I can't breathe in this cold." He got in, and so did the guy.

That was when John made that breathless call to me saying he was with a nice young man. When he recovered his breath, John asked the guy, "You got the wallet on you?"

"No, sir."

"It was here," he patted the console, "when I picked you up."

"You better stop leaving your wallet out where anybody can grab it."

"Watch it, son. Once you're in it, the prison system is a trap that won't let you loose."

"You call the cops?"

"Not yet."

"So it's my word against yours."

"Who'd believe you?"

The kid shrugged. "Who was it you told I was a nice guy?"

"My wife."

"You been married long?"

"Twice as long as you've been living. Don't ruin the rest of your life."

The guy shrugged.

"I'll give you $100 to give me back my wallet and save yourself from a wretched life."

The guy pondered, looked sideways at John, then said, "Okay. Drive to that trash bin."

John drove to a black hulk on the edge of the lot. The young man opened his door, and John opened his. Regardless of his knit cap, wool scarf, thick gloves, and a well-padded barn coat, John gasped in the cold as he watched the young man retrace footprints in the snow.

John saw him lean over the bin, retrieve a torn, wet cardboard box, and grab something from inside it. Then he got back in the car.

"Why'd you hide it?"

"Wanted to be 'clean' in case you called the cops." He handed John the billfold. "Now you got a fresh frozen wallet!"

John took it and counted the cash, which was not in the order John had left it but was all there. John counted out five cold twenty-dollar bills. "Get yourself a decent coat. And be well."

The guy pocketed the bills. "Thanks." Then he slid his hand across the console onto John's thigh. He reached for John's crotch. "Want a blow job?"

"No, but thank you," John replied, pushing the guy's hand away. "You'd pleasure me more if you stayed in school, out of trouble."

The fellow nodded. "You're a beautiful old man."

"Next time you say a prayer, pray that you keep out of prison and I keep breathing."

The young man opened the door and paused to say, "Bless your soul. I mean it." He stepped out but leaned back in. "Don't turn a cold eye on others just 'cause of me."

As the man began closing the door, John throatily voiced, "Bless you too."

After John had finished telling me all this, I asked, "Will you ever pick up another hitchhiker?"

He looked up from the kitchen table and grinned. "Sure. I'll hide my wallet though."

I leaned down to kiss my beautiful old man's bald spot.

Amid this spring's news of disasters, manmade and natural, winter's bout with snow now seems tame, remote. But it too caused havoc and also brought out the best in some people.

That was a rather lame ending but all I could manage at the time. John now approved the story. He said the guy had not tried to keep him from falling, but I'd made a good addition. It made the fellow more human, as perhaps the "Want a blow job?" line, though true, did not.

By the time I'd written the last line, forsythias and tulips had begun blooming. Cardinals, goldfinches, and chickadees did not return in their usual numbers. In the previous fall, we'd taken down the bird feeder after flocks of starlings regularly colonized it to gobble up the little birds' food. I'd go out on the deck and yell, "Bad birds," which chased them away only so long as I was outside yelling. John said those starlings were like a motorcycle gang in some sleepy little sheriff-less town. They invaded, stole, and pillaged, and left the town in rubble. Little birds had had to do without our offerings of sunflower seeds, but at least they hadn't had to protect themselves against big black starlings.

I emailed "After the Cold" to the *New York Times*. I heard nothing. I knew that my story wasn't right for the Sunday *Review,* but I wanted to do something with it and had no time to check out suitable magazines. By then no one would have wanted to read about sickness in the past winter anyway.

I thought again of escaping South. "Is it just that you still have some kind of thirteen-year itch?" John asked. I said no, but I still felt that a road trip South might mean leaving sickness in the North. John said a road trip to Savannah or wherever would require too much energy. Besides, Princeton was warming up.

Later I discovered that, on the notepad where I wrote down the email address of the *Times*, I also scribbled down an address for short-term rentals on Wisconsin Avenue, near Georgetown University Hospital. Those notes meant that when I sent the story to the *Times* in March, Hannah was already seriously lobbying for us to move to DC.

Back in graduate school at the University of Texas's School of Information, Hannah had organized a symposium in 2003 on "Information and the War on Terrorism," which John and I had attended with pride. Her symposium readily earned her an internship at the Congressional Research Service of the Library of Congress. After she received her master's degree, the CRS hired her, first as a Presidential Management Fellow and then as a permanent staffer. John and I were delighted to have her move so near to us. In our frequent visits back and forth, we'd gotten to know our daughter as an adult, a special one. In the eleven years she'd lived in the District, Hannah had become an authority on Congress, an expert at mapping world conflicts, and an advocate of most things Washingtonian. In the spring of 2015, that advocacy turned into a campaign for better healthcare for her father. She wanted us to move to DC to be near its best hospital. I was game.

I wanted my beautiful old man restored to himself and to me. Of course, I didn't think of John as old. He'd been so young and vibrant just this past Christmas, so invincible, we'd thought.

And he was, and always had been, a beautiful man.

8

IT DOESN'T MATTER

Our leafy neighborhood was transitioning from medium-sized houses, like ours, to giant ones, thanks to a series of teardowns. It was a quick bike ride and not-so-quick walk to the center of Princeton along peaceful and charming streets. Though John was not keen on leaving for DC or anywhere South, he admitted he did not want to spend another frozen winter in Princeton. Still, he thought we should sell our house before contemplating a move. A realtor gave us an upbeat assessment of sales prospects. Moving would, however, mean leaving behind good friends and would require major packing, which John feared he couldn't do. We did downsize a bit, readying some furniture for Reid and Hannah. From shelves and drawers, I packed up glassware, knick-knacks, and several sets of bookends—serious heavy quartz ones, silly ones with monkeys reading books, and sentimental ones with my bronzed baby shoes resting on platforms of books.

Curious Maggie sniffed about inspecting my work, which disrupted her sense of order. Whenever anything was out of place or strange, even a leaf that blew in from the deck or a blueberry that rolled off the counter, she would check it out. Our family joke was that John and Maggie must be kin, for he too noted if anything was out of place—computer files, his stack of mail, an opened drawer. Contributing to the joke, John had begun lamenting, "Oh, meow," when he suspected disorder. As he watched me doing minor packing, he channeled Maggie, "Oh, meow, oh, meow." It would distress him to sit and watch as I boxed major china, silver, and books. Movers can pack for you, but John didn't want the uninitiated to touch his collection of Jonathan Swift's original early-eighteenth-century publications. I hated to think what they'd charge for packing the huge amount of stuff we'd accumulated—rooms full of furniture, including Mother's antiques, and all the many purchases we'd made ourselves, especially bookcases, reading lamps, serving trays, wine glasses, and of course a seemingly infinite amount of books.

Back in the 1980s, John and James Woolley had launched a project for a corrected edition of all Swift's poems, with an electronic archive explaining the variations in each line in different eighteenth-century publications. Because the English crown put bounties not only on Swift's head but also on the heads and ears of his printers, different versions of each poem circulated by hand and then were printed by authorized and unauthorized publishers. Thus, straightening out what Swift actually intended to print was a mammoth undertaking. John sometimes laughed that he and James could take their time because this work was so arcane no one would scoop them on it.

Instead, a major press scooped James for a new complete edition of all Swift's works. James, not John, was to edit Swift's poetry. James explained that John was excluded because his PhD was from Florida, not Yale or one of the Ivies. But another Swiftian told me that the true reason was that John, in a powerful review, had exposed sloppy research methods used by the man now heading the new edition of Swift. Like the jealous poets Swift wrote about in "Verses on the Death of Dr. Swift," that man would not forgive John. On the other hand, John had schooled himself in forgiveness, especially after converting to Christianity. He did not want the rest of his life poisoned by resentment. Though excluded from the major edition, John continued his work on Swift. I, however, excluded everyone associated with the new edition from a personal cocoon I'd been weaving almost since I first knew John.

At the fourth symposium on Jonathan Swift in 2000 in Münster, Germany, John presented a stunning take on Swift's longest poem, "Cadenus and Vanessa." Arch Elias surprised everyone with a talk on Swift as dictionary-maker. That was the summer when John and I took the train down to Rome after the symposium. It was also the summer of an unprecedented heat wave in Germany. Audience members, clad in Germany's usual June wools, were near heatstroke at several presentations. One afternoon, Susan Elias, a descendant of Abigail and John Adams, went with me into the town center, handsomely restored after World War II bombings, to buy cool cotton tops for ourselves and our daughters. Back in the States, we two couples were becoming close friends, until Susan became seriously ill and died of breast cancer in 2002. We remained friends with Arch, as he and John shared their opinion of the state of Swift studies. Arch also revealed more to John about his presentation on Swift's single foray into dictionary-making, written in a vocabulary book Arch had described as "now in private hands."

At that 2000 symposium, Arch had kept it a secret that those private hands were his own. In 1976, he—back then a wealthy Yale PhD— had bought Swift's dictionary at Sotheby's, which had been copied by Swift's young friend and protégé Esther Johnson. Planning someday to publish the vocabulary book, Arch was in 2000 investigating Swift's debts to other dictionary-makers. Then Arch, a lifetime smoker, contracted lung cancer. When he knew he would die, Arch invited John to take over editing and publishing Swift's *Word-Book*. We visited Arch's Philadelphia home on several occasions and picked up rafts of papers and electronic files so that John could continue the project of publishing what was, so far as anyone knows, Jonathan Swift's only unpublished work.

At Arch's funeral in the summer of 2008, John reflected on the honor of having Arch trust him with his life's work, writing that mattered greatly to Swiftians and to anyone who cared about language. John was quite aware of the fearsome responsibility of undertaking a project on which there could be no slacking (not that John ever slacked on anything). He embarked on this project with fresh zeal. He planned to publish the *Word-Book* with facsimile copies of some original pages in Esther Johnson's hand. Introducing the book would be essays by John to add to Arch's on Swift as dictionary-maker. There would be a preface, appendices, and extensive notes. It would be an arduous but rewarding scholarly undertaking. By 2015, John had been working on the project for seven years and hoped to complete it in another.

On 8 March 2015, I attended a CWW program on state parks, which John said he felt too weak to attend. At home, I later discovered, he had written a scholarly "will":

> Despite being goofy with Prednisone, I will offer as much guidance as I can to whoever attempts to pick up my efforts to prepare Esther Johnson's copy of Swift's Vocabulary for the press. My efforts have been almost entirely solitary and so may be worthless. In that case, my successor may choose to begin again, starting with the project as it stood when Arch Elias passed it on to me.

Of course, John's efforts were far from worthless. In that "will," John also generously guided his successor through his vast collection of computer files and papers. I did not even know that he was thinking of a successor. I did not know he had written a "will," a mere eight weeks after the warning in the Walmart parking lot. Later my friend Jane Goette asked me when John knew he was dying. Maybe it was earlier, but certainly on 8 March 2015 John knew or feared that he was dying. When I found the "will," I had to wonder why he didn't tell me, why he didn't demand that we find him a different doctor who might have cured him.

In his 1978 *On Swift's Poetry*, John had argued that meditations on death provide our strongest moral instruction. His conviction about how to die had not changed, though as he was doing this scholarly work his understanding of Swift himself changed some.

For the sixth Münster symposium in 2011, John had produced an essay on the history of the *Word-Book's* provenance, detailing its passage through various hands until it arrived in Arch's possession. John's was the lead talk at that symposium and was printed first in a 645-page collection by thirty-five world-class scholars. After writing that essay on the book's provenance, John had begun more personal investigations of the book's background. He'd become intrigued by Swift's puzzling relation with Esther Johnson. The two had met in the establishment of Sir William Temple in 1689 when he was twenty-two and she not yet nine years old. In 1694 and 1695, Swift was ordained deacon and then priest in the Anglican Church in Ireland. Temple died in 1699 and left Esther a decent inheritance. In 1701, Swift, then thirty-three, convinced Johnson, then twenty, to move to Dublin with an older companion to live close to but not with him. She must have expected him to marry her, but almost as soon as she came to Ireland, Swift left for England. He would become a hero for his satires on English oppressions of the Irish and for his criticisms of England's drawn-out war with France. (Although published anonymously, no one doubted who wrote the brilliant satire on religious and government factions in "A Tale of a Tub.")

From England and back in Ireland, Swift informally continued to guide Esther Johnson's reading. Since she had not been schooled in Greek or Latin, difficult words in various books, including *Paradise Lost* and his own "A Tale of a Tub," apparently baffled her. Back in college, I'd had the same reactions, so I empathized with Esther's mystification while also pitying her unrequited love for Swift. He dealt with her ignorance—but not with her romantic frustration—by writing for her edification over several years an "Explanation of Difficult English Words."

When John had returned to those facts after 2011 to write another introductory essay on the *Word-Book*, he was struck by the absence of letters or indeed any writings actually by Esther Johnson. Swift had noted every letter she wrote to him, yet none survived. In his *On Swift's Poetry*, John had endorsed Swift's assurances to Esther, that, as she aged, "she had made of her life, childless spinster though she was, something of value." John had been amused by Swift's injunction in a birthday poem to Stella, as he by then called Esther, to "be not troubled, / Although thy Size and Years are doubled ..." Rethinking *On Swift's Poetry* in the new millennium and informed by our own love story, John found Swift's assurances to Esther less charming and in fact downright unkind. John began a new essay called "Pygmalion Reversed."

In the winter of 2015, my talk of escaping South exasperated John. He said, "Okay, you pack up all our stuff and make the move, then you can ship my corpse to Naples, Florida." I didn't know what to say. I did not want to sound like a Pollyanna. But maybe, when I accused him of being too pessimistic, I was being too optimistic. Avoiding such discussions did not help. Still, with spring in the air, moving South seemed less of a priority. We disappointed the realtor by not putting our house on the market after all.

On 20 March, though my X-ray showed clear lungs, my new doctor ordered a CT scan for me because I still had a bad cough. No Princeton doctor had yet ordered one for John. Why did a new doctor take my cough more seriously than any of our other doctors took John's? Apparently they thought they already knew what was wrong with him and did not care to rethink it. Or perhaps the new doctor hadn't gotten the message about not over-ordering expensive procedures. Dr. G. wanted John to start pulmonary rehab but was unwilling to put him in the hospital because "hospitals are terrible places, and the food is awful." When we reported to Hannah Dr. G.'s opinion of hospitals, she threatened to come up and strangle the guy. I should have done so myself, but I was too tired to notice how illogical that statement was. I suppose John was so weary he was glad to avoid the exertion physical therapy would require. Hannah suggested later that there was a connection between sticking by Dr. G. and picking up a hitchhiker: She thinks that John took risks because he no longer valued his life.

I value most of my brilliant daughter's opinions, especially about her beloved father, but here I disagree. I think John did still value life. Certainly he cared about what happened to his work on Swift's *Word-Book*. And he definitely cared about what happened to me and to Hannah. I think that he picked up the hitchhiker out of kindness and also a sense of hubris: he still felt too strong, too quick on his feet to worry about the guy becoming a threat. Maybe he felt something similar about Dr. G., as if he were capable of evaluating the man's character and skills. Perhaps, though, illness had sapped John's judgment, along with his stamina—not that he or I admitted this.

On good days, John rechecked all references to letters, poems, and bits of prose or verse that Esther Johnson was supposed to have written. He assured himself that no creative composition was truly hers and that all the letters she wrote to Swift were truly gone. No conclusion was possible except that Swift himself had destroyed them. John was deeply disillusioned with Swift's relations with Esther. John even briefly permitted himself to wonder if he'd devoted his scholarly career to a man unworthy of his devotion.

On the night of 25 March, cold weather got Princeton back in its grip. The forsythia blossoms shriveled. Still, we went to see *Baskerville*.

I drove and parked near the theatre. We did not eat or drink beforehand, so we wouldn't need to leave our seats to go to the restrooms. John seemed to enjoy the clever farce, with a few actors playing all the parts in fantastically rapid succession, but afterwards he wanted just to sit in the lobby until the crowd departed. I said I would bring the car, but he said he could walk. I'd parked barely over a block way, but we took a very, very slow walk, because John needed to hold onto every lamppost and parking meter to catch his breath in the chill late-March air. At last I realized the desperateness of John's condition.

Results from my CT scan showed my lungs were healthy. John's lungs definitely were not. Still, both of us tried to trust the doctors, as if there were no other options. I took John to the GI doctor the day after the theatre. Incredibly enough, that doc still saw a simple cause-and-effect chain: a clogged esophagus caused aspiration, aspiration caused lung irritation, lung irritation caused coughing, coughing caused poor breathing, poor breathing caused weakness. He did not address the fact that, thanks to his procedure, John's esophagus was no longer clogged yet he still could not breathe clearly.

John was losing stamina. One night he was too tired to go to a meeting at the town hall about plans to repave and add new sidewalks to our street, a disappointment to neighbors who'd grown to count on him to speak up, protecting our properties, including our trees, from destruction. On lazy mornings, John and I used to cuddle together, John wrapping himself around me and holding in his left hand my right breast, the one that had had multiple operations for possible cancer. (These unnecessary operations had found no malignancies but had managed to deflate my right breast.) But by this time, lying on his right side had gotten painful, so we turned over and I held him. Then John had just to lie flat, and our cuddling had to end.

John saw Dr. G. on the last day of March and asked about getting a handicap tag to save me from driving. Dr. G. agreed but did not write the request. He offered suggestions in such rapid fire John asked him to write them down. I have the list. He started with inhalers; John was to stop Advair and take Breo once a day, as well as ProAir every four hours, as needed, to stop the urination problems that these medications cause. He was to up the Prednisone back to 60 mg a day. If he wasn't better, John was to decrease the Prednisone. That advice was not complicated when written down, rather than spoken all in a rush. It was also not very perceptive. All that the doctor really advised was to alter the inhalers and to switch the dose of Prednisone either up or down. He did not order a CT scan. Nor did he order oxygen, which can come in a handy carrying case. He should have told John that the problem was beyond his expertise. He didn't. How the urination problem is connected to inhalers I still don't know, but there is a connection. Dr. G. did not follow up even by writing to endorse a handicap tag for John or by having a nurse call to see if the new inhaler improved John's breathing or his urinary problem.

The phrase "fog of war" refers to the difficulty of making military decisions in the midst of conflict. John and I were afflicted by a fog of illness. His doctors had made up their minds and were not reconsidering. John and I did what we were told, but we were exhausted. We did not ask why I got better treatment than John. We did not question why the doctors hypothesized that John's problems were mild COPD and aspiration. We had no idea what was the matter with him. We knew that heart attacks, strokes, aneurysms, and even cancers can appear rapidly, without warning, but John's illness was different. COPD is normally a slow, wasting disease. Something else was squeezing John's strength away in a pincer-like grip.

On the first of April, I dropped John at the dentist for a routine visit. When I picked him up, he said that the dentist had refused to clean his teeth, lest the bacteria generated by a cleaning aggravate John's lungs. "I'm sorry you had to sit there for an hour while I went to my Pilates class," I responded. "Couldn't someone have driven you home?"

"It doesn't matter," John replied. He had read the news on his smartphone and claimed he wasn't bored. The John I had loved for forty years had always resented interferences with his scholarly writing or time lost to anything except studies or duties or pleasures. How could he have said it didn't matter?

John did not say, "It didn't matter," which might have meant that he was tired anyway and had an hour to spare. He said, "It doesn't matter." I know he thought love, learning, freedom, forgiveness, kindness, social justice, and faith matter. So, I wondered, what "does not matter"? Maybe he believed that his life's work on Jonathan Swift no longer mattered. Of course Swift mattered: In "A Tale of a Tub," he'd exposed the absurd factionalisms that threatened to destroy the Christian faith; in "The Public Spirit of the Whigs," he'd hastened the end of England's long-drawn-out costly war with France (and also hastened the temporary demise of the Whig government); in the "Drapier's Letters," he'd instigated a boycott of worthless coins (and other exports) foisted on Ireland by the English; in *Gulliver's Travels*, Swift set about, in Arch Elias's terms, "Reforming Mankind"; and in his innocently titled "An Epistle to a Lady," Swift actually exposed the shenanigans of the king and prime minister of England. John never doubted Swift's brilliance or importance, though he had begun to question his relationships with women.

That evening at cocktail hour, I asked John if he'd meant that Swift doesn't matter.

"Heavens, no, Panthea. Remember that epitaph about his being a 'champion of human Liberty'?"

"Remind me."

"I'm too tired to recall the Latin. Yeats wrote a terrific translation."

I found my copy of *The Collected Poems of W. B. Yeats*, and read the poem titled "Swift's Epitaph":

Swift has sailed into his rest;
Savage indignation there
Cannot lacerate his breast.
Imitate him if you dare,
World-besotted traveler; he
Served human liberty.

I closed the book. "Yes, that 'savage indignation' did, does matter, even today."

"I've spent my life believing so. But let's watch the news."

So I never got from John as explanation of what he meant by saying, "It doesn't matter." Later Hannah and I talked about it. She thinks John meant: "I am dying and it doesn't matter."

I reread John's essay on Swift's "Verses on the Death of Dr. Swift." John first quoted Swift on the absurdity of thinking death an evil. Then, John had written that "the central tenet of all meditations on death" is that "in the sickness and death of our friends (and of ourselves) is our strongest moral instruction." When I'd pondered John's recent "It doesn't matter" remark, I had thought he meant his life didn't matter, but later, looking back over his words on Swift, I concluded that he meant that death itself did not matter. How he faced it did matter. Like writing his scholarly "will," John's equanimity before death suggests that he had taken those ominous lung spasms in the Walmart parking lot as premonition. He and I were rather like Raymond Carver and Tess Gallagher; as she says in one of her poems, "we don't know yet that you are dying." John had not said, "Dying, Panthea, dying," but we both were beginning to fear he was.

If Hannah couldn't get us to move to DC, she could at least get John to see a doctor there. She made an appointment for him with her allergy doctor, with the understanding that the allergist would probably send him to a Georgetown University Hospital pulmonologist. John agreed to this plan. Nevertheless, on Monday and Tuesday, the 13 and 14 April, I belatedly tried to see if John could get into a closer hospital, said to specialize in lung and heart conditions. I printed out its admission forms, only to discover that that hospital requires elaborate records and referrals weeks before admission. We lacked time for such procedures. The calendar on John's desk still read January. Three months had passed since the Walmart parking lot incident. John's skin looked like a larger man's hand-me-down bodysuit. His breath sounded like a motorized lawn mower running out of gas. He would not recover unless we took action.

John's notes say that between 6 and 13 April, Dr. G. took him from 60 mg of Prednisone a day down to 30 mg. When he kept an appointment with Dr. G. on 14 April, John told him he had decided to go to DC, finally, to get a second opinion. Dr. G. said he wanted John to feel his best, and so upped his Prednisone dosage back to 60 mg, arbitrarily I thought. He also ordered another swallowing test. John faltered on the walk down the long halls between the clinic and the hospital, but no one offered a wheelchair. Nor did I try to find one. I walked slowly with him, sometimes holding his hand, appalled at how weak he'd become.

While he went into the outpatient clinic to retake the swallowing test, I called Hannah to say that her father had hardly enough "puff" to walk.

"Oh, no, Mom!" Her voice on the phone was loud enough to hurt my ear. "I've got to call Georgetown. Bye."

We both knew how much John's life really did matter.

9

SAVE THE LIFE
OF MY DAD

The waiting room beside the outpatient clinic at the Princeton hospital was almost empty and very quiet. I looked at the statues in the lobby and turned pages in magazines. The sofas and chairs were pleasant and comfortable enough and the light was soft. I, however, was uncomfortable. I couldn't think what would happen next, what I should be doing. Then Hannah called me again. She had rung Georgetown University Hospital and spoken to the head of pulmonology there, saying, "Please, please, save the life of my dad." Dr. Reichner had obliged with an emergency appointment for the next day at 2 p.m. "Oh," I said, "I fear that's too early."

When John emerged from the outpatient clinic after the swallowing test, he sat down by me. "How was it?" I asked. He shook his head and wouldn't speak. Then I held his hand and informed him that he had an appointment at Georgetown University Hospital the next afternoon at two.

"I'll never make it," he said.

Then Hannah called to say that she'd gotten the appointment

changed to 3 p.m. "Oh, Hannah, thank you, thank you," I whispered into the phone. Then I told John that his appointment was now at three. I said we could and would make it.

John had consented to the idea of starting with an allergist and, if necessary, being referred to Georgetown. That plan's very orderliness served as a buffer of sorts against acknowledging how sick he really was. Changing the plan must have threatened to make him face his sickness. He invented excuses. We wouldn't have time to pack or make arrangements for Maggie. His gut problem would not let him out of the bathroom early enough to make even a 3 p.m. appointment in DC. His condition was not serious enough to call for the attention of Georgetown's head pulmonologist. I at last knew better. With Hannah's support, I would not give in, and so John finally consented.

At twilight, John and I drove through the New Jersey countryside where sprouts of corn and beans were daring to emerge from the just-thawed soil. After we left Maggie at the Cats Only Inn, we came home to pack our bags and stow them in the car, leaving only toiletries and his scholarly papers by the door to stash in the car's backseat early in the morning. I think I ate cheese and crackers for dinner and John had a taste of cereal. Insisting that driving along I-95 wastes no breath, John took the wheel for the first part of the trip, crossing the Delaware Memorial Bridge. I have a mild bridge phobia, so I did not begin driving until after we got into Delaware, hiding my anxiety at having to keep to our tight lane in the Baltimore tunnel as giant SUVs roared along beside us.

We stopped at a Maryland welcome site just before entering DC. As we walked down the slope to the facilities, John said, "Oh, no." He said he dreaded going back up that incline. I promised to get out of the ladies' room in time to repark the car low on the slope. The timing worked, for as I drove into a new parking place John was leaving the men's restroom and walking toward me. Seeing him from a distance gave me a shock. He looked like his old mentor and friend Aubrey Williams the last time we'd seen him before his death at eighty-six—extremely thin and too frail to walk steadily. John appeared more like a scarecrow than himself. At least, I thought, we were headed for Georgetown University Hospital where Hannah believed superior care could save her father.

On Wednesday, 15 April, we got to the hospital just after 2 p.m. after all. We bought something neither of us ate much of at a snack bar and found our way to the pulmonology division of the hospital. Dr. Reichner spent no more than ten minutes with John before she sent him to the emergency room for a massive run of tests. He was too sick, she said, to think of leaving the hospital or being out on his own anywhere.

Her assistant, not an aide but an MD, eased John into a wheelchair and pushed it down halls and into elevators, with me following behind. A storm of emotions raged inside me: a hint of vindication (*I knew you were sicker than you'd admit*); a gripping fear (*This sounds really bad*); relief (*At last we have a doctor who knows what she's talking about*); and hope (*If anyone can save John, I believe that Dr. Reichner can!*). As I followed John through higgledy-piggledy hallways, formed by different buildings cobbled together, hope became my predominant emotion.

Despite its rather ramshackle construction, Georgetown University Hospital was spotless. When we got to the emergency room, John was whisked away for tests. After he was returned to me in the ER, teams of physicians and medical students soon began visiting, offering hypotheses about his CT scan, X-rays, and blood tests. Clearly, John had COPD, but there was another underlying problem.

Hannah and Michael arrived in the ER at the end of their work day. When she saw her father for the first time in months, Hannah wept. A born writer, she started keeping a log:

> Dad says he would cry with me but is afraid of making his condition worse. I say that I'll stop crying then, and I do. The nurse is very

nice—from Alabama. She tells us that at the hospital where she worked in Alabama, they had hotel-size bottles of liquor for patients who were regular drinkers, but they didn't have any such thing at Georgetown. Dad's overnight in the ER had been made much more comfortable by a really good eye mask, and the nurse found extra ones for me and for Mom. There's lots of joking about Dad's LSU watch and about how it's good she's not from the University of Alabama—I think she was from Auburn. Various theories about Dad are proposed, including interstitial lung disease because of the "clubbing" in Dad's fingers. However, the pulmonology team disagrees and says that he has pneumonia. They start him on IV antibiotics and breathing treatments, but the treatments seem to make him worse.

She also recorded, "They do see something in the CT scan, but what it is isn't completely clear."

I spent that night alone in the motel room on Connecticut Avenue Hannah had reserved for us both. Early the next day, Thursday, Hannah wrote that she and Michael got to the hospital to try and "catch the docs on their early morning rounds." To avoid the morning's rush-hour traffic, I arrived later and drove to the Pasquerilla Healthcare Center entrance, the same entrance to which John had driven us the day before. I had to ask how to get to the ER, and was told to follow a green line through Gorman Building, a blue line through Bles Building, then to turn the corner to the Concentrated Care Center building and follow a red line to the Emergency Room. These different buildings are not all on one level, so I also had to watch for inclines and declines patching the buildings' floors together.

That afternoon, John was moved to a corner room overlooking the soccer fields of Georgetown University. "The best room in the hospital," several people said. It was accessed from the hospital's original rather elegant entrance, with flower urns and marble floors. When I went out that elegant door, I was surprised to discover that the cafeteria was just across the parking lot, while the entrance I'd used earlier was way off to one side. When I'd arrived that morning, I'd gone back to the Pasquerilla entrance because it was the one I knew. A different perspective, however, revealed how inconvenient that entrance was. Just like me, our doctors in Princeton had just followed the path they knew, without even considering going beyond it or trying something different.

We weren't sure whether John got the privileged room by accident or because he was the sickest patient or because he was the most entertaining. When teams of doctors came to visit, they chuckled at John's ironic take on current events. When they heard that John had been an English professor, a surprising number of nurses, interns, and doctors seemed to crave talking with him about their favorite authors and poets. One man sat on the foot of John's bed for nearly fifteen minutes talking about Kurt Vonnegut. Hannah said, "We hear that Americans don't read, but these medical people loved reading. Maybe they wouldn't have talked about books with anyone except Dad."

On Friday, Michael dropped off Hannah then drove to Arlington, where the home office of United Way Worldwide is located. Michael is Director of Technology there. In their five years of marriage, Michael had been wonderfully supportive of Hannah in the autoimmune problems that threaten her health. Now he was supporting her father and me as well. He returned for lunch with us. Hannah recorded:

The breathing treatments still seem to make Dad worse, though they've changed the meds in them. A resident proposed that Dad is having trouble with the breathing treatments because he is anxious, a ridiculous suggestion for Dad, whose problem is obviously physical and not psychological. We all tell the resident so, and he says that it has to be psychological because the breathing treatments open up the lungs and that's all there is to it. After he leaves, we all agree that he's the worst person we've seen, and Mom asks if there's a place to report him. Dad says, "If there's a place to report incompetent people, please let me know. I've been looking for it all my life." Dad really wants to take a shower, which he does, but then is much worse immediately, as the steam has really irritated his pneumonia.

I think this was the first day Michael got a tuna melt at the cafeteria, which all of us got at some point. I think about it as the iconic food of the time. Dad would sometimes eat the hospital food, but more often than not we would bring food in for him and he would eat some of it—often soft things, like part of a tuna melt; once I got him a chocolate pudding.

As I drove back to the motel, I recalled John's line about looking for the place to report incompetence. It did seem he was too witty to be gravely sick. And besides, the Georgetown doctors had given me hope.

Navigating neighborhood streets on the way to the hospital the next morning, I noted charming brick Georgetown homes on small elevations. It seemed time for us to try living in a city like this, I thought. But now steps promised to be more of a problem for John than for me. After two nights at the motel, I moved to Hannah and Michael's tall old town house on Capitol Hill, where John and I had often stayed in their guest room, stuffed into their sofa bed between bookshelves.

On Earth Day, Saturday, 18 April, the Global Poverty Project staged an all-day concert on the National Mall. Famous bands and entertainers performed in support of ending extreme poverty and combating climate change. Pedestrians jammed all the streets near the Mall, so Hannah, Michael, and I were diverted from our direct route to Georgetown, as Hannah wrote:

We end up getting rerouted to Virginia, then the GW Parkway, then the Chain Bridge. It's a beautiful day though, and Mom and I do a little real estate speculating. We get to the hospital around 1:30 p.m. Dad seems maybe a little better. Dr. Roberts, a full-time faculty doctor, has arrived in our absence—he's got a Texas affect, but when he gets really interested, the affect goes away and he's clearly really smart. He has proposed that Dad has gunk locked up in the nonfunctioning chambers of his lungs. When the treatments open up his lungs, they release so much of the gunk his lungs can't deal with it all at once. Dad thinks that that sounds about right, and we all agree that you can train stupid persons to be doctors (like the resident the day before), but you'll never get real doctoring out of them. All this time, along with very good doctors, nurses have been outstanding and have mostly allowed Dad to be off his monitors except when he has to be checked for oxygen and heart rates. They treat him like an adult. He wears his own nightclothes. He was so intellectually alive that his hospital room began to feel like he was hosting people in a hotel room—I began to worry that he would fool people into thinking that he was well. I told the doctors my worries, but they assured me that they know he is really sick.

On Sunday, in slower traffic, Hannah and Michael again drove me to the hospital, this time as a tutorial for maneuvering our car around monolithic marble and stone government buildings, museums, and monuments. I was not a great pupil, for I kept getting distracted by cherry blossoms, monuments, and crowds. That afternoon, Hannah wrote, "Dad seemed to turn a corner today and to be a bit stronger. Mom and I went out to look at two condos." One, owned by an embassy, was impossibly expensive; the other, in an attractive 1960s building with a central courtyard, was convenient, affordable, and accessible, thanks to an elevator. I took the flier back to John, telling him that we really could live there. John feigned interest, though it was hardly a time to contemplate moving. He and Michael had intended to watch a Nationals baseball game but had ended up turning off the television just to talk. Michael asked John if he could call him Dad and me Mom. Michael has such a deep sense of family, it was an honor to be addressed as parents, without, as he explained, disrespect for his own parents or their religion.

Now that I was staying on Capitol Hill, after Hannah and Michael left for work, I carefully double-locked their front door and walked along an irregular old brick path, past the deep red tulips Hannah's friend Michele had sent, opened a little iron gate, and found our car nearby. John and I had sometimes talked of moving to this convenient, charming area, but had concluded that the row houses had too many steps for my bad back. Now, such steps seemed too daunting for John's lungs. I set out driving down their sleepy street, past parents pushing strollers and shoppers walking to Eastern Market. On Independence, I drove past the Madison Building, where Hannah was working, by the Capitol, past the National Conservatory, and along the Mall and the famous Smithsonian buildings on my way to Georgetown.

On those days, John and I felt very close. We were mostly alone in his hospital room, except when teams of visiting nurses and doctors arrived. John had a theory that we'd gotten the same infection back in January and just kept swapping germs back and forth but that they were harder on his weakened lungs. We kissed passionately, though not on the lips, and looked forward to making love again back in our Princeton house. We held hands and remembered fun times from the past, including marvelous days in Portugal, England, Germany, Rome, and the Shenandoah National Park. When he got well, we planned to take that long-delayed Southern trip, if it wasn't too hot. A better plan was to go to the Reid Orchards in Kentucky, my true home, and then drive to Chicago, where John had lived as a boy. We'd seen some of that DVD he'd picked up at Walmart, but it mostly showed the nine cousins visiting their grandparents in Surfside. I wanted to see where the Fischers had lived in Chicago until John's tenth year. After Chicago, we planned to drive West and see spectacular national parks. Then we would return to Princeton, and John would finish the Swift *Word-Book* project. I began writing friends, letting them know that John was in the hospital and I was by his bedside.

When I told John I was about to write Herb Rothschild, he said, "Not now." Like many old friends separated by thousands of miles, John and Herb talked on the phone, exchanged Christmas gifts, and planned get-togethers, but they hadn't seen each other since Hannah and Michael's wedding. I had often laughed thinking that whenever they got together the two men would resume the same arguments about radical political solutions that they'd left off at their last meeting. John conceded that he wanted to talk to Herb but "not till I've recovered." When Hannah arrived, I told her what John had said about not calling Herb. She took her dad's hand and said, "If he's really your best friend, he'll want to know how sick you are now." He seemed to concede her point, so that night I emailed Herb to say that John had a mysterious illness that had landed him in the Georgetown University Hospital. Much to my surprise, I got an immediate message back saying that Herb and Deborah were in DC at that very moment. I told Hannah but not John.

It seemed such serendipity that Herb was in town. Hannah and I hoped that Georgetown University Hospital could not only bring his best friend to visit but also could save John's life.

10

VERY, VERY MY DAD

The next morning was bright and cheerful. When I got to the hospital, I found John wearing one of his own sleep shirts and standing by his window looking out over the Georgetown soccer fields. One group of students was taking turns kicking, another taking turns being goalies. I stood beside John, my arm around his waist as we watched the sides change places below us. Cell phone reception was better close to the window, and he had just connected with Hannah on the phone when I turned toward the door. "John," I said, "you have a surprise." He looked back and saw Herb and Deborah in the doorway of his hospital room. Tears sprang from his eyes.

Hannah could hear the tears she couldn't see: "I was on the phone with Dad when they came in. Mom told him to turn around, and he said, 'Well, my goodness,' and was so delighted. I said I would hang up now and he said, 'But do you know what has happened?' I said I did know and was so happy."

Herb was a bit grayer and balder than the last time we'd seen him, but his intensity hadn't dimmed. Deborah was as ever tall and elegant with reddish curls and a wide cheerful smile. John didn't seem to be eating much of his lunch, but we couldn't interest him in the salads, complete with grilled asparagus, we brought back from Georgetown's salad bar. (Here I disagree with Hannah: the iconic meal of our time in Georgetown University Hospital was not tuna melt but grilled asparagus in a varied salad.) We had a wonderful day, full of reminiscences and plans. An iced tea bottle cleverly disguised a cup or so of bourbon, and so late in the afternoon, after Hannah and Michael arrived, we drank nips of bourbon to John's health. He didn't drink, saying he couldn't handle the whiskey. I drank his cup as well as mine. Herb and Deborah invited us to visit them in Oregon. They said a cheery good-bye to John, who seemed happy but tired; then they took the rest of us to dinner. Hannah wrote, "We had a lovely dinner with a great view of the magnificent thunderstorm that broke that night. Herbert was shocked at the idea that Dad could have died before getting to Georgetown and that he, Herbert, would not have seen him for a last time."

John's private bedroom had a bathroom with a shower, but the steam made it difficult to breathe, so he decided to take sponge baths holding onto the sink in his room. He asked a nurse to print a sign he could tape on his door: "Do not disturb. Patient bathing self." Before he shaved, he put a towel under his feet to collect stray hairs. Hannah wrote that such fastidiousness "was very, very my Dad."

With the nurses and then me, John practiced walking up and down the hall, an oxygen tank in tow, wearing aqua hospital socks that had rubber anti-slip dots on their bottoms. His newfound sprightliness also seemed to Hannah to be "very, very my Dad." The doctors thought he'd beaten back the pneumonia. *Hope,* I thought. *That's what I feel now.* I tried to recall Emily Dickinson's poem, "'Hope' is the thing with feathers." I remembered that the bird of hope "sings the tune without the words." So though I didn't remember all the words, I felt hope fly into my chest.

Dr. Reichner released John on 21 April, after six days in the hospital.

Hannah thanked her for saving John's life and started to cry while the doctor graciously said that the whole medical team had enabled John's recovery.

He and I spent the night back at Hannah and Michael's, careful to bring in only a small case with changes of underwear and a bag of medications. But we were not careful enough. John was too tired to go out to dinner, so Hannah ordered in something to eat. The many stairs up to the bedrooms in their Victorian row house are steep, but John climbed them and then insisted on going downstairs to the half-bath during the night. Getting back up them must have been a struggle, but he didn't complain, or perhaps I was too dead asleep to hear him. It was very, very like John to insist on making it down and up those steps by himself.

After a week away, we missed our home and our cat. We set out for Princeton late the next morning, and John insisted on driving, remarking again that it took no more oxygen to drive than to ride. When we pulled into our driveway, we both tackled unloading the car, though I begged him to take it easy. I got my suitcase out of the car trunk and into the kitchen, then I dumped the dirty clothes in the basement. When I came back to the kitchen, John had taken my case upstairs. I said he shouldn't carry suitcases, but he said he didn't have a bad back, as I do.

"But I don't have pneumonia and COPD, as you do," I replied.

As Hannah wrote, in this way, "My Dad was not a very good patient—he had a hard time adjusting to the idea that he would need to get others' help and to rest for a long time." Here is where I must fault the Georgetown doctors. In their release, they should have made explicit to John and me that there were to be no stairs, nothing to carry, no cars to drive, nothing to do but rest. But I should fault myself more than the doctors. If I had only asked, I'm sure our neighbor Colin Von Vorys and his son C. J. would have been pleased to carry for us suitcases, dirty clothes, bags of Swift scholarship, and the bag with a jar of peanuts and a bottle of bourbon, which John and I always took on travels. But I didn't think to suggest it. If I had, John would have refused anyway, embarrassed to ask a younger man to carry his stuff for him. Refusing to ask for help was very, very John.

We still had time, late on the afternoon of 22 April, to pick up Maggie, who purred all the way home. The Cats Only people claimed she ate well while we were gone, making us fear that her poor appetite was indeed a simpatico reaction to John's bad cough. Despite our fatigue, John and I left Maggie at home and made a trip to the grocery store, where John looked for something sweet and full of calories and found chocolate bars, brownies, and a crumb cake. After I roamed the aisles for other food, we met at the deli. John hadn't bought our usual sinful brisket sandwich with cheese and barbecue sauce, but instead a whole-grain loaf filled with turkey and cheese, lettuce and tomatoes, which we could slice into cross sections for dinner. John was so exhausted from standing and waiting a few minutes that he was holding onto a display case. He looked as frail as he had back in that Maryland rest stop just the week before. He hadn't recovered after all.

For dinner, John ate terribly small sections of sandwich. He said that his chest cavity had a limited size, so food filled up his stomach, leaving little space for his lungs to expand. I didn't argue, since that was how it felt to him. He did eat brownies, cut in tiny pieces, and bits of the crumb cake. I tried and partially succeeded in keeping him from unpacking everything that evening. Maggie slept in his half-unpacked suitcase.

We both must have rested the next day. Maybe I washed clothes—I can't recall. That evening, when I handed John a screw-top wine bottle, he twisted it open, despite his weakened condition. "John," I laughed, "you can't leave me. I'd never be able to open another bottle of wine."

"I'm sure you'll manage," he replied with a grin.

Even chocolates with or without bourbon and other sweets didn't supply enough calories for him. From a normal weight of 150 pounds, John now weighed in the mid-120s. Still, we might or might not have made love once in that period, tenderly. I don't remember that but I do know that we cuddled together, avoiding any strain on his breathing. By then, I was giving Maggie baby food to get her to eat something, as she had stopped eating again. Maybe I should have tried it on John.

Just twelve hours after his last dose of Azithromycin, John said he could feel himself backsliding, as if he were "fighting this monster and fighting it alone." He called Georgetown, where the on-call doctor prescribed more Azithromycin three times a week, but the "medicine men" of Georgetown overruled the doctor and ordered that John take a very strong dose, 250 mg, every day for pneumonia, not just for COPD. Hannah told me that at Georgetown they call the medicine specialists at their hospital "'medicine men'—Dad kept saying that he was on the verge of calling them 'heap big medicine men.'"

Our nearby pharmacy had no Azithromycin, so on 25 April, in weather now bright and clear, I drove out to Princeton Junction, the train stop, where the pharmacist had a thirty-day supply waiting for me. Maybe I imagined it, but he seemed to have tears in his eyes, as I did. The instructions said to "Take 1 tablet by mouth daily," but "Stop if you experience palpitations/lightheadedness." John had neither of those problems, but he must have still had pneumonia. I told Hannah, as she recorded on 26 April, "New prescription seems to be working. Dad feeling better." The Georgetown pulmonologists expected that with the Azithromycin, John would be okay until his appointment on 6 May with Dr. Reichner.

John was not better for long. I often woke in the night and watched him breathe. His chest rose and fell heavily, heaving. His inhalers continued to make urination difficult, and he had no appetite. I don't recall talking very much to Hannah about John's problem urinating, but I said enough for her to write that "needing to get up in the middle of the night to go to the bathroom is beginning to be a real problem." I called Dr. G., who prescribed another different inhaler that, as Hannah wrote, "only made Dad's bathroom problem worse. He's getting up more in the middle of the night, isn't getting much sleep, and his pulmonary problems are worse again."

When she wasn't answering questions from Congress and plotting maps of Iraq and Syria and other trouble spots, Hannah busied herself on an urgent search for short-term apartment rentals near the Georgetown hospital. Her plan was for us to spend a couple of months there, where John could be under the care, daily if necessary, of the Georgetown pulmonologists. He was skeptical, especially after two rental ads turned out to be of the send-us-your-money-first sort. John was sleeping poorly, thanks to the urinary problem that awakened him with the need to pee but then prevented him from peeing. He went back to Dr. G., who wasn't thrilled to hear about all the tests the Georgetown doctors had administered. With no more imagination than before, he prescribed higher doses of Prednisone. For the first time, John went to pulmonary therapy in the outpatient section of the hospital on Thursday, 30 April. That was the only time after he became sick that I did not drive him there. I figured if he was going to be put on a treadmill, he could walk across a parking lot. But I was wrong. When John returned, he was too worn out to talk for a while. Finally, he told me that a nice woman named Loretta worked with him. He would not talk about the therapy itself. That too was very, very John.

His sleep was ever more interrupted. He moved into the guest room so as not to disturb me with his frequent bathroom trips. I thought it just as well, because my bursitis was acting up. Rolling over on my back or front or onto either side, I couldn't find a comfortable position for my left leg. Had John been beside me, I'd have kept him awake, when he didn't keep me awake.

For our upcoming temporary move to Georgetown, we packed our suitcases so that we would have enough clothes to last us a month. We made arrangements to take Maggie back to the Cats Only Inn on 5 May. On the first of May, we had several interruptions at home. Guys from a moving van company came to haul away my mother's piano and the French provincial bedroom suite I'd been given when I turned twelve, both on their way to Reid in southwest Virginia; they also took a nineteenth-century china cabinet for delivery to Hannah and Michael in DC. John was bothered by having to sit and watch all this. Later that day, our handyman contractor came, as he did each spring, to talk about house repairs, going over a list John and I had made together some months before. John didn't feel like going outside to check soffits and shingles and talk about plugging the hole a diligent woodpecker had pecked in a fascia board. It distressed John to be just an observer, so very John, but he did let himself nap after those hardy guys left.

At seven the next morning, John appeared in the bedroom doorway. "Panthea, dear, I hate to wake you, but I can't pee and have to get to the emergency room." He felt that urine inside him was building up, poisoning his system. There was no question of getting to Georgetown in such a crisis, so I drove to our Princeton hospital in fifteen minutes. I dropped him off, as usual, parked the car, and came in to find him waiting, looking miserable.

"Darling, are you okay?" I asked.

"No," he grimaced.

I told the attendant they should see John right then. It was an emergency. She said they were going as fast as they could.

Oh. Lord, I thought to myself. *Here we are back where all this started.*

We weren't in the Walmart parking lot but near the offices of our regular physicians in the Princeton hospital. These physicians had taken my cough more seriously than John's, had convinced themselves that John's problem was a clogged esophagus, not pneumonia, had never put him on oxygen, and had not even ordered an X-ray or CT scan for a better look at his lungs. They had their theory and were sticking to it. Now we were back in their territory, not saved by Georgetown after all. John looked terrible, not ashen but jaundiced. I supposed that he really was being poisoned by his own urine.

Finally John was put on a bed with curtains drawn about it and catheterized by an emergency doctor. I saw him grimace in pain, but then he was much relieved to have his bladder drained. I tried not to stare, but I saw how quickly his catheter bag was filling. When they rolled him away for some tests, including his first X–ray at Princeton, I left to get him sleeping clothes and toiletries. I suppose the hospital could have given him a toothbrush, razor, comb, and such stuff, so I suspect I was so distressed I just wanted to get out of there for a while. Driving away, I ran over the curb on one of those grassed islands that mark the ends of parking lanes. *You idiot,* I thought to myself. *It won't help John for you to tear up the car or yourself.* I feared I'd wrecked our car, but it sped along, taking the jolt in stride.

At home, it was hard to gather supplies for him without bursting into tears. I fed Maggie then put her on my lap and called Hannah. When I told her that her dad was in the Princeton hospital, she seemed not just to sob but to scream. Later Hannah told me she had choked up when she recalled what our friend Al had said, as he was dying unexpectedly of lung cancer: "The Princeton hospital is a nice place to go if you're ready to die."

She said she and Michael would be on their way soon. I put Maggie down and cleaned out her litter box. I put out more food and water for her then stopped in the doorway. "Bye-bye, Maggie. You be a good cat. I'll be back before too long. Don't you worry. You're my very favorite kitty cat." She seemed comforted when I spoke to her in such a sing-song voice. She was fine. I was frazzled and frightened as I drove back to the hospital.

John's life had not been saved after all.

11

THIS IS OUR
ANNIVERSARY

Princeton's hospital is beautiful and brilliantly designed, inside and out. Unlike the patched-together buildings of the Georgetown University Hospital, this is a place that was carefully thought-out and planned to be efficient and tasteful—a true meeting of form and function. The elegant hospital was made to feel welcoming to its patients, to make them feel safe and cared for, but its calming aesthetic and lovely architecture did not reassure me, nor did the grimace I'd seen on John's face.

Hannah wrote on that Saturday morning:

Mom calls me at around 9 a.m. As soon as I get off the phone, I start screaming, crying. I think I know then that my Dad will die. I feel that I have planned wrong. Great legislators get legislation passed through a combination of two things: 1. Policy—having the right policy at the right time; 2. Personality—taking an accurate measure of the personality of the people around them and understanding what it will take to get those particular people to support the legislation. I had managed the first part—I had engineered a good policy of coming to Georgetown, where the medical care was clearly superior to the care Dad had been getting previously. What I had not done, however, was adequately taken into account Dad's personality. Dad was never going to make the call to go to the emergency room a day before he needed to go. Further, he hated the idea that the social and medical network that he and Mom spent over a decade putting together in Princeton was going to fail them just at the moment that they needed it. And finally, he was an amazingly forgiving and loyal person. I think, even then, he trusted Dr. G., though Dr. G. had missed his pneumonia and had put him on an inhaler that landed him in the hospital.

Hannah and Michael arrived by late afternoon. By then John had been moved to the hospital's critical care unit. We sat in a waiting area next door to John's room while some procedure took place. On the wall hung huge blown-up photos of orange and yellow irises, reminding me of Georgia O'Keefe's paintings. After we were allowed into his room, John grew talkative and, besides the catheter bag, seemed almost his normal self.

Once I saw passing along the hall the GI doctor who'd advised us to stay in Princeton rather than to drive South. The doc did a brief double take upon seeing John in the ICU bed with me beside him, then he kept on walking. John did not see him and I was in no condition to run out and talk to him. Anyway, what could I do? I just vowed never to go back to him or to his medical group.

When an intelligent nurse took over that evening, she told us the weekend on-duty doctor had ordered IV antibiotics, but our medical practice doctors had replaced that order. Hannah wrote, "They still thought Dad just has COPD, not pneumonia." The nurse said she could see the pneumonia on the new X-ray, so, at Hannah's urging, the nurse herself authorized one more round of antibiotics.

Thanks probably to the medications, John remained upbeat over the weekend, and on Monday, 4 May, he was transferred down the hall to the telemetry wing of the hospital, where patients on cardiac monitors stay. Hannah wrote that "Dad has to stay on his monitors at all times, is treated more like a child, the nurses don't change the sheets or wash him every day or, indeed, at all, without being reminded." His arms bore purple patches, the color of eggplant skin, where so many needles had been stuck. I showed John that I had developed some sort of rash on my arm, out of empathy, I said tenderly.

Hannah recorded, "Dad is feeling better. I swear it was the antibiotics. He is so much better that he and the doctors believe he will be discharged tomorrow." We planned to drive John back to Georgetown on Tuesday, using both cars, for his appointment with Dr. Reichner on Wednesday the sixth. John's catheter was removed but he was weak. Hannah told him she wanted him back at Georgetown: "With a certain amount of irritation, he said, 'So be it.'" When Hannah, Michael, and I went home that Monday evening, we packed, planning for John's release. They took our houseplants outside to let the elements care for them. We gave John's keys to the Von Vorys family across the street.

John, however, was too weak to be released on Tuesday, then that night was very bad for him. Hannah wrote, "He seemed much worse when we got to his room early Wednesday morning." He was not discharged, nor was he on his way to Georgetown. When Dr. G. came to John's room on his rounds, Hannah wrote that he said, "Essentially, Dad had COPD and basically nothing could be done for him." Hannah said, respectfully, that she "thought he was wrong—among other things, I thought Dad's WBC [white blood count] had gone down with the IV antibiotics, even though Dad's Prednisone had continued, but Dr. G. wouldn't let me finish my argument. He said 'Oh, I've had discussions with families before,' but he wouldn't debate with me. The whole thing left me shaken up, though Dad seemed pleased—I'm still not sure why." I'm sure John hoped for harmony or at least understanding between his daughter and his regular pulmonologist, whom he still liked. Maybe he did not want to think we should have fired Dr. G. Maybe John was simply being generous. Or maybe, as Hannah later suggested, John no longer valued his own life very much.

I called Dr. Reichner at Georgetown to cancel John's appointment. She hoped to see him when he recovered enough to drive to DC. I also canceled Maggie's reservation at the Cats Only Inn. I'd already cancelled my Pilates exercise class and postponed more theatre tickets. Michael returned to DC, needing to run office meetings, but Hannah stayed with me. John had told us to put his crucial work on Swift by the front door so we could load it into the car on 5 May. I occasionally told him that his writing would be safer at home than in the car, but John always wanted backups in case the house burnt down or was vandalized. (He also joked that no vandal would want his Swift notes or books, though his books are certainly far more valuable than televisions and CD players.)

At the Princeton hospital, the paintings on the walls, tastefully chosen from local artists' works, represent soothing scenes in varying degrees of abstraction. I could tell where to turn for the visitors' elevator, because it was opposite a pale orange weaving of silk and cotton threads. The turn for the restroom was signaled by a print of a sunset. Each nurses' station had its own color scheme. The one near John's room used color-coordinated shades of yellow ochre. Sometimes I got cups and straws from there, ignoring the caution for John not to drink from a straw, issued by doctors who believed his problem was aspiration.

I finished Marilynne Robinson's *Lila* and began rereading her *Gilead,* finding comfort in its acceptance of death. I brought in Sir Walter Scott's *The Heart of Midlothian* for John, but he read it only briefly. "Too depressing," he said, though his mind was still alert to responsibilities. He told me, "When they're tearing up the yard, why don't you transplant that volunteer cedar that sprouted by the front walk. It deserves a better home." Hannah and I promised to do so. On Wednesday, garbage day, he thought to ask how I was going to deal with a heavy bag of dirty kitty litter. (How a cat who ate so little could create so much poop, I didn't understand.) Her litter box in the basement had to be emptied and cleaned, the weighty bag carried up and out once every week.

"I'm hiring C. J. to be my handy man," I explained.

"But he's only a kid."

"He's fourteen, and so were you when you worked summers in your dad's dress factory, started smoking, and I think first got laid."

C. J. had been born on 27 May 2001, the very week we moved to Princeton, and the day after John had turned sixty-one. I continued, "He is plenty strong enough to carry that bag up the stairs and into the garbage can." In truth, I wondered how John had been able lately to do that chore himself. But he would have died, figuratively, before he admitted he needed a kid to take over his job.

John finally conceded that hiring C. J. was a good option. "Get him to do the lifting whenever you need it," John instructed. C. J.'s parents, Colin and Laura Von Vorys, wanted him to help neighbors without thought of recompense. Now, though, they agreed that he could earn a very modest "salary" for helping me. I started paying C. J. and, whenever I cooked, sharing my largesse, more than I could eat, with his family, as they shared with me.

I later found out that on Monday, 4 May, John took a selfie. He must have put the phone on the nurse's tray-table above his bed and then stared straight at it. Maybe Hannah and I were in the cafeteria picking up lunches when he took the picture. His rumpled hospital gown reveals still-black chest hairs, and his mustache and short beard look mostly dark. His sleep mask is raised above his forehead and he is not wearing glasses. Oxygen tubes emerge from his nostrils. He shows no emotion, but looks ready to confront whatever comes next. Except for the oxygen tubes, he looks almost normal. Staring straight at the camera, he seems to be thinking: *Here am I, John Irwin Fischer. This is how I look on 4 May 2015, when I am not quite seventy-five years old.*

By this time, John must have really known he was dying.

He did not look almost normal for long. Every day he seemed to be getting frailer. I tried not to stare at the ever-growing purple bruises on his arms where more IV needles had punctured his skin. Hannah was busy teleworking from the family respite center, answering the complicated questions that senators and congresspeople refer to the CRS. Once I heard Hannah promising a Senate staffer that she'd get a map and relevant information to him within thirty minutes. She held a conference call, partly in John's room, all very professional, giving no sign that she was near despair over her father's health. Once he said to a nurse, "And this one has been wonderful!"

I turned around to look. "Which one?"

"You," he answered, I think to me, but maybe not. I doubted I'd been wonderful. I just did what I thought I could in an unquestioning stupor. Hannah, however, was indeed wonderful.

In the hospital room, she tried to entertain John with tales of her plans to go at last on a wildlife safari. She said she'd become obsessed with safaris and was buying books on African wildlife and taking animal photography classes at the National Zoo. I think her plans eased John's mind about reneging on his long-ago promise to take her on safari ourselves.

The Princeton hospital offers a tempting menu from which patients may order meals. Once we got John to order the dinner of the day, to no avail. Once he got an egg salad sandwich, once a tuna salad sandwich. He just nibbled on their fillings. A nutritionist suggested Boost, the same dietary supplement John had bought to keep his frail mother going until she almost reached 100 years. He wouldn't touch it, and I later gave his unused Boost to a food bank. We started ordering ice cream and fortified milk shakes for him. I brought him granola bars and the new-to-me Kind bars, offering 200 calories apiece. John tasted them and approved but couldn't eat but a crumble. I asked myself what I could do for a man who was wasting away. His weight by then, a nurse confided to me, was under 120 pounds. "Pretty soon, I'm going to be the family heavy-weight," I tried to joke. When Hannah and I drove home, we often found that Maggie hadn't touched her mixed grill paté. "Not you too, Maggie," I said as I threw the old food away and opened a jar of baby food with a side of savory salmon paté.

Sometimes, if we asked, a nurse technician bathed John. I'm sure he found it humiliating, but they were professional and efficient. "What if I need to take a crap?" he asked. "I'll get you to the toilet," was the response. Nursing requires a good bit of strength, as well as professional distancing, so his beautiful body, as it had been, was just an impersonal bit of flesh for them to care for. I had had no desire to care for his mother in such ways. After she was moved into the nursing care unit of her facility, I thought she had lost so much of her mental faculties that it didn't even matter whether John or I came to see her or not. He said that the staff knew, so he would keep on visiting her regularly, as he would do over years, even if she did not know he was there.

Though I wouldn't have bathed and diapered his mother, I could have done this for my dear John, though it would have violated our roles as rather fastidious but passionate sexual and equal partners. He would never, however, have wanted such care from anyone, certainly not from me. Also, I think he did not want to live in a debilitated state, hauling oxygen tanks, relying on people to help him with the simple chores of daily living. Perhaps here too is another reason John climbed stairs and carried suitcases. He did not want to live as an invalid.

This was the time, when we were alone, that John said to me, "This is our anniversary."

"But we weren't married until Thanksgiving 1976, after I finally got my divorce."

"Yes, but our real anniversary was in May of 1975 when we first made love."

I kissed him on the forehead. "I do remember."

At home that night, Hannah and I conferred at length. She wrote: "We're desperate to figure out something to do. Since Georgetown seems out of the question at the moment, we decide to reach out to a pulmonologist Mom's friend Leslie has recommended, Dr. Barton, who Leslie said once saved her son's life." We looked up Dr. Barton on the web and found that he had written scholarly articles and had won academic prizes. In truth, I didn't know if doctors had protocols preventing them from interfering in each other's cases. In hopes that they did not, I left a message with Dr. Barton's answering service.

I called again on Thursday morning, 7 May, when Hannah recorded, "Dad continues to get worse." I didn't hear back and was about to conclude that this Barton was just another callous MD who cared more for medical camaraderie than for helping patients when my cell phone rang. Dr. Barton's receptionist called to say he would be in John's room within the hour, as a consultant. In ten minutes, he was there, shaking all our hands. Hannah noted that Dr. Barton was "the first doctor who sat down with us so far in our stay at this hospital. We told him the whole story, and he ordered a boatload of new tests." After Dr. Barton left, we asked John what he thought of him. "Handsome," was his single word.

"But do you trust this ruggedly handsome doctor?" I asked.

"Yes. Honest," John replied, in a throaty whisper.

Dr. Barton proposed doing a bronchoscopy, as they had talked of doing at Georgetown. Sending a miniscule camera into the bronchial tubes would allow Dr. Barton to see the vicious infection, treat it, perhaps cut it out, and restore John. When he heard that there was a CT scan from John's time at Georgetown, Dr. Barton ordered another one for comparison. Hannah and I spent a busy Friday afternoon, in between her teleworking, on the phone with the Georgetown radiology department. Staff members there said they would cut a CD and overnight it to me, if I had a FedEx number. With some hassle, I paid for my own FedEx account and placed the order. After all this work, Hannah wrote, "I'm really proud of us."

At 7 a.m. on Saturday, exactly a week after John had awakened me needing to get to the ER, a FedEx man rang the doorbell at home to deliver a padded bag with the CD in it. We rushed it to the hospital. Hannah wrote:

> Dr. Barton told us to take the CD to radiology, but doing so turned out to be a nightmare—as is so much with this hospital. I asked for directions to radiology at the nurse's desk and they said they'll take it down for me. Two hours later, I asked about it again, and it turned out that they gave the CD to a nurse. It had to go through some kind of proper procedures, and now a resident had to take it down. I said I'd take it down myself, but then they wouldn't give it back. After Mom said it's her property, not theirs, a resident finally showed up to take it down. This took up much of the day. Dr. Barton came by to say that many of the blood tests are coming back normal. Dad is upset that he has to wait all weekend in the hospital—he says he is miserable. He does take a good walk with a very cheery physical therapist, however, who walks him up the

stairs as practice for going home. It's nice to have someone who is genuinely cheery—as Dad says, the hospital is full of people with a lot of "gloomth"—gloominess, sometimes covered by a false feeling of chipper theory.

That was Saturday, but soon John was in such discomfort that he had to be recatheterized. Michael drove back up, and we three went out to dinner in a real restaurant, not a hospital cafeteria, but I couldn't eat much.

On Sunday, John was worse. No one tried to get him to walk. He said he needed to have a serious conversation with Hannah and me.

I half expected him to talk about organ donation. Instead he spoke of Swift's *Word-Book*—so very John. He described the headings for the electronic files and their backups and told us where the disks were located. He told us he had made out a set of scholarly instructions to pass on to the person who took up the project after him. The book should begin with the four sections of introduction: three essays by John, including the paper he'd presented in Münster in 2011, and the one Arch presented in Münster in 2000; then a transcription of Esther Johnson's vocabulary, along with a few facsimiles of her actual pages; then appendices to John's and Arch's essays. I said that maybe I could ready the first parts for publication, with Hannah's help. He thought I might possibly handle that but not the last parts, which would involve endless academic discussions of every word in the book, arcane matters of interest only to eighteenth-century scholars. I took notes on his instructions. Their complications were endless and overwhelming, yet another reason for saying, "Don't die, John, please don't die." We spent a glum evening and left John early, hoping he could rest. At home, I found John's scholarly "will," as I've called it, on his desk. I shuddered to find it full of technical computer instructions I could not follow.

We were back in the hospital early on Monday, when Hannah wrote:

> The day starts with Dr. Barton coming in and saying that many of
> the tests are back and are normal. It seems that hope is almost gone.
> We start talking seriously to the hospice people. Michael returns to
> DC. Then, at the end of the day, Dr. Barton comes back, looking
> exhausted. I think he's maybe had a fight with the in-house doctors
> who, when we ask about Dad's thirty-plus-pound weight loss, say
> things like, "Well, he's been in and out of hospitals lately, so that
> can happen."

The on-call doctor from our group of physicians made that ridiculous
excuse for a medical explanation. I should have said, "You don't lose
thirty pounds just from a couple of stints in bed. What is wrong with
him? And what is wrong with you?!" But of course, there was no point
in confronting her, and I lacked the energy to do so anyway.

The radiologists finally compared the two CT scans, and they
found that the mass in John's right lung had consolidated and enlarged.
Dr. Barton said that a bronchoscopy would let him take a sample in
case, as Hannah wrote, "it's a weird infection that could be cured with
targeted antibiotics. Dad has some hesitation, but agrees. Mom and I are
elated." Actually, both Hannah and I hid our reactions; we wanted John
free to make his own decision. Hannah continued, "We think this is
going to be the solution. Dr. Barton thinks he probably can't get a room
to do the bronchoscopy until Wednesday. He warns us that people are
often worse afterwards because the operation will stir up the infection.
We don't care. Dad asks for his 'veins to run with morphine' if things go
wrong. Dr. Barton agrees."

I was just sitting in the hospital room, unable even to read, when,
from beneath a pile of covers, John raised himself, pulled down his
Georgetown eye mask, and said, "Can't talk." Wires and tubes ran

out of the puny hospital gown that half covered his shrunken form. He pointed to his middle saying, "Pain equals" and then collapsed. I pulled the covers and mask up and tried to figure out what he meant that his pain equaled. Something very bad. I rang for a nurse, but by the time she arrived, John had subsided into a deep sleep. I still wondered what his pain equaled.

Because the mass in his right lung—which none of the Princeton doctors had even known about—was consolidating, Dr. Barton managed to get an operating room on Tuesday afternoon after all. When the healthcare services called to say so, John heard my response and rasped "Procedure today?"

"Yes, my dear," I replied.

"Dad, remember how happy we were bicycling in France?" Hannah asked. He nodded, just before they sedated him and put him on a stretcher. We followed it through staff elevators, one hall turning into another in a Kafkaesque maze ending in the ambulatory surgery unit. I recognized it as the very place where the GI doctor had given John a colonoscopy and endoscopy and then had dilated his esophagus, ages ago it seemed. Hannah and I waited quietly in a windowless room while the surgery took place. We were told that John came through it well and that we could wait for him back in his more comfortable room in the telemetry unit.

12

WHAT ST. PETER
WILL SAY

Hannah and I sat in John's room, side by side on the hospital sofa, holding hands and, I think, both praying. John's hospital bed, with clean smooth sheets, sat empty across from us. Even the bells and chimes and dings of hospital procedure seemed to have stopped in several suspended minutes of silence. Then a resident rushed in, his rubber soles squeaking on the floor tiles. In an agitated voice, he announced that John had crashed! He said that the doctors needed our permission to intubate John. (I didn't even know the word, but it was easy to figure out.) John's health directive and every instruction and conversation he'd ever had with staff said he did not want to be kept alive on feeding tubes. He had even joked of having "no code" tattooed on his chest, unavoidable instructions not to revive or resuscitate him. Explaining that John had refused to answer questions without us, the resident insisted that we should get back to ambulatory surgery right away. We followed him through the maze again, each of us terrified and nearly panicked. After we got there, as Hannah recalled, "It's all in-house doctors and staff crowded around Dad's bed. Dr. Barton has gone."

The "crash" meant that John's oxygen level had sunk to the low 70s. (A normal oxygen absorption rate is in the mid-to-high 90s.) They'd given him pure oxygen and temporarily upped his level back to the 90s. Hannah wrote that the in-house doctors were "all hectoring us. 'We don't understand,' they say. 'If you wanted hospice, why did you do a bronchoscopy? Don't you want us to intubate him?' We again said 'no.' Dad shakes his head 'no.' I ask if there isn't anything else—all we were being offered was hospice or intubation, and I was still looking for treatment. A nurse was hugging me. 'Am I making the choice to kill my father?' I asked."

Hannah and I were disgusted and frustrated with the original Princeton doctors who hadn't been able to help John. Our switch from these doctors to seeking treatment at Georgetown and from Dr. Barton had been an apparently audacious move—almost as outrageous as hoping that John could be treated, even cured. Hannah thought those doctors and staff members were punishing us for our audacity to seek other opinions. Forgetting John, they were determined to prove us wrong, themselves right:

> Dad, who was still perfectly sentient when he got back to his room, agreed with me about the motivation. It was only later in the evening that he became loopy—hallucinating, trying to take the O2 tubes out of his nose, etc. I'll never know if it was some kind of bad mix between cough medicines and morphine or what, but I really do regret this phase. It wasn't at all what Dad had envisioned by asking for his "veins to run with morphine." He was anxious and miserable. At times, however, he would be sentient. I asked him, "Dad, do you think Porgy finds Bess?" He smiled and said, "Of course I do."

I was not very sentient myself during this time. Somehow, the whole experience numbed me. It was Hannah who asked the questions and drew the conclusions. The reason I've relied so heavily on Hannah's memory of the bronchoscopy's aftermath is because I pushed it out of my mind, like so much else. Once I looked at a strange set of keys in my purse. "Where did these keys with the ugly orange plastic tab come from?" I asked.

"Mom, don't you remember, you had them in DC to let yourself into our house," Hannah scolded. I truly had forgotten. I guess fear can act like a delete button. I worried that fear and stress might take my mind along with my memory. Something else seemed to be taking my husband then, but I tried not to think about what was happening to my beloved John.

Again, John pulled down his sleeping mask. This time that stare that could look into me seemed to turn on me with accusing eyes, as if asking, "How could you do this to me?" John might have been thinking that I was the cause of his pain. I grabbed my chest, as if to protect it. I felt stabbed in the heart by my true love, no doubt just what John was feeling too. He pulled the oxygen tubing out of his nose then cried out, "Can't breathe." After I put the oxygen tubes back in his nostrils, his distress subsided and he became peaceful. His eyes focused kindly on me and on Hannah, who'd come to his bedside too. "Where am I? What world am I in?" he asked. He drew figures in the air. At times, Hannah wrote, "he seemed to be pointing at lovely things in the sky. I asked if he were comparing texts, and he said he was. I asked if they were different, and he said, 'Oh, yes,' as if he saw something beautiful in them—like the golden text I saw once in a dream." Once he said, "It's like different streams of consciousness. I see pictures of them. Flowers too." He seemed to be passing into a new existence.

I slept that night in his room, in my clothes on the hospital sofa, under blankets that stuck together, almost Velcro-like. When Hannah arrived in the morning, John took off his sleeping mask and said, "I worry about elephants."

A nurse, busy laying out medications, laughingly asked, "Elephants?"

As part of her talk about safari plans, Hannah had read him a *Smithsonian* piece before his surgery about the plight of elephants, killed by poachers for their ivory tusks. Later, she worried, "I shouldn't have read that to him."

All this time in the Princeton hospital, John had worn the pathetic standard-issue hospital gowns, with open backsides and mismatched snaps, to accommodate a heart monitor and various wires and tubes. On Wednesday, a hospice nurse and a social worker visited us and suggested that John might be ready for in-hospital hospice care, which keeps the patient comfortable but no longer attempts to cure him. They assured us that hospice can be reversed when, or if, the patient improves, a consoling option. So Hannah and I agreed that all the wires and tubes, except for the catheter, could be disconnected from John's body. Days before, I had brought in a nice yellow nightshirt for him. At last a nurse took off the pathetic hospital gown and wires and put him in the fresh shirt.

I said, "You look quite fetching."

He replied, "Just what Saint Peter will say."

I blew him a kiss. "You clever guy."

When John slept, I began writing an account of his progress, or lack thereof. When he woke and saw me writing, I fear he thought that I was at my eternal scribbling, perhaps turning his situation into another short story. Instead, I was writing a letter that I headed "devastating news" to send to our friends. That same Wednesday, a day after the bronchoscopy, Dr. Barton came to sit with Hannah and me while John slept. He said that the procedure did not reveal any strange disease, though results of the lab tests would not be in for days. Besides, John was wasting away. Dr. Barton seemed resigned, having done his best, the best possible, too late. He said to Hannah, "You realize that your father is dying."

The hospice nurse and social worker talked us through the process of entering in-hospital hospice that day and going home the next. John was sometimes sentient, often not. He hallucinated about being put in front of a firing squad. Once he tried to cram all his fingers in his mouth. Once he said, "Just kill me now." I wrote that horrible remark down, and then forgot it. In a clear sentence, he also said, "I don't want you to build a self-sustaining structure." I think he meant that he didn't want me to live without being close to Hannah or Reid. Hannah and I were distressed at his misery but we knew not what to do.

A hospice chaplain came to John's room. She said that there were five things people needed to say to each other at a death: "I love you," "Thank you," "I forgive you," "Will you forgive me?," and "Good-bye." Hannah noted that we had already said a lot of "I love you's" and "thank you's," but not the others. John asked Hannah to forgive him, but she said he'd done nothing to call for forgiveness. He said of course he had. Hannah first thought of his breaking his promise about taking her on safari but she had long since understood and forgiven that. Then she recalled that when she was about fourteen, a friend committed suicide, but neither John nor I had been very sympathetic to her schoolgirl anguish. Now she forgave us both for it. Hannah wrote that John had "taught me how to live for the living. I asked if he would forgive me, and he said of course. He didn't make me say for what in front of the cleric. We didn't say good-bye."

An hour later, the hospice nurse appeared, asking me, "Do you want him to die at home?" It was still almost impossible to think of death, but I answered, "Yes, of course," in tears again.

Hannah called her half-brother Reid, sobbing as she told him we were taking John home to die. "I've got my bag packed and am on the way," he replied.

Reid had had an uneasy relation with John. After the joint custody compromise, Reid spent the school year with his father and Christmas and summer holidays with John and me. Although Reid grew to adore his half-sister Hannah and treasured his summers with the three of us, he would arrive for his visits rather surly, filled no doubt with his father's diatribes against John. By the end of the summer visits, however, Reid was a civilized kid, very fond of John, delighted to hear him talk, but still reluctant with open affection.

One summer in Baton Rouge, Herb Rothschild campaigned as the liberal Democrat for Congress against the entrenched Republican representative of big business. As Herb's treasurer, John gave Reid a summer job, paying him to work for the campaign. Herb did not defeat the incumbent, but Reid learned much about computers and John, whose conscientiousness was a model of good business practice. That summer, John had a basketball hoop set up by our drive and shot hoops with Reid most evenings while Hannah walked Lucy down the sidewalk and I made dinner. Sometimes we went out to a favorite dive called Ruby's. Companionable memories of politics, basketball, and hamburgers were part of Reid's memory bank too. And since the birth of his own son, Reid had grown to love and respect John even more.

As soon as Reid heard Hannah say that her father was dying, he set out for Princeton. He arrived at 3 a.m. on Thursday, 14 May, after a freak closure of the Pennsylvania Turnpike. With little sleep, he came to visit us in the hospital and kissed John's forehead. Then Reid went home to help ready our bedroom for John's return. The paramedics delivered a bed, oxygen machine, wheelchair, potty chair, and more stuff to our home at midday. Everything came sealed in plastic, but there were no sheets. I suppose that no one in such a situation wants to use someone else's sheets. Anyway, I told Hannah where to find one of our green flannel sheets, which I'd finally taken off our bed as the temperature warmed, and she tucked it over the narrow hospital bed's mattress. Reid had worried that, from our bedroom, John might get up and fall down the stairs. After he and Hannah acknowledged that John was not getting up, they busied themselves arranging our bedroom, pushing aside chairs and book tables to accommodate all that equipment. I rode home in an Able Ambulance, seated next to the driver due to safety precautions while a medic monitored John's vital signs. I made small talk with the driver about the various improvements on Princeton's streets. I could not talk about John. My stomach felt queasy, but I could not let myself throw up whatever I had eaten that morning, not with John so very sick on the stretcher behind me.

That Thursday night, Bill and Ilse Goldfarb came by our house to pick up theatre tickets for the second show I'd postponed. I asked if they wanted to see John but gave them a choice. On the one hand, I knew John would hate for them to see him so debilitated. On the other hand, out of love and friendship, they might want to say good-bye. They chose to do so and went up to our bedroom. When they came downstairs, both were in tears, as were Hannah, Reid, and I.

A hospice aide arrived to spend the night by John. Hannah and Reid thought that John's breathing could be eased, and the aide agreed. So my two very different children went out together around 10 p.m. searching for Mucinex. Hannah said she was still thinking "that if we take very, very good care of him, he could live." When they returned, she started reading Shakespeare's sonnets to him. At first he seemed to enjoy them but then lost patience. She wondered if "they were too on the nose about the passing of time."

I belatedly realized that the chaplain should visit John one last time. The hospice team had supplied me with phone numbers, so I called and she arrived after eleven, bringing a pocket Communion kit in her purse. John and I took the thin wafers and drank the juice, the Body and Blood, in Christ's name, and the chaplain blessed John. He knew he was "dying, Panthea, dying." At last, I did too. Hannah tells me that we then invited the chaplain for cookies and tea or wine in the living room—she had tea, I wine. She stayed until after midnight. Fear pushed the delete button again, and I forgot about entertaining her. I only recalled asking the aide if she needed anything. She did not, since aides are expected to bring their own provisions. I said goodnight to Hannah and Reid, changed into a nightgown, and climbed into bed. John was beside me under the green flannel sheet on the hospital bed with the aide sitting in a chair near his feet. I felt like a zombie, incapable of feeling any more.

The hospice nurse arrived in mid-morning. By 10:30, she told me, "His heart is racing, trying to keep him going. He won't last much longer. It might comfort him to hear you read." She raised his bed so it was on a level with our high antique one and pushed them together. I stumbled into the hall like a zombie wondering what to read in John's last hour: the New Testament? Jonathan Swift? William Butler Yeats? Then I recalled looking up Yeats's poem, "Swift's Epitaph." I shook myself out of my zombie state, retrieved the book from my study, and crawled up across our bed to lie close beside John. Reid stood in the doorway. I reached out to clasp John's hand and began reading in as strong a voice as I could manage Yeats's "Sailing to Byzantium."

I knew John had liked the poem, but when I came across the line "Consume my heart away; sick with desire / And fastened to a dying animal," I thought I saw him exhale a slow breath. I feared I'd made a poor choice of reading material, however poignant were Yeats's lines. When I'd finished reading, I was about to turn to "Swift's Epitaph" or Yeats's poem "The Folly of Being Comforted." But as I started flipping pages, I glanced up and saw both the aide and Reid shaking their heads. I dropped the book and rolled toward John, throwing my arm across his chest. "John," I whispered, "don't leave me. Please don't." Beneath my hand and that yellow nightshirt, his ribs were utterly still. He hadn't lasted long enough to hear all thirty-two lines of the poem. He was gone, his soul no longer fastened to a dying animal.

Reid went downstairs to tell Hannah, who was out on the deck talking to a therapist. She wrote that she had been "already crying about how my plan to save my Dad hadn't worked, when Reid came outside. He patted me on the back, but I said I was on the phone. He leaned against the railing of the deck so I could see his face. 'He's dead,' he said. I screamed and wept." She dropped the phone, and she and Reid "held each other and wept—neighbors must have wondered what was going on." Then Reid returned upstairs.

The hospice nurse asked if I had another nightshirt for John, since grape-colored cough medicine had spilled on the yellow one. I got out a fresh blue nightshirt and wondered how someone with the quick wit and presence of mind to make that remark about St. Peter could be dead two days later. It wasn't logical. It wasn't right. It should have been otherwise. But there was no denying that John was really dead. He would not have liked knowing that the hospice nurses stripped the bed with him in it, pulling back the green sheet to reveal his penis, with a white tube running from it into the catheter bag, in front of me and Reid, before pulling the sheet back around John's body.

After the nurses had left, we each spent time alone with him. Even from downstairs, Reid and I could hear Hannah sobbing over her father. She regretted that she did not insist he remain in DC so he could have continued treatment at Georgetown University Hospital. She blamed herself, not John, who said he didn't want to be hauled back and forth down and up I-95 like a slab of beef. Probably she mostly blamed me because I didn't fight to make him go back quickly enough. I too blamed myself. Though hospice care publications and other materials on grief all advise you not to blame yourself, I would continue to do so for at least a year, as did Hannah.

After lunch on the day he died, I went up to sleep with him. I told Hannah and Reid the story of Miss Emily Grierson from Faulkner's "A Rose for Emily." Having poisoned her lover lest she lose him, she kept him for years in an upstairs room where, the town discovers after her death, she slept with what remained of him. "Now that's what they call 'Southern Gothic,'" I explained to my chillun. I wasn't ghoulish, but I did want to hold John in my arms one last time. As Tess Gallagher says, "We were dead a little while together then, serene and afloat on the strange broad canopy of the abandoned world." After I awakened, my arms still around John, I kissed him, one last time. I found myself paraphrasing Janice Joplin, "holding John's cold body next to mine."

That afternoon, Michael once again arrived back in Princeton. We four gathered beside the hospital bed. "John," I said, "We have one daughter and two sons here mourning you." Whenever I touched John, he seemed to get colder, if that were possible. His chest swelled up. His mouth fell open. When Maggie-the-Cat came upstairs, I held her up so she could see John. She hopped away and ran downstairs. I think she knew that the Daddy-Cat was dead, really dead.

Late that afternoon a huge black hearse, from the funeral home a hospice counselor recommended, drove slowly up our street and turned in our drive. Two men brought out a stretcher. I delayed them at the front door, while we each went up to say a last good-bye. The funeral guys were nice enough. A black man in a suit, a white one without a jacket having trouble keeping his shirttail tucked in. "Sorry for your loss," each said, several times, as they shook our hands. Hannah, Reid, and I left the room and walked out to the driveway, holding hands.

Soon the men came out the front door carrying a stretcher. On it was a long red rubber body bag zipped up tight. Inside was John, so small, so flat, so dead. I was glad not to see his face as they loaded the stretcher with the zipped-up bag on it into the hearse and drove slowly away. The words are "inexorable and irrevocable." There was no way to go back and change anything, not anymore.

I later learned that those impersonal body bags are regulation procedure for mortuaries. I assume they don't reuse them. The name for these men is not "funeral guys" but "undertakers." I wondered if there was another name when they put the body not under the ground but in the crematorium. Hannah and I had decided that John's body should be cremated, so that I could take him with me if I left Princeton, rather than have him buried there. At some point, which I don't remember, the paramedics took away all that equipment, of which John only used the bed, oxygen tank, and catheter.

That night, we four went to dinner in Hopewell at the Brothers Moon. We drank the bottle of the Honig wine John had put aside for a special occasion, and we used John's birthday card for a free dessert in the month of May. "Whose birthday is it?" the waiter asked.

I had to say that it was my husband's, who'd died that morning. The waiter was at a loss for words until I said, "It's all right. He was here in spirit, his soul was with us."

"Maybe he enjoyed the dessert," Michael quipped.

My diminished family stayed until Sunday, doing chores for me, replacing one toilet seat and screwing in another, breaking up the ice in my freezer, buying me gizmos to help my arthritic hands open jars and bottles, even purchasing a more efficient clothes dryer. Reid and Hannah were apprehensive about my living alone. Some eight years before, I had fallen rushing down the steps into the garage and landed on my head atop the concrete floor. That was before the Princeton hospital had moved, so John had gotten me to their ER in five minutes. John told the physician, "Panthea needed this like a hole in her head."

The doctor replied, "She has a hole in her head." (I later wrote up the story as "How I [Almost] Lost my Mind" for *Newsweek* online.) Falling and getting a resultant concussion left me subject to minor dizziness. Once I lost my balance on Reid's un-banistered front steps and called out, like a Victorian maiden in distress, "Catch me, John." Instead Reid, who was beside me, caught me. Now I assured my son and daughter that I always held onto railings and never, ever rushed up or down steps, and that I would be careful on my own.

My chillun left on Sunday, and then I had only Maggie-the-Cat for company. She was grieving too, and maybe angry at me. Or maybe Maggie was canny enough to calculate that if she turned up her nose at the dinner on offer I'd doctor it up with baby food, or cheese treats, or a new supplement in a tube called Cat-Cal, mightily improving her din-din.

I told her, "It's just us girl-cats here now. How're we gonna get along?" Maggie had no answers. Nor did I. I'm sure I overuse the word "alas," but I had to fall back on it again: ALAS.

I kept wondering what else I could or should have done, what St. Peter would say to me.

13

OTHERWISE

On Monday morning, 18 May, the doorbell rang at seven. In our doorway stood a suntanned man in a yellow jacket with orange stripes. The morning sun glowed on his reddish brown hair. He smiled at me, "Letting you know that we're working on your side of the street today. Belgian blocks for the curb. Gotta move your car across the street."

"Thanks, but no thanks," I replied, pulling my robe about me. "I'm not going anywhere." Except for emptying the trash, I stayed inside for a week, courtesy of Princeton's street engineers. The weather turned surprisingly cold, and I encased myself in an Irish cable-knit sweater of John's. I must have looked like a shivering refugee in a hand-me-down, but my shivers were from John's absence as much as the weather. Dogwood buds opened, even the one struggling in a thicket of root-choking bamboo. Rhododendrons boasted great pompoms of lavender blooms. Our center-hall colonial lacked the flamboyance of the Baton Rouge house I'd bought, but John considered our Princeton house his sort of place. How sad, I thought, that he couldn't relish the prettiness of our "New England cottage," as he'd called it, banked by flowers in the delayed spring.

When they'd been here on John's last day, my chillun had turned up the air conditioning. In this suddenly cooler weather, the cat and I were freezing. It took me some time to realize that I had options other than sweaters and covers. I belatedly turned on the heat and wondered if I'd become brain dead. We'd had a DVD of *From Here to Eternity* sitting around for months. "Is that the oldie with the kiss on the beach?" Hannah had asked. It was, but without John, I had no desire to watch it. Finally I put the red Netflix envelope out in the mailbox. A day later, I had a Netflix envelope again. I thought delivery had speeded up until I realized that this was the same envelope I thought I'd sent away. I didn't know how many times I'd removed disks from those envelopes and repackaged them for return. My brain had deleted the memory. Once I left the chandelier burning in the dining room all night. Twice I left the door to the deck unlocked. I recalled Emily Dickinson's "After great pain, a formal feeling comes." For me the feeling was numbness.

I became a slob. I skipped flossing my teeth. I avoided trimming my toenails. I didn't bother with vitamins or nightly showers. When I did shower, I lacked the imagination to search my closet for something different to wear. John and I had always made the bed together, a private ritual closing over our place of love. That winter we'd begun leaving the duvet and covers in a tangle, amused that Maggie would burrow under the warm duvet and look cute peering out from the tunnel she'd made. Since John had died, Maggie had not come into our bedroom. I sometimes spread the bed covers, but usually I left them alone. I didn't bother to open the shutters and let in light. Our bedroom became a dark den for me, alone.

I also became a snob. A friend brought me a vegetable salad in a glaring yellow plastic bag with red letters. After a day or two I chucked the salad, which smelled. I put the cleaned bowl back in its bag, but I hated those ugly colors jarring my kitchen harmony of pale shades of yellows, blues, and greens, so I stuck the bag out on the garage landing where I wouldn't have to look at it. I was invited to go to a movie and dinner one night. The thought was revolting, especially the dinner part. I was irritated with town workmen who seemed like silly boys playing with giant construction toys. Policemen zipping down the empty street in reverse also seemed like kids. I hated jackhammers, sounding like a thousand woodpeckers and making the house shake. I wondered if workers' jacket colors bespoke some protocol. Was there a meaning to the lime green shirts? Lime green with orange stripes? Just plain bright yellow shirts? Maybe there was no meaning at all to the brash colors they wore. Maybe there was no meaning to anything. But if there was no meaning, why live on?

My mood improved when I recalled John's great love, which had sustained me for so long. One week to the exact minute after his death, just before 11 o'clock on 22 May, I lay down in our bed and read "Sailing to Byzantium" both silently and aloud. But I had no hand to hold. I heard robins, catbirds, and daddy cardinals chirping in the trees, caught in that sensual music, the dying generations of Yeats's poem, which I now realized was indeed the right poem to have read to him on his deathbed. I hoped John had found the artifice of eternity beyond the decay of life, some solace in, as Yeats ends the poem, "what is past, or passing, or to come." I also fervently hoped my soul could join John's someday soon, "over Jordan" as another song goes.

On Saturday, 23 May, I awakened twice in a state I'd never experienced before. I knew not where or indeed what I was. I was floating in a black void. A cynic might point out that I was wearing a black sleeping mask, but I'd been doing so ever since the nurse at Georgetown gave us those masks. This felt different, floating free of my bodily form. It happened twice and then no more. I believe for just a while I was floating out of this universe with John's soul. I needed for him to speak to me, to tell me where we were, to explain the universe.

But there was only a black void, no sound, no explanation, except perhaps in Yeats's great poem: "Once out of nature I shall never take / My bodily form from any natural thing."

Later that morning, after a fit of coughing so violent I could hardly get my breath, I called the Saturday clinic of Dr. Barton's medical group. I got an 11:45 appointment, before they closed at noon. A doctor listened to my chest and prescribed a generic form of Ceftin. He also gave me an order for a chest X-ray. A nurse measured and weighed me. I was only five feet tall and weighed 108 pounds. At least, I thought, the jeans I wore at Christmas, when I weighed 116 pounds, should fit now. To Reid and Hannah, I described myself as the "incredible shrinking granny." I had not driven since Tuesday, 12 May, when I first slept in John's hospital room and Hannah took our car home. On 23 May, I thought I'd forgotten how to drive. The problem instead was that driving seemed a sacrilege, a violation of John's place behind the wheel. I could hardly bear to think that he was dead.

As consolation, I began writing down what I was doing, what was happening. Those diary-like jottings were just a way of remembering, a way to help my shattered brain get a focus on my grief. I had company on Friday, but they irritated me by talking about travels I wouldn't take and exhibits I wouldn't see and also by swallowing words at the ends of sentences. When they left, I wrote angrily about people who don't speak up even after being asked to and who avoid mentioning the great gap in our lives that John left. When the Goldfarbs came over, they spoke so clearly I could easily hear them. They asked how John died, and I didn't mind telling them. Bill had in his wallet a copy of Jane Kenyon's "Otherwise." He read it to Ilse and me that evening. In short, condensed lines, Kenyon speaks of her pleasingly ordinary day, which "might have been otherwise." She ends: "But one day, I know, / it will be otherwise." My face scrunched up as I sobbed. "Oh Bill, that's just right. Please read it at John's memorial! You know, I think it might have been, could have been otherwise. It certainly should have been!"

The morning of Sunday, 24 May, I had my first sexy dream. John and I were feeling up each other's bodies and trying unsuccessfully to find a private place to make love. Later that morning I went to church, thinking then more about the spirit than the flesh. The woman next to me in the pew leaned over to ask how I was doing. "John died," I sobbed. Later, I asked for a blessing on "the beautiful soul of my husband John Fischer, who died on 15 May." Then I broke into tears again. People I didn't know came up to hug me, including a woman who had also lost her husband suddenly, about a year before. That afternoon, I attended a CWW meeting. Of the many comments I received, among the most touching was one woman's comment, "It was a privilege to have known John." For me too.

I was so tired, I let my crooked spine get the best of me. Standing up straight seemed too much of an effort, and my scoliosis twisted me to the side. I meant to practice walking but didn't. Our street was too muddy and sludge-covered. Or I was too lazy. When I finally went out to the grocery store, I looked at pear-shaped women my age and thought, *They are old.* I wondered if they'd ever had sex, or enjoyed it. Or maybe, I realized, they looked old because they were sick or had endured operations that I was lucky enough to have avoided. *Where's your compassion, Panthea,* I asked myself.

Hannah and I talked almost daily on the phone. Planning memorials at least gave us some diversion from our grief. We decided on having two of them, the first in the august Princeton University Chapel, the second in the Arts Council of Princeton's eclectic building. Hannah printed up a classy black and gold email invitation to the dual memorials. I got a call from literary scholar Pat Spacks, whom we'd known first through John's mentor Aubrey Williams. She told me that a doctor long ago had told her that, in grief, it is necessary every day to have face-to-face encounters with live persons. Phone conversations won't do. You may talk to a sandwich-maker or yardman, but you had to talk to a human being. I invited people over, partly to test Pat's advice and partly to help me consume the supply of eats via FoodyDirect that Michael's family had sent.

Next-door neighbors Hinda and Norbert arrived late one afternoon. Their visit was a blur of plans for a dinner party I thought of giving before the memorials and of questions from Hinda. She wondered why our grass was so green. I was so brain-dead I couldn't answer, and it was only later I recalled that John had planted grass seed, religiously, after a huge tree from the yard on the other side of ours crashed across our yard after Hurricane Sandy. Hinda also wondered if my loss was like that of a mutual friend. I responded vehemently, "No." Our friend and her boyfriend didn't have children together, didn't even live together. Her house didn't look much different after he died, except for a few paintings she inherited. Her man was a part of her life but never really a part of her house.

On the other hand, I insisted, "This house we are sitting behind was ours, both of ours." I told them I couldn't open a drawer or a cabinet or a closet or look at bookshelves without encountering John. When I got in the car, I had to push aside his driving moccasins. On his desk, I'd discovered a contraption that looked like a pitcher with a tube attached. He was to blow into it hard enough to suspend balls on his breath. I'd opened the kitchen-table drawer and found an odd-shaped green plastic bottle, another breathing aid. The kitchen counter reproached me for not keeping it as spotless as John did. So did the car, which he kept washed and waxed, its insides vacuumed. John was everywhere, as were reminders of his illness.

Once when Lynn invited me over, I scraped the side of the car, trying to park between her car and her fence. I suppose if he saw our scratched car, John would say, "Oh, meow!" I did renew his library books online at Princeton University's Firestone Library in a process he had meticulously described to Hannah and me a few days before his death. As I was typing in his bar code number on our old computer, it occurred to me that John's borrowing privileges would expire by midsummer. I was sitting on a rickety chair in the basement, which felt like it might crumble beneath me. Even there in the basement, there were books everywhere, including the library's complete edition of Sir Walter Scott's letters, which John checked for footnotes he needed for the *Word-Book*. I didn't know what would happen to the *Word-Book* or to these library books. The old chair didn't crumble, but I felt I might.

"Five-twenty-six-forty." How many, many times over the last months had I given out his birthdate to technicians, orderlies, nurses, doctors? I couldn't count. But I did know that on 26 May 2015, John would have been seventy-five. I got a note from our German friends, Hermann and Erika Real, recalling John's fiftieth birthday when they, colluding with Hannah, then eleven, had surprised John at breakfast. He sat down to one of those huge German breakfasts of rolls, cold cuts, liverwurst, butter, cheeses, and strong coffee, not noticing a balloon over his head. With nods from Hermann and Erika, Hannah, who had been concealing a needle in the palm of her hand, punctured the balloon. Cascades of confetti spilled over John's hair and the liverwurst, to his complete astonishment. The Reals that day took us to a country fair. In Soest, a medieval town with an impressive Romanesque cathedral, dating from 950 AD, we had a lovely outdoor lunch and took a picture of John, who rarely ate desserts, actually eating cake. Giving up sweets was one of his ways of keeping trim, until his last months, when he ate almost any sweet in a desperate attempt to counter the weight loss that was zapping his strength.

I wondered what I should do for John's seventy-fifth birthday.

I mostly cried and drank bourbon with Leslie. But first I drank ice water with Deborah Blanks, Associate Dean of the Princeton University Chapel, where Hannah and I planned the first memorial service on 14 June. Dean Blanks and I talked about our backgrounds, especially John's. Bringing samples of past memorial programs, she pointed out all the arrangements I'd need to make: what music to choose for the prelude and postlude, what verses were to be read by whom, what hymns were to be sung and in what order, what to do about contributions. I was glad to tell her that our old friend David Lange, who had baptized John and Hannah back in Baton Rouge, had agreed to fly in from Texas to give the eulogy. That seemed a Grace, as did an offer from our CWW friend Nora Sirbaugh, who teaches voice at two local colleges. She volunteered to sing from Shakespeare's *Cymbeline* "Fear no More the Heat o' the Sun." Imagining how my Shakespeare-loving husband would react to her singing, tears welled up in my eyes.

The next morning, after I had a chest X-ray taken to send to Dr. Barton, I couldn't get back in our driveway because a giant Komatsu front-end loader was tackling the stump of our old maple tree, removed to make way for the new sidewalk. I parked in a nearby office building parking lot to walk home. I saw the front-end loader grab the tree stump in its maw and heave it down on the driveway, a mangle of twisted roots and growth looking like some medieval trap.

Rather than smartly waiting until the pavement workers took a noon lunch break, I dumbly walked out at 11:45 and started driving the car back. One giant machine was scooping up gravel and dumping it in the back of a truck blocking the turn into our road. I stopped, but a brazen guy motioned me on. I crept along, terrified that I'd scrape the right side of my car again, or drive my left wheels into the ditch for Belgian blocks. I managed to skirt such disasters, but I came inside quite shaky and calmed myself with a vodka tonic. I wondered if I was becoming a drunk. Probably I was, but who cared? I didn't. But when I left a message for Hannah on the wrong phone and set out the wrong vitamin pills at the wrong time, I did care to find a way to rescue myself from ineptitude. A natural scribbler, as well as former English teacher, I hoped that words might help me get control of my addled brain, make order out of my misery.

Later that afternoon, I saw the monstrous front-end loader again tackling our uprooted, creature-like tree trunk. Its giant maw pulled it up and hurled it down, again and again, most of the afternoon until the machine finally demolished it, leaving roots all over the drive. In the past, John would have been out yelling, "What the hell do you plan for me to do with this mess? Don't tell me to place my branches in neat piles by the roadside." In the spring of 2015, he'd hardly had energy to go outside, much less to yell. It occurred to me that I needed to yell, not at the workmen, but at doctors, smokers, incompetents, and myself.

Jotting down my experiences helped clear the cotton wool from my mind so it could focus better. I realized that those experiences might also be building blocks for a memoir that would help me with my grief and maybe others too. Still, I wondered if anyone would learn much from my steering between a truck and a ditch. And I doubted that people would want to read about the interminable chores that reproached me for neglect. John's still-packed suitcase, for example, had been sitting on the floor in our bedroom ever since we'd planned a move to Georgetown, thinking to leave on 5 May to see Dr. Reichner the next day.

The Goldfarbs visited again, bringing leftovers from a Memorial Day feast they'd had for neighbors. I had one barbecued rib. It was good, but I didn't want to eat much of anything. Cheese and fruit and the whitefish salad the Pincks sent were more my style. I drank a vodka tonic and then wine with dinner. I received, via UPS, a living tulip ready to flower if I could follow the instructions. Meanwhile, I discovered poison ivy on my leg. That seemed impossible, since I'd hardly been outside, but there was no denying the itchy, stinging rash of blisters. I wondered if writing about that could help me survive. But then who would care to read about my poison ivy?

I found a tube of some old anti-itch cream bought years ago at the beach in Mathews, Virginia. Even that plain little tube brought back memories of being with John in Mathews's old-timey drug store, with its wooden floors and helpful pharmacists, a husband-and-wife team. Those good times in the sleepy little town were bygone recollections. Instructions on the tube said to apply to affected area. That was me, all of me. Maybe, I thought, people might care to read about that after all.

On the morning of Thursday, 28 May, I found the kitchen aglow, not just with sunshine but with our many-bulbed kitchen light fixtures. I apologized to John's ghost, since John never would have gone to bed without checking lights. I expected to be delivered from the burden of heavy chores, but then I listed the little chores and found that I had a whole page (and a whole day) of them ahead of me: calls and email messages to readers of Bible verses, the administrator at the Chapel, the printer for the Chapel, the florist, the sexton, the organist, other possible participants, thank-yous to write to people who'd sent food and tulips, and a call to the undertaker. My message for him was that I'd lost my husband and didn't know where he was (or his ashes were). All these various chores were unavoidable, most but not all of them boring. They did keep me from subsiding into sobs and wails. I tried to stand up straight, most days. Hannah and I continued speaking regularly. With her anonymous stories about inside workings of the CRS and Congress, she offered diversions. I was not so comforting to her, I'm sure.

I wish I had read then Atul Gawande's *Being Mortal*, especially his chapter "Letting Go." with comments on the "modern tragedy" of our inability to accept death. Instead, I Googled the five stages of grief. They seemed to have nothing to do with "letting go," and none sounded like me, except guilt. I keep thinking about the many ways I'd failed John. I could not explain why I didn't get him away from Dr. G. and the docs who wouldn't rethink their hypotheses. If I'd only asked earlier for recommendations of pulmonologists, maybe I could have found Dr. Barton sooner. Or perhaps I could have gotten John to the heart and lung hospital in New Jersey or to Georgetown in February. I knew that grievers are not supposed to dwell on regrets, much less failures, but I faulted myself for all that I might have done but didn't. Writing about it clarified my thoughts but brought more tears.

I had been putting off calling Express Scripts, from which our health insurance insisted we order prescriptions by mail. At the end of other chores that same Thursday, I did call. To my surprise, I talked with a live human being. She cancelled John's policy but wouldn't let me send back the meds that had arrived after he died. Express Scripts had sent Atorvastatin for John. The hospice team had ordered a large drug bag, overnighted via FedEx. The drugs, which must have cost a fortune for the insurance company and the taxpayers, arrived the day after John died. The bag included Haloperidol and Lorazepam for anxiety or agitation, acetaminophen suppositories for mild pain or fever, Hyoscyamine to prevent secretions to the lungs, Prochlorperazine for nausea and vomiting, Bisacodyl suppositories for constipation, and morphine, enough for fifteen days to treat pain or shortness of breath. I was thankful John hadn't needed all those heavy drugs, which was hardly a bright side to dying so quickly, so unnecessarily.

When I walked down nearly to the end of the block, I imagined neighbors whispering, "Isn't she wearing those same turquoise-colored pants she wore the last time we saw her out?" I also imagined headlines, "Grieving widow walks, somewhat tipsily, on unfinished road of stones, gravel, and silt; trips, falls, and perishes." I did not perish but came home with mosquito bites on the top of my head, where my hair was thinning. I took a long shower and scratched the bites with John's ginger shampoo. In March and April, John had repeatedly opted for a washing-up rather than showering. I'd thought he was just too clean to need a complete shower. Later, I realized that, at home as in Georgetown, the steam from hot showers had made breathing difficult for him.

Maggie still refused to go upstairs. I supposed she recalled seeing John dead on the bed beside ours. Maybe she thought I killed him. Maybe she missed the news, because without John, the house was very quiet. I felt I should go back to listening to news and music. I tried turning on the TV, but it didn't work. I mentioned this problem to Hannah as part of the long list of things I didn't know how to do without John. She paused and then confessed to unplugging a cord by the TV while she'd been here and forgetting to replug it. I was relieved that I hadn't exposed my incompetence by asking Colin to help me fix the television when all it needed was plugging in.

One night Maggie did come up to our bedroom, perhaps because I turned on the air conditioning, flooding her pallet with cold air. She noticed John's still-packed suitcase, sniffed it, and settled in for a moment. Then she hopped out. Perhaps the scent in even his clean clothes brought him back to her, or rather reminded her that the Daddy-Cat couldn't come back. Or maybe she felt that she was violating John's special space. Anyway, she scurried downstairs. Thinking in slow motion, I moved her downstairs pallet away from the vent that was sending out cold air.

Maggie's brief sojourn in John's suitcase reminded me that it was past time for me to unpack it. I hadn't wanted to encounter something else so very John—his clothes, so carefully folded they looked ironed. At last, I lifted them out and put them in his chest of drawers. Placing his neatly folded polo shirts, nightshirts, socks, and underpants beside his orderly arranged swimsuits, shorts, and the other casual clothes that he'd worn at the beach reminded me, yet again, what a handsome man he'd been before that disease ravished his body.

One night, I opened the kitchen table drawer and this time found two pairs of glasses and a prescription for new lenses from the past October. I had encouraged John to buy progressive lenses rather than switching between glasses, one pair for reading, hanging around his neck on a lanyard, the other one often lost. He seemed to think that progressive lenses were fine for me, too expensive for him. I wondered if he thought that he wasn't worth them. Or perhaps he thought he wouldn't live long enough to get his money's worth out of them. I wondered if he'd had a premonition.

Such reflections might indeed be raw material for a memoir, if I correctly understood memoirs—why people write them and why other people read them. I knew that many memoirs are self-aggrandizing, usually ghostwritten, designed to validate or enhance the author's or the subject's fame and fortune. (Jane Mayer's *New Yorker* article "Trump's Boswell Speaks" offers a harrowing example.) And there are hangers-on memoirs, of the "I-knew-him-(or her)-best" sort. Such memoirs hope to capitalize on or to create fame. In our celebrity-saturated culture, people often try to participate vicariously in fame and fortune through reading about movie stars, athletes, politicians, or other celebrities. John was no such star. His fame as a brilliant and conscientious Swift scholar was not something on which to capitalize. So I considered that perhaps no one would care to read about him or me. I also realized, though, that there are memoirs other than the celebrity variety, memoirs that engage and even inspire readers. I wondered if I could write one of those. For now, I was content to jot down my thoughts and memories, raw material that I could continue to shape and revise into a manuscript with the passage of time.

After all John's frugality, I planned to spend a minor fortune on memorials for him. I had decided to have a dinner Saturday night at our home for mostly out-of-towners, small enough recompense for their travel to be with me. Then two memorials were on Sunday afternoon: a service in the Princeton University Chapel followed by a less formal remembrance at the Arts Council of Princeton. I hoped John would approve. He was different about money from most people. He was frugal, hating to spend money to buy good clothes when old jeans would do. (I think wearing jeans was another reaction to those years of dressing in a suit and tie to look the part of The Chairman of the English Department. He figured his good clothes hadn't earned him much respect, so he might as well be comfortable.) He also did not want to hire a gardener, much less a landscaper, when able-bodied people like us could plant, weed, mow, and shovel. But the same John, who hated to spend a little money to hire a gardener to help outside, was glad to hire a maid to help inside, and really loved picking up the tab at family dinners, hotels, and weeklong holidays on the beach. I suppose that was being a paterfamilias. He was glad to be a big spender for the family, not for himself, so he didn't like it when Hannah or I paid for a surprise he thought extravagant. "How much is all this costing?" he'd ask suspiciously.

For our seventieth birthdays, Hannah and Michael gave us a fabulous present: an open-air feast offered by Outstanding in the Field, which travels the country staging food and wine events with local farmers, fisher folk, vintners, and chefs. Ours was in early September 2010, on the sands at Rehoboth Beach, Delaware. While we nibbled on appetizers and drank an aperitif, people gave talks about their methods of growing, fishing, pickling, baking, braising, harvesting, fermenting, and so on. The group brought tables to the farm, instead of the other way around. The multicourse dinner lasted hours, and was extraordinary. When he found out how much it cost, however, John was appalled. His reaction was to pay for "the kids'" room that night and to buy tickets for both cars to ferry across the Delaware Bay to Cape May the next day.

In the motel that night, I poured us each a nightcap of bourbon. I handed him his and sat by him on the edge of the bed. "John, my dear, these 'kids' are grownups. They make nice salaries, probably bigger than our pensions. This was their gift. You don't have to treat them."

"Yes, I do," he smiled, joking at himself, a bit.

I laughed and patted his knee, under one of the sleep shirts I'd bought him. Then I leaned to kiss his cheek. "I understand, I think." So I did not object when he picked up the bill at lunch for the four of us in Cape May the next day.

I understood that John wanted us to save our money so no grandchildren of ours would be denied a first-rate education, as he had been. He had been told that there was no money to send him off to school, though five years later his brother got sent to MIT. John stayed home to attend Ohio State, but actually ended up getting a very good education in its new honors program. He was admitted to several prestigious graduate schools, including Yale, but could not afford to live in New Haven with his first wife. Besides, he got an NDEA fellowship to go to Florida and study with Aubrey Williams. How studying Jonathan Swift's poetry could qualify under our National Defense Education Act remained an enigma, but Florida made John happier than Yale ever would have. John didn't want any grandchild of ours to have to turn down a great education because she or he couldn't afford it. Our only grandchild is Reid Jr., no blood kin of John's, as it seemed that Hannah's health was too risky for bearing a child. Do I dare say "alas" again? Still, John wanted to provide for the younger Reid's education as he wished his grandparents and parents had provided for his. We made a modest gift to a college fund for Reid Jr. when he was just a baby. It has nearly doubled in value since then.

As it was, I began telling Maggie that we were wealthy lady cats. But even the fanciest of cat food doesn't cost that much. The money that John and I put in young Reid's college fund may actually have limited his ability to earn a scholarship, so I didn't want to give Reid any more college money then. There were so many good causes needing money that I began giving more generously to humanitarian aid, environmental causes, and political ones too. Still, I remained unsure which charities John would most endorse, which ones would make him proud to know I was trying to preserve his identity as a paterfamilias. I began thinking of setting up a small foundation in John's name to help support underprivileged children, but I felt that I needed his advice.

However much ideas of sharing John's generosity brightened my days, one thought still darkened them: It could have been otherwise.

NO WAY

On 29 May, two weeks after John died, the doorbell rang. I pulled on my robe and scurried downstairs. This time the early morning light shone on the silver hair of Karl, the plumber. Having investigated clogged-up filters, a broken toilet, and a lightning-struck air-conditioning unit, he'd gotten to know us over the years. In fact, when I'd made the appointment months before to have our air conditioning checked, I'd requested Karl.

He asked the usual, "How you doing?"

"Poorly," I said, holding the door frame.

"What's the matter?"

"John died," I said.

"No way!" was his reply. That was exactly how I felt.

There was no way the sun wouldn't rise and set, no way the moon wouldn't wax and wane, no way John could have died. But he had.

After Karl left, at 10:50 I lay down on John's side of our bed, without a hand to hold, and read "Sailing to Byzantium" aloud. I kept wondering how I might have saved him. I went through another litany of should-haves. I should have insisted we go South in February, ignoring the GI doctor's restrictions. I should have been more frightened by John's difficulties breathing in the mornings. I should have distrusted his near-normal afternoon breathing. After he was released from Georgetown, I should have insisted that we stay in a motel with no steps instead of at Hannah and Michael's with its steep steps. I should have kept John from carrying suitcases up our steps. I wondered if, as John lost strength, I had too. Perhaps I had regressed into being again something of a timorous mouse, after all those years.

I knew that memoirists must believe that parts or the whole of their life stories are worth preserving for others. Historical memoirs include astonishing, priceless experiences of surviving slavery, an arctic voyage, the Holocaust, a Pacific voyage, and other such harrowing experiences. Enormously popular travel memoirs allow readers to participate in adventures without the risks and expense of travel and also to plan for their own best possible travel experiences. Memoirs may simply be family reminiscences, "I-was-there" or "I-knew-your-great-grandmother" remembrances. They can keep bits of the past from being lost and thus may serve as legacy memoirs. Many memoirists write self-explorations, which can become social commentaries and often spiritual journeys. And there are cautionary tales, implying, "Don't make the mistakes I did."

I felt I'd made so many mistakes of omission or commission that my story was a cautionary tale. My guilt obsessed and so nearly paralyzed me that Hannah took a weekend off to check on me. We busied ourselves going to the jeweler who'd downsized John's wedding ring for me to wear stacked above my engagement and wedding rings. We looked over the Arts Council, that remarkably lively building designed by Michael Graves on Paul Robeson Street, transformed from the old YMCA. Its displays included a quilt showing people and places from the old neighborhood, children's paintings, and even art created from trash. That night Hannah roasted asparagus she'd bought on her way into town. We ate it with ribs the Goldfarbs had left for me, all tasty enough to give me an appetite. Almost anyway.

John used to say that I'd be better off if he died first, not that he was planning on doing so. I'd contradicted him, knowing that my areas of domestic competency were easier to learn than was his expertise in electronic, financial, and mechanical matters. John did avoid knowing much about household appliances. When I was away, he ignored the washer, dryer, and dishwasher. In the past, I'd been the cook, he the cleaner-upper. Sometimes I'd thought he cleaned too much: "You're not leaving anything for the maid to do."

"There's plenty left to do," he'd insisted. "I'm not mopping, dusting, or scrubbing tubs and toilets. I'm just keeping crumbs from getting tracked all over the house."

John's expertise in many matters seemed, on the other hand, impossibly complicated. I had conveniently avoided knowing anything about car maintenance, lawn mowers, sump pumps, our "water commander," or computer maintenance. On finances, I'd written the checks and done a monthly tally, but John had had a complex system of checking my tallies against an ongoing budget by which he calculated each month's overage or underage. His care with the finances could have made him our broker's favorite client, but John also checked to see why some investments did not meet the S&P average, why several didn't perform as advertised. I couldn't do that. No way.

When I repeated to Hannah John's remark about how it would be easier if he died first, she thought my explanation about learning the other's skills was irrelevant, even ridiculous, and thought John's remark was yet another instance of his failure to value himself enough. He knew he would be devastated if I died first, but his would have been emotional devastation, not a matter of learning to cook or do laundry. My dear John had not envisioned how emotionally devastated I would be by his death.

On 31 May, Hannah and I had a visit from Tamara, widow of John's first cousin Paul, who died of the same disease that had killed John's brother, Jeff. We had long feared that acute myeloid leukemia was lying in wait to pounce on John too. I suppose John did have a better death—at least a quicker one, if that's any consolation. Tamara brought her new beau, and they took us to brunch at the Brothers Moon. I had an omelet with caramelized onions and goat cheese, asparagus, and home fried potatoes, food yummy enough to bring my appetite back, almost. I saved half of mine, and Hannah saved half of hers, which she left behind when she departed later in the afternoon. I suppose she feared I'd starve without a little more sustenance.

Graduation at Princeton was on 2 June. Everyone on my list connected with the Chapel was busy. I needed to find accommodations for out-of-town guests. The Nassau Inn, ideally placed downtown, would be full on the weekend of the memorials, and so I tried to think of places out on Route 1. I recalled a motel, which I'd passed too many times, opposite the highway from the Princeton hospital. I got reduced rates for guests who mentioned either John's name or mine.

Seemingly endless chores still awaited me. I could pull weeds and repot the tulip gift, but it still seemed too wet and cold outside. Besides, men in bulldozers, dump trucks, and front-end loaders were all over the street. I didn't want them to see me working on the lawn, lest they realize that I lived alone. I could have neatened my study. I could have drawn a map for out-of-town guests. I had a box of Mother's early-twentieth-century Alabama postcards that I had promised to donate to the University of Alabama Library that I could label and package. Or I could pay bills. Maybe I could sort John's medical records. Maybe I could go back to bed. I looked forward to noon, when I could pour myself a glass of wine to drink with warmed-up omelet and then take a nap. I recalled that John and I had napped often in his last months, I from fatigue and wine, he from fatigue and, I belatedly realized, insufficient oxygen.

A police truck with flashing red and blue lights drove into our driveway. I hoped the front-end loader hadn't damaged some gas line. I wouldn't have known, since I hadn't used the gas stove since long before John died. The truck was full of orange cones, the sort Governor Christie joked about putting out to close the George Washington bridge. After the truck left, the cones dotted our street. I gathered energy to put out the green bin of organic recycling materials, mostly of uneaten food, both mine and Maggie's. She still seemed to be grieving for John, as I was. I managed to group the historical postcards into labeled envelopes and sealed the assortment into a sturdy wine box for mailing. No matter how many chores I finished, others surfaced and seemed to multiply. I understood the phrase "sick and tired." That was how I felt.

The only upside, if you could call it that, to this tragedy was that the daily mail brought private, handwritten letters, not just a flood of junk mail. The handwritten notes I was then receiving were true condolence letters. Many were on conventional Hallmark cards with personal remarks added about how much John had meant to people. Many recollections were portals into past adventures John and I had shared with a variety of people. Many cards were unconventional, artistic reproductions: a William Morris pomegranate print, a photo of marshlands, a cat imprint on heavy handcrafted paper, an Andrew Wyeth painting of an open window with sheer curtains blowing inward. On that card, our friend wrote, "You and John opened many windows to experiences and now I imagine a window is always open to the flow of his spirit." I doubted anyone would have such fond memories of me. I am not so kind as John, but one friend pleased me by calling us "PanJohn— one funny, elegant, perfectly balanced duo." Being only half of a well-matched pair meant, however, that I was out of balance, in several ways.

From my study window, I watched a man propelling an almost cute little two-roller compacting machine up and down the newly cleared space on the other side of the street. Via remote controls, he made vibrators inside it jiggle the soil until it flattened, ready to have asphalt poured on top. Just a few years ago, a sidewalk had been laid on that same strip. In 2015, it had been torn out and replaced with an asphalt bike path, while my side of the street was getting its own concrete sidewalk. Princeton could afford all this, thanks to heavy property taxes, but I suddenly recalled that John had been glad the old sidewalk was across the street; so he'd not be responsible for keeping it shoveled. *Oops,* I thought. *Now I'll have to shovel snow on this side, unless C. J. can do it.* C. J. kept a wallet, where he put the $5 I paid for his kitty litter duties. I figured he ought to be glad of a bigger salary so I wouldn't break my back shoveling snow.

I still had no death certificate, no proof of John's death other than my memory of holding his cold body next to mine and seeing them take away that zipped-up red body bag. I didn't even have a bill for cremation. I began to wonder if John's ashes could get mixed up with someone else's. I worried that they could stuff ashes from a fireplace or a burnt building into the cherry box Hannah suggested I order for John's ashes. I didn't know if a person's DNA remained in his ashes. Clearly, I believed, his spirit did not, but where was it? "What world am I in?" he'd asked. It was still hard to believe he was no longer in my world.

When I backed out of the driveway on 3 June, preoccupied with not running over our recycle bin, I did run into the giant front-end loader, doing no damage to it or our Honda, since I was only inching along. I drove to nearby Rocky Hill to mail the box of postcards to the University of Alabama Library, but the postal clerk said the law prohibited putting a wine or whiskey box in the mail. When I ran a few other errands and returned with the rejected wine box, workmen were lined up on the curb opposite our drive, like birds on a wire, each eating a sandwich out of a blue and white cooler. Maggie had thrown up by the front door. John had been so good about cleaning up her messes, as if he wanted to protect me from them. Now I got paper towels and disinfectant to erase the mess myself.

On the kitchen phone was a message from Loretta, at pulmonary rehab. "John," she said, "I'm inquiring about how you're feeling and wondering if you have any plans of returning to rehab." *Oh, Lord,* I thought. *How can I answer that?*

Sometime back I had made an appointment with Dr. Barton, though by June his partner's prescription for generic Ceftin had worked magic on me. *Suppose our GP had prescribed it for John last January—maybe he'd still be alive. Then maybe we'd be happily sunning ourselves on the beach at Mathews, Virginia. Or maybe we'd be house-hunting in St. Augustine.* Like so much else, such ideas were too painful to linger over. I no longer needed to see a doctor, but I kept my appointment with Dr. Barton to ask about John. I complained that no one had prescribed Ceftin for John. He pulled up John's chart and showed me that John had actually gotten Ceftin, but only after he arrived in the Princeton hospital. I said, "Too late." I recalled that Hannah had written that a comparison of CT scans had revealed that "something, probably pneumonia in Dad's chest, has consolidated and gotten bigger." Dr. Barton did not renew that observation, probably to keep me from despair. After all the suffering and bad timing and grief, there seemed no point in confronting the one doctor who had used his imagination to try and save John.

At home, I went up to my study to renew my jottings, now less like a diary and more like a fledging memoir. I was recording my devastation and my ineptitude, but I'd also begun asking myself how I might survive and why. Later that day, I opened a soft calf's leather wallet sitting on John's dresser. I'd bought it for him and had the initials JIF embossed on it. The middle fold had frayed and it lacked a transparent window for his driver's license and multiple pockets for credit cards, so John hadn't used it recently. Leaving for the Princeton hospital's ER, he'd left behind his more day-to-day one with a Velcro closing and a stash of credit cards and cash filling its pockets. Later he'd asked Hannah to bring an old one to the hospital, and so she'd found this monogrammed one and taken it to him. When we'd left the hospital, it was among a few things in a tote bag that I'd returned to his dresser.

On that June afternoon when I opened it, I saw, on the stiff, yellowed ID card inside, evidence of our past. John had crossed out our Baton Rouge address and phone number and inserted the Princeton information. He had changed my last name when I resumed using the name Reid. And on the bottom line he had crossed out the name of a former doctor and had written in "Barton." John had only met Dr. Barton on 7 May. Thus near the very end of his life, whatever he feared or intuited, John had hoped to change doctors. Perhaps he simply wanted Dr. Barton, not the others, to sign his death certificate. I couldn't know, but I thought the ID card provided concrete evidence that somehow John had, after all, hoped to live.

Working with the caterers, the Arts Council, and the Chapel staff took days, off and on. I actually enjoyed drawing a rough Princeton map ("NOT to scale!") for out-of-towners, highlighting the major spots they'd need to get to. I mailed it to them all, using stamps of a flower, outlined in black with a little red heart on the side, a "forever" stamp that echoed the fact that my love and mourning for John would last forever. Dean Blanks from the Chapel called to say that I hadn't included a prayer in my plans for the memorial service. I did say the Lord's Prayer most nights and asked for a blessing on John's soul. I couldn't think why I didn't put a prayer in the program, except that there seemed no way I could cope with all the burdens I was carrying without dropping some. My inspiration to survive threatened to implode.

On 4 June, I saw the garbage men pick up my trash, including the bag of drugs, which would all be, I hoped, crushed. I couldn't imagine any danger of someone searching through such bags to find pills and a bottle of morphine among soiled kitty litter. Still, why I didn't just pour out the morphine remained a mystery, even to me, except I didn't know where to pour it.

I erased twenty-seven missed calls on the answering machine without listening, since most of these "private callers" are just automated recordings. Some leave no message, but some say they want me to buy new insurance, build a patio, or refinance my mortgage (though I don't have one). I had no desire to hear whatever they had to say. I finally got up the nerve to leave Loretta the therapist the message that John was dead. She soon called to express her regret. She also said that when she worked with him at rehab, he told her again and again how much he loved me. He had struggled valiantly at the exercise machines, but she thought that, back on 30 April, he was too debilitated just to have COPD. Loretta also said John's weight loss meant he had no reserve to fight whatever terrible infection was eating him alive. She recalled that during his one exercise therapy, he was wheezing, and they struggled to keep his oxygen count up to 90 percent. She thought his pneumonia had not been cured. Maybe if Dr. Barton or the Georgetown pulmonologists or she had been on the case when John had strength, he could have been saved, at least for a year or so. I'd have taken that year, as would Hannah, though it would have been harder on John. As it was, he escaped the long painful declines from leukemia of his brother and his cousin.

Talking with Loretta made me belatedly realize that I should not have let John drive himself to the rehab center on 30 April. Whatever understanding and wisdom I'd arrived at had always been too late, as my repeated used of the adverb "belatedly" proved. Every time I wrote the word, it stood as a warning to me and to others: do not wait or postpone or avoid. In troubled times, seek help; act to find solutions; make them. Do not remain a timorous mousie accepting the doctors' dominion. Of course I could not have known how much difference such actions might have made, but at least if I'd tried harder I wouldn't have been so ravaged by guilt.

On 5 June, a large official envelope from the state of New Jersey arrived. Inside were ten long copies of the Certificate of Death for John Irwin Fischer. The certificates carried Dr. Barton's name as the "certifying physician." Artistic scrolling decorated the bluish paper along its edges. The bottom right corner of each copy bore the seal of the State Registrar of the Office of Vital Statistics and Registry. John's demise was now official.

Also on 5 June, three weeks after John died, I again lay in bed stretching out my hand to him, as I did on the fatal Friday the fifteenth. For at least two months before his death, when he'd looked in the mirror at his shrunken body and loose skin, John had shuddered. Once he'd even said, "Auschwitz," exaggerating, but not entirely.

"You are still beautiful to me," I had tried to reassure him. And he was: *my beautiful guy*. On 5 June, I read "Sailing to Byzantium" once again, supposing that the lines "An aged man is but a paltry thing / A tattered coat upon a stick" might also have gotten some reaction from John a minute or two before he died. I was sure that Yeats's lines "Consume my heart away; sick with desire / And fastened to a dying animal" actually did resonate with John in those last moments. Maybe they reified his sense of letting go.

Daily nuisances continued. One morning Maggie had diarrhea and also threw up in the basement. I took care of the unpleasant cleanup, grateful that her poop and vomit at least weren't on Persian carpets. Redoing that box packed with historical postcards, I disguised the wine labels by enclosing the heavy box in cut-up brown paper bags, a surprisingly tedious job. I found myself exhausted from that and the cat cleanup, not ready for gardening, not even for a walk. At this point the only things I liked doing were talking with Hannah, writing about John and my loss of him, and drinking whiskey or wine. Drinking numbed me, while talking with my daughter gave me courage. Writing was like a lifeline, helping me hold on. I asked Hannah if she would share with me the log she had kept in the hospitals. She too had found that writing helps one survive grief. I think that's also true for non-writers; just making notes in a calendar or a diary is an act of control, of rising above devastation, just for oneself.

On Saturday, 6 June, I woke up early enough to do several morning errands. I took the heavy box of old postcards back to the post office. A cheery woman of about my age came in calling, "Hi, Grace. Everything okay with you?" Grace is the grumpy Chinese clerk who actually scares people, especially at tax time when she runs down options for receipts, telling people how to sign for certified mail in a rough quick voice with no articles (like "the") and few pronouns. ("You take, sign two sides, return. Come front of line.") John liked her for her efficiency. Today, she was all smiles for the cheery woman, who thanked a young man for holding the door for us. "Watch out," she teased, "there are twenty-one more women behind us." She walked faster than I, so I saw her husband, who'd circled the post office, pick her up. What an efficient couple, sharing chores, just as John and I used to do. I got into my car, weeping.

We too were a loving, efficient couple. On Tuesdays (senior discount day), he'd drop me off at the grocery and circle the shopping center to pick up cleaning, cat supplies, and, increasingly often, medications. Then he'd go back to the grocery and buy flowers. If I got to the deli first, I'd order a sandwich for lunch and then sliced meats, cheeses, and prepared salads. He'd do the same if he were there first, until I appeared, my cart full of provisions for the week. We'd get home in time to watch Andrea

Mitchell on MSNBC and eat our sandwich. The routine pleased us in its very predictability. After John's death, I did miss excursions to galleries, theatre, and dinners, but I also missed sharing mundane, everyday tasks, like grocery shopping and even bill paying with John. Such tasks formed the net that caught us when our high-intensity publishing and traveling acts threatened to drop us.

Hannah and I needed to decide about the hymns to be sung at the memorial service in the Chapel. Years before John had suggested we list songs for our funerals. I knew where the file was, rather lugubriously placed alphabetically just before purchase "Guarantees" in our household file drawer. His first choices were "Amazing Grace" and "Lord of the Dance." The latter was not in the Princeton Chapel's hymnal, and Eric Plutz, the organist, didn't know it, so I feared he wouldn't play it. When Nora rehearsed her solo with him, though, she loaned him an old Methodist hymnal that included it and he agreed to play it.

On 7 June, four weeks and a day after John died, for the very first time I did something unrelated to death. I watched American Pharaoh win the Belmont Stakes and the Triple Crown. That victory was not a cure for my sorrow but rather a diversion from it. Though I at first felt guilty or disloyal, I soon realized that diversions from grief can be healthy, even restorative. Hannah and I continued talking almost every day. Conversations were more necessary for me than for Hannah, who could share her feelings and thoughts with her husband. I had no one except Maggie-the-Cat, a good listener but not much of a respondent. Hannah emailed me her written account of John's last month in the hospitals. It brought back, once again, all that agony and anger and sadness, as we jointly for a while had believed there was "no way" John could die.

I approved the Chapel memorial program, which featured a beautiful picture Hannah had supplied, cropped as a bust shot of a beardless John, his eyes looking at someone intensely and kindly. It predated 1998, because in the uncropped shot, John was holding his pipe. Hannah and I asked for the picture to be reproduced in color on the program cover. She wrote a marvelous poem about the difficulties of communicating with him. His spirit seemed like a bird beating its wings against her window, trying unsuccessfully to speak to her.

I thought of asking C. J., his little brother Aaron, and Reid Jr. to get up and dance to "Lord of the Dance." Both Hannah and Reid said that was a terrible idea. Probably I conceived of it after drinking more than a wee dram of whiskey. I mention it only to suggest how little judgment I had left.

I made an effort to reconnect to world events, but TV coverage seemed to be only about murderers who escaped from a New York prison. My cell phone had a text message reading "you look so good I could eat you off a plate." I erased the words but didn't know how to prevent more revolting spam from getting into my electronic mailbox.

When I met people at the grocery or on other errands, they typically asked how I was sleeping. My answer was quite well. When a homeless woman, used to nights in a cardboard box under a freeway, gets a quiet secure place and a bed with clean sheets and blankets, she sleeps and sleeps. I was like that, not homeless but harried, worn down by each day's troubles. Or maybe I just drank too much. I felt guilty in the mornings, having slept so well. It would have been better to say to others that I'd been up all night crying, but that was not true. I'd just been awake all day crying.

At four o'clock one morning, I heard John calling to me. Nothing more, and I went back to sleep. When I next awakened and remembered hearing him, I was furious with myself for not calling, not reaching out to him, not trying to lure his soul into close contact with me, however fleeting. Clearly I was sleeping too soundly.

Betty and Marge, both recently widowed, insisted on taking me to lunch on 9 June. They had empathy and good advice, like, "Don't feel you need to give away his clothes yet." Marge promised to bring pots of flowers to put on the steps and deck for my outdoor dinner party. Later Betty sent me an article from the *Washington Post* by Anne Bernays, who'd recently lost her husband of sixty years. After he died she too felt "numb and raw." But she found some pleasure in living alone, as I began to: a different evening routine, sorting the mail while the news played, as John would never have done, flinging a leg across the bed without worrying about bothering him, eating fewer sandwiches and more salads, not cleaning off counters and tables until I felt like it, leaving the bed unmade. Those modest consolations of widowhood were in no way compensations for heartbreak. Early one morning, I woke up sneezing. I grabbed tissues, hoping I hadn't awakened John, but then I remembered that John was gone. *My true love is dead.*

What I heard from the widows and read in the *Post* had little to do with the intensity of my relationship with John. From the beginning, it had been almost a fairytale romance. After I had given up fighting to keep Reid from his father, I was glad we could have him on predictable terms. And I was relieved to be for a while alone with John, whom I loved absolutely. Reid fared well enough without daily contact with me. He made good grades, cooked for himself, and even ironed his shirts and chinos when required. His father's behavior became ever stranger, preparing Reid, I joked, for living with another crazy person in adulthood. Sometimes Reid agreed, wryly. He became a caring son and a devoted father as well as a terrific lawyer.

Hannah's birth had not fractured the emotional space John and I shared or disrupted our romance. Of course, babies do complicate their parents' lives and drain their time and energy, but John and I managed so well (having resources for nannies and nursery schools) that we felt little strain. She was such a charming, beautiful, and bright little girl that she enhanced our lives. Friends debated whether she was more like me or John. She was really a fulfillment of us both, and a joy. Even in churches and libraries, on international airplanes and visits to aged scholars, she could sit quietly reading a book. And at the London Zoo, she raced about exuberantly, calling us to catch up with her to see toucans, or giraffes, or cheetahs, or red pandas, her favorite.

Our absolute love mellowed some. John quickly discovered I was neither Stella, who turned out not to be so docile after all, nor the fiery Vanessa. John was always my rescuer and hero, but his irritability could aggravate me. Over the years, we survived quarrels, achieved more balance between us, developed tolerance for our different families, and managed irony about each other's foibles and literary tastes. From our beginnings, we'd agreed about the power and importance of Swift and Faulkner, but I hadn't related to *Zen and the Art of Motorcycle Maintenance*, nor did he get much out of *Franny and Zooey*. Later, John distrusted Virginia Woolf's brilliance and what he considered her snobbishness; I could barely keep awake reading John Dryden.

Still, our literary disagreements were few, none of them professional. They had almost nothing to do with who was invited to speak more or cited in more journals or got a better salary. We wrote side by side— not literally, for John read aloud as he wrote, making it impossible for me concentrate in the same room, but metaphorically, writing mostly at the same times then later reading and critiquing each other's works. Sometimes John would say, "Panthea, I don't know where you're going in this paragraph. Is this relevant?" He could find every sloppy phrase or example of poor reasoning I ever wrote and point them out without offending me. My editorial remarks also helped him, especially in clarifying the complexities of what he was saying and in adding conclusions. Sometimes he'd lay out the evidence like a lawyer and then stop, as if smart readers could jump to obvious conclusions. I assumed the role of a juror who wants to be told what the evidence means. I wanted him to draw conclusions for folks, like myself, not so knowledgeable as he. So we had a relationship of books and love, as he testified in the talk he had given in Münster in 2000 on Swift's "Cadenus and Vanessa."

In that talk, which I've only briefly mentioned before, John recalled writing, in the summer of 1975, his chapter in *On Swift's Poetry* about the flirtation between Swift (Cadenus or the Dean) and Vanessa. By 2000, John could say that, back in 1975, his "domestic circumstances" had been in chaos. He did not explain that that chaos was a result of leaving his wife while I was wrangling over my divorce and custody problems. After twenty-five years together, in 2000, he revised his opinion of that poem and of love. He said, "Love emerges as unjudgeable by reason. But individual relationships can and should be judged by reason." He ended that talk with a dedication to me. (No wonder a former colleague said it was almost embarrassing to see how much we loved each other.)

As I've suggested, people often read memoirs to participate in the lives of the rich and famous. More profoundly they want to explore an external landscape or an inner self, to discover lost chapters of history, or maybe to uncover their own backgrounds. They want to understand how it happened on a battlefield, a playing field, a Civil Rights struggle, a political tussle, a conversion, anywhere forces were marshaled against each other, especially the forces of innocence, good, and decency against those of oppression.

As I revised my jottings into a possible memoir, I cross-examined myself. I knew people would want to hear details of John's astonishing personality and the wonder and excitement of living with him. And they would care about the inept medical care that hastened his death. They'd also be interested in reading about my slow healing process. But I wondered if they would care about our pets, street repair, front-end loaders, morphine disposal, cat poop and vomit, memorial planning, and all the other chores that preoccupied me after John died.

Brenda Peterson and Sarah Jane Freymann say in *Your Life is a Book* that a memoir is all about "giving to your readers the pleasures, dramas, and insights from your unique life story." But memoirs aren't just about pleasures, they are also about sadnesses. They must include drama, but at first I wondered how much drama there could be in doing or avoiding chores. The drama of John's death lay in the conflict between appearances (what the doctors saw) and a worsening reality (which I was slow to see). Still, I realized that the counterpoint to the high drama in my tale of intense love, horrid loss, and gradual healing was the low drama of everyday chores and the business of everyday life. Almost without my intervention, everyday details formed themselves into recurring motifs, the background to my story of John's death and my grief and slow recovery.

In 2015, thinking back about John's dedication to me at the close of his essay on "Cadenus and Vanessa," titled "Love and Books," I considered the ways our love had greatly deepened as well as slightly mellowed. In my despair, I had felt that no one could be as devastated by loss as I was. The so-called "grieving memoirs," though, testified otherwise. I was hardly the only person to feel deep loss and to write about it.

The best grieving memoirs, I came to realize, provide both a powerful feel of the person lost and sharp insight into the writer herself. The double focus means that the writer is himself or herself a character in the book. However curious people may be about the lives of the rich and famous, when they turn to grieving memoirs, readers are quickly put off by artificial or conventional expressions of grief. They yearn to read heartfelt reactions to loss, honestly presented, even if the writer has to admit some unlovely responses. Such reactions may sometimes be comic, lightening the tone of the memoir, but they must not be faked.

Grieving memoirs tell a personal story where the writer and their lost loved one(s) must be fully realized, rounded characters, so that readers can come to know enough about them to understand the writer's grief. Reading about someone else's loss reminds us of our common humanity and helps us cope with our own losses. Though everyone's pain is unique, it is comforting to know that we are not alone.

Seeking a distraction from grieving, I picked up *The Annotated Alice*. As an English teacher, one of my pet peeves had been students' writing "it" or "that" without a clear antecedent, so I was much amused to read that when the Mouse said that the Archbishop found "it" advisable, the Duck asked, "Found *what?*"

The Mouse said, "Of course you know what 'it' means." The Duck said that for him, "it" is usually a worm he's going to eat, but the question remained about the "it" that the archbishop found advisable. (I do hope readers have found no ambiguous "it" in this book!) The conversation between the Mouse and the Duck, however, reminded me of John's dislike of imprecise English. As a distraction from loss, then, *Alice* failed, because, like almost everything else, it just reminded me that I'd lost John, my true love.

I'd been about to quit Pilates classes and let myself decline into out-of-shapeness, but instead, I called the studio to say I was returning after two months. Janell, my teacher, was waiting for me beyond the row of machines called Reformers. We embraced and wept. Even during exercises on a Reformer or a Cadillac, we each teared up. She reminded me to lengthen my right side, rather than collapse into crookedness. After that strenuous but healing class, I busied myself with clearing off our cluttered kitchen counters, where the caterer would lay out Saturday's dinner. C. J. came over to carry out the kitty litter and garbage. I invited his parents to talk about arrangements for Saturday. While I was putting out nibbles for them, I started making cookies and, now that Maggie had gotten her appetite back, fixing dinner for her. This was the sort of multitasking that would have driven John nuts. Nevertheless, I fed the cat without putting chocolate chips in her dish or cat food in the cookies. I finished stirring up the dough, difficult without John's strong arm to mix dried fruit and chocolate chips into the batter. I used a little cookie scooper to get almost uniform bits of dough on the pan, put out snacks for the guests, and poured myself a vodka tonic. The Von Vorys and I counted the chairs and tables we'd need if we dined outside on 13 June. C. J. and Aaron came over to say they wanted to help and I hoped these boys would be a good influence on Reid Jr. I grimaced over the 60 percent chance of rain forecast for the next Saturday.

That night, though I couldn't bring myself to bake more cookies, I did write a few more pages. By that time, I'd begun telling people that I was writing a memoir. I expected it to evolve into a book but considered that published memoirs seemed to require happy endings. I could not imagine one, so I decided to put aside the writing and get some sleep.

After I had my hair cut, I recalled that John had liked it longer and hoped his spirit didn't take offense at the new cut. When I decided to make granola, I could hear John whispering over my shoulder, "Why?" I replied to his ghost that I hadn't yet put away the pots, pans, and measuring equipment from making cookies. John's ghost reminded me that groceries sell granola. *True, but it's not as good as mine.* My recipe, gleaned from various friends, involves coconut, wheat germ, various seeds and grains, and dried fruit but takes a long while to cook. I confess to having a yen for being an expert at many things, like Pat Spacks, former chair of several English departments, president of the MLA, a prolific scholar and author, and an excellent cook.

John long ago accused me of trying to be at once like my two favorite Reid first cousins, each a generation older than I: the maiden Marian Gillim, Chair of Economics at Barnard and advisor to the Truman administration, and Katherine Reid (Kan Dickey) Cox, a beautiful woman who looked like Lauren Bacall and cooked like Julia Child. That night I was weary enough to concede that I'd tried to do too much. Still, one of my additions to the granola recipe was applesauce. I used two little cups left over from the hospital, where it had helped John swallow his pills, thus making it his granola too. The chance of rain for Saturday went down to 40 percent.

I called the Goldfarbs, asking them to pick up my former dissertation director Weldon Thornton and his wife, Barbara, at the Trenton airport. Weldon said the Goldfarbs could identify them as probably the oldest couple on the plane, which they were. Late Thursday night Hannah and Michael arrived. The chance of rain on Saturday was down to 10 percent, so we decided to dine outside Saturday night. At home, we three sat at the dining room table viewing Hannah's slideshow of John's pictures, so beautiful, so intimate, and so sad.

Saturday was a model of efficiency that would so have pleased John. Our pest control company sprayed for mosquitoes. Our new lawn man mowed the grass. Reid, who'd driven in at about 2 a.m., appeared with little Reid. Michael and Reid went with Norbert to pick up more tables and chairs. Our forest of bamboo had shed its brown leaves and was sprouting new green ones, but the dogwood tree that grows in their midst had cracked a branch. You couldn't walk between the lower deck and the bamboo thicket without pushing it aside or breaking it off. Michael went to the hardware store and got a strong rope and some tree seal, with which he painted both sides of the broken branch. He and Hannah strung the rope around the branch, and little Reid shimmied up the dogwood trunk. He pulled the rope higher and tighter until it lifted the branch off the ground. I watched from my upstairs bathroom window, thinking it would have made a great picture, except that all of them were hidden in a virtual forest of bamboo spikes.

Late in the afternoon, when I got out of my shower I looked out the window and wept at the beauty of our backyard. The grass that John had so carefully planted and tended was a bright, well-trimmed green. Hannah's friend Johnny, whom she'd met at LSMSA, and her Emory friends Matt and Michele had arranged the extra chairs and tables with tablecloths on the lawn. It looked like pictures I've seen of weddings on someone's estate. I hoped John's soul was hovering above, watching.

Reid and Matt brought up from the basement the galvanized tub we'd bought for large parties back in Baton Rouge. They put it on the deck and filled it with ice and bottles of refreshments. Reid Jr. labeled and put out bins for recycling and trash, Matt did a second spray for mosquitoes, and Michele arranged platters of fruit, cheese, crackers, and such. I had a moment fearing the caterer had gotten the wrong day, but soon two women arrived with platters of grilled tarragon chicken with blueberry salsa, Moroccan seared salmon with honey mango sauce, and roasted tomato tart with caramelized onions and cheddar, along with a kale salad and one of watermelon and feta cheese, all beautiful food, which they spread on the kitchen counters while they put little desserts in the fridge. Ann called, just in from Virginia, wondering if I wanted her, with husband Rick and sister Jane, to arrive early, on time, or fashionably late. I said, "There's no way I want to wait for you to be fashionably late. Come as soon as you can get here."

There was no way I could have staged this party without such wonderful help, everyone there to honor John, my darling guy who had also been theirs too.

Despite the fact that everyone was gathering at our home now to honor his life, it still seemed like he was about to join us. It felt like there was no way he could have gone away in that zipped-up red body bag, lost to all of us, especially and most painfully to Hannah and me.

15

DINNER ON
THE GRASS

Below the back deck, tiger swallowtails flitted among thicket of plants whose arched stems earn them the name goose-necked flowers. Hannah's friends were exchanging news and photos with each other. Friends of John and mine arrived separately or in small clumps, affording me time to greet each one privately with a mix of joy and sadness. When they got out to the deck, the young people pointed the guests to the cheese and fruit platters, the tub of wine and cool drinks, and the bottles of gin and bourbon on the table.

Herb and Deborah arrived at the front door in a huge Tacoma pick-up. Herb hugged me tight and we both wept. He confessed that John's death had rattled him. More particularly, Deborah said that Herb "kept telling people he will never have another friend like John." He took comfort, she said, only in "remembering our visit with John and you in the Georgetown hospital and dinner afterwards with you, Hannah, and Michael. What a gift that visit turned out to be for us." For the trip here, Deborah had left travel arrangements to Herb. He'd forgotten to rent a car, which explained their arrival in a pick-up.

When next the front doorbell rang, I saw through the storm door another Aubrey Williams grad student from the University of Florida. I hardly recognized John's old friend Earl with silver gray hair. He wasn't his former boisterous self, but instead a subdued one. "I can't believe it happened," he said.

"Nor can I," was my reply, four weeks and a day after it did happen.

Betty and her husband, Bing, also came to the front door. I'd first met Betty in the third grade after my parents and I made what I considered our tragic move from our Kentucky home to Alabama. Betty now has completely white hair, cut short and sensibly. Though a docent at the National Portrait Gallery and accustomed to speaking publicly to small groups, she had declined to read at the Chapel memorial. Gael Fischer, widow of John's younger brother, Jeff, appeared with her new man and her two sons. She wore white, the color of mourning, she said.

Out on the grass, I rushed to meet Ann, who always greets me as "darlin'." She and Rick brought more wine, as if we needed it. Her sister Jane hugged me and then engaged upon a serious conversation with C. J., asking him about what books he was reading and recommending similar choices. The sun was settling in the west, and Jane moved about as the sun did, trying to keep the glare out of her eyes and to meet the guests, whom she later described as "my people too." People began serving themselves in the kitchen. Many stopped on the deck to pour themselves wine or water. While waiting in line, they tasted the food.

"Mmmm," someone said. "What's the sauce on the salmon?"

"I can't remember," I admitted, replenishing my wine glass.

Hannah was nearby and explained that the spices were Moroccan, the sauce honey mango.

"And who'd have thought of putting blueberries on chicken breasts? They're great," someone else said.

Reid arrived with his charges, helping Louise balance on spiked heels.

He served them both, telling little Reid that the tart was like pizza. Then Reid settled the little one at a small table with the boys from across the street and placed Louise at the end of the table beyond the garage, where I had moved. Reid soon returned with a full plate and sat by Louise. I ventured into the kitchen, serving myself salmon and salad, and then returned to their table. When I saw Barbara and Weldon rounding the side of the garage, escorted by the Goldfarbs, I rushed to them and wept. Weldon held my hand for some time. Long ago, when I was in graduate school, I'd had a crush on him, as I would tell John years later. John had reminded me of Weldon, especially in earnestness and honesty and brilliance, though John beat Weldon in handsomeness. Weldon and Barbara went inside and then brought their dinners to my table. Weldon told the folks there that this was the one-hundred-and-fiftieth anniversary of Yeats's birth, suggesting that more than one disembodied spirit was among us.

Having all our friends assembled with Hannah and Michael, their pals, and our local friends—Hinda and Norbert, Leslie and Stuart, Bill and Ilse, Trudy, Colin and Laura and their boys—seemed to round out all the stages of our lives, John's and mine. Hannah and Michael sat at a table with their young friends. I heard Hannah and Michele tell stories about sharing an apartment during their senior year at Emory. One of their aims had been cooking creatively. They laughed as they recalled that at their first dinner party, they hadn't known that prepared Mediterranean food was available in groceries. From scratch, they'd made hummus, baba ghanoush, stuffed grape leaves, and banana curry. The latter was such a hit, Hannah said people still ask for the recipe. Hannah's shared resourcefulness with Michele, not just in the kitchen, had always seemed to John and me vindication of our confidence in our daughter.

Soon people began switching places to visit with others. I was just happy to have with me my dear friends Ann and Rick, Herb and Deborah,

Weldon and Barbara, my son Reid and, of course, his Louise, who did not speak. Reid spent much of the evening tending to his charges, getting up to serve them both seconds and desserts, which someone had gotten out of the fridge. Laura Von Vorys did the same for her two boys. At a table by themselves, the three boys developed camaraderie and independence. At our table, Ann told about the program she and Rick launched for indigent children in Giles County, Virginia, where kids used to show up for school having never held a crayon or a book and lacking even a notion of what a meal was.

"What do they live on?" I asked.

"Mostly potato chips," Ann answered.

People wore what they pleased; older men in coats and ties, younger ones more relaxed, having, as Trudy said, "more sense," as did elders who soon removed their jackets. Women wore cool summer dresses in muted colors, often with artistic necklaces and bracelets. Trudy wore a silver wrap-around bracelet, which Louise complimented. (Later Trudy and I sent her one like it.) Most guests went inside for second helpings of chicken, salmon, and tomato tarts, and then for desserts, pretty little cups of kiwi cheesecake and chocolate pots de crème. While the adults were eating and talking in muted voices, young Reid and the two neighborhood boys raced about the yard playing some sort of tag fantasy game, yelling "You're captured!" They used as base our giant rock, a glacial erratic left behind when the last glacier left what's now New Jersey. They paused to eat desserts; then Laura accompanied the boys across the street to their house, where the three boys played Monopoly for hours.

In our backyard, people seemed to float about in patterns of subdued colors, mostly black, gray, navy, and white. After the harsh glare from the west that had sent Jane skirting the sun, the light melted into evening softness. The sky became a pale blue, the color of our kitchen cabinets. For me, the evening blurred happiness with terrible unhappiness.

Earl sat with the young people and was impressed by Johnny's account of the great impact John had had on him as a youngster, when John's words and deeds encouraged him to think freely for himself. Hinda and Norbert also joined the table of Hannah's friends, who were talking about people they had lost. I came over to and heard a young woman talk of losing her mother. During the time of their deepest mourning, she said her father had looked out their window and pointed to their bamboo, weighted down with snow. He said, "We're like the bamboo, almost breaking under the weight. But spring will come, and slowly, the snow will melt and the bamboo will stand straight again." I thought that hopeful statement had little to do with me. This gal was young, and maybe her father was comparatively so too. I suppose they have righted themselves and gone on. I couldn't imagine righting myself after losing John. My basic reaction was that their love was not so deep as mine, but then my loss was recent, my grief a raw sore. Perhaps someday, I hoped that I too could right myself.

Hannah commented that she had never been a very good writer of love poetry, and it had bothered her not to write love poems. "I've always written about death, with regret, because it made me feel that I didn't really love the people I knew I did love in my life." Now it seemed to her that writing about death was, indeed, writing about love. "Loving someone beyond the grave is the hardest relationship we can negotiate," she said. Jane watched Hannah struggle between her hosting duties and a "trip wire of grief," her face fighting for control. Michael held her hand.

The sky turned a pale pink beyond our back fence, silhouetting our neighbors' tall red pine and white oak trees. Jane and Deborah were talking about writing as our way of connecting with people we don't know. Jane said she once wrote Bill Moyers a letter of gratitude for his reporting. He wrote back saying that he was keeping her letter in a file for his grandchildren. I thought of all the letters John and I had gotten over the years thanking him and me for our writing and teaching (he got more than I). I'd kept some of them, but John had always thought that the memories were enough, we didn't need proof.

At another table, the discussion got political. I think it started with complaints about Princeton's high taxes but quickly turned to broader issues. I heard Earl howl when he found that Colin was a Ted Cruz supporter. But both liberals and conservatives harmonized as they deplored, as John had, the corrupt influence of big business upon government. Earl tried to enlist Herb into the conversation, who just said, "I've lost my dearest friend," and moved away.

Betty told about my Alice in Wonderland party when we were ten years old, saying, "Panthea of course was Alice." (I could imagine John too saying, "Of course.") Trudy had just seen an exhibit in the Bronx of new Gee's Bend quilts. Betty surprised Trudy by being an Alabama-raised white woman brought up during segregation who knew and cared about Gee's Bend and the quilt-making culture there. Their talk expanded around the table to a discussion of cross-cultural sharing. Trudy remarked that John had been terrific, the best she'd known, at bringing together people from all sorts of different backgrounds.

Leslie and Stuart live a block behind us on another street in what is essentially our house with the blueprint reversed and a larger garage. Shortly after we moved in, Leslie heard that a literary couple was occupying her twin house. When she saw a couple standing in front of her house, pointing out one side and then the other, Leslie burst out of her house, exclaiming, "You must be the new literary couple on the next road over." We were. Later she became my editor for my Olsen biography, and Stuart would write lovely tributes to John. But at the party it was just a funny story about similar houses and similar interests, including England, Jonathan Swift, William Morris fabrics, the Bloomsbury Group, and our shared absorption in literature. Telling a funny story was Leslie's desperate cover for what was really in everyone's mind and heart: how much everyone there missed John.

John and I were never especially gregarious people. Mostly we had each other and a few really good friends whom we'd accumulated over many years in many places. Many of those good friends showed up that evening, from far and wide. Each brought heartfelt expressions of sorrow and of kindness. And many reached out literally to touch me. It seemed strange to feel someone else's hand brush my cheek or pat my shoulder. For all those years, I'd hardly been touched, except in the most formal way, by anyone but John. These touches made my skin quiver, recalling the gentle touch of the rough skin of John's fingers.

As the pink sky faded into pale gray, most adults were still eating and drinking. I lit a large citronella candle in a bucket on a table. Its lemony fragrance floated beyond the table, enveloping everyone. I reflected upon the common thread in all our comments—disbelief that John could be dead. And there was something else that made the evening different from any other, a presence beyond the smell of citronella. Leslie later confided to me that, despite being an atheist, she said she and everyone else felt John's spirit with us there in our backyard.

I thought and still think it was his soul. Praise be!

As dusk closed in, fireflies came out to flit and flicker among us. I lit the nine blue candles I'd stuck in the brass candelabra my Methodist grandfather brought back from his 1923 trip to the Holy Land, as it was then called. In the evening breeze, they burned unevenly, sending large and small cascades of blue tallow dripping on the iron table and the deck floor, looking like multiple blue volcanoes.

I proposed a toast to John, and everyone raised a glass. Deborah recalls that I stood with my back to the light from the kitchen window with the candelabra before me, its flames shooting about wildly. I shared with the guests a recent dream. Deborah remembers what I said better than I do and wrote to me: "In that dream you were in a very dark place, perhaps a black void, and suddenly John was there beside you. You told us you knew you would have to go on, but at that very moment it was difficult for you to conceive how you would manage without him. Finally you said, 'John Fischer was the love of my life. There will never be another man like him.' That was the moment I felt your loss most keenly."

Apparently, my words made some folks worry that I might do something drastic to myself. I assured them that I wouldn't, since I have my dear chillun to live for. Still, Earl asked Hannah to take care of me, though he later worried that that was too hard a burden to put on her. With fireflies blinking on the lawn, the candle flames settled or went out. It seemed that everyone was hugging me.

Thanks to the kindness of our friends and daughter, I didn't have much to do with the cleanup. Michele did a marvelous job of washing up platters. (Jane later told me that she'll never forget Michele, who was "selfless and tireless and super-organized and devoted to Hannah.") Friends expressed their concern for me by putting leftover chicken and salmon in separate baggies that made meals for me for months. Ann found my rarely used blender and made soup out of leftover kale salad with yogurt she found in my fridge. Clearly I'd have much to feast on, both literally and metaphorically through the memories of this beautiful evening that John would so have loved.

I don't know about Yeats's soul, but I really did feel John's soul hovering near me that evening.

16

MEMORIALIZING JOHN

On Sunday morning, I stayed at our house, though calling it so seemed strange by then. I'd often been irritated by people's overuse of the first-person possessive, as in "my son" or "my house." I'd always spoken of Hannah as "our daughter," as had John. I could not call this New England colonial "my house." It was ours, with its crazy assortment of rolling, turning, and stationary bookshelves, desks and desk tables, oriental carpets, nineteenth-century antiques, William Morris upholstered chairs, literary posters, Indonesian flowers made from banana leaves, paintings by friends and my grandmother, and stacks of books and papers from our unfinished writing projects. I sipped a glass of wine and ate some nibbles from the night before. Then I went upstairs to read "Sailing to Byzantium" one more time for and to John before I dressed in a black top and a longish skirt in shades of black and brown.

I later learned that Betty and Bing had taken my hand-drawn map and scouted Princeton streets and parking places, sites I'd highlighted in yellow. Then they'd met the guests staying at the same motel at the next-door restaurant and offered commentary on the map and on driving in Princeton. Michael's family had appeared briefly at our house, and then the Pincks went out to lunch at Bon Appétit, where Hannah met them after sharing more time with Michele and Matt.

Hannah came home to change and then dropped me at the Chapel while she parked the car. I went into the awesome cathedral to find David Lange in the front row, waiting for me. David's strong athletic arms embraced me. We both wept, and David apologized that family commitments had kept him away from dinner the night before. We surveyed the chancel where our service was to take place before the Great East Window of Love, a fit spot for a memorial to my beloved John.

Betty and Bing were stationed at the front and back doors of the Chapel, handing out the beautiful programs. I met people as they came in, shaking their hands, embracing, and often weeping together. Eric Plutz and I had agreed that Bach, a contemporary of Swift's, was right for the occasion. Eric played cantatas BWV 654 and 147, "Jesu, Joy of Man's Desiring," a favorite of John's. In the chancel we sat where the choir usually sits on elaborate pews, which had been carved, I later learned, from wood originally set aside to make Civil War gun carriages. I sat with family members on the south side, watching the sun stream through the handcrafted stained glass windows opposite and above us, offering a holy blessing. Michael read the Twenty-third Psalm as a responsive reading, and Nora sang "Fear No More the Heat o' the Sun." We sang three verses of "Amazing Grace," and Hannah read the Beatitudes.

David Lange began his eulogy with a "Mourner's Kaddish": "It is a fearful thing to love / what death can touch." He said that, contrary to Flannery O'Connor's "A Good Man Is Hard to Find," I had found an "exquisite" good man. David addressed John: Jonathan Swift had "clearly engaged your beautiful mind and you as a scholar not only elucidated his work internationally, but exceeded his satirical assertion that we have just enough religion not to love one another." After canonizing "Saint John Irwin Fischer," David addressed John further: "You never met a paradox you couldn't love. You probed the contradictions of conventional either/ or thinking and judging, parsed the particulars with carefully balanced precision, and, with elegant grace, married the differences into the perennial wholeness of what we each experience in our own ways yet still call 'the universe.' You not only loved and worshiped the ultimate paradoxical Mystery, you lived by it uncommonly, authentically, and compassionately—a righteous son of Abraham and a baptized brother of Jesus, before the Holy One of Israel and in the Cosmic Christ!" Throughout, David continued to emphasize John's mixed Jewish and Christian heritage. "We sang 'Dayenu' at Passover with gusto and prayed fervently at Eucharist together." This remarkable eulogy was the best I'd ever heard or ever hope to hear.

It took people a few moments to get into the rhythm of "Lord of the Dance," it being so joyous and unlike most hymns, but they did. The postlude was Bach's "Sheep May Safely Graze," from Cantata 208, which Eric played heart-wrenchingly on the Chapel's great organ.

I had engineered this memorial—cutting the number of verses sung and insisting that the readings and the eulogy be short—so that people could get to the Arts Council of Princeton by 4 p.m. Most drove, but some walked, including Weldon, who not long before had been crippled with fibromyalgia, but not that day. I had asked Betty and Bing to drop him off at the ramp to the Chapel's back door and then drive him to the Arts Council. He was having none of it. At eighty, he outwalked the rest of the crowd.

Hannah dropped me off at the Arts Council, where the slideshow she had prepared was already playing and a crowd had gathered in the auditorium. I let the slides run through one more rotation and then stood to welcome all. I thanked John's friends and family, who came from Oregon, California, Texas, Arkansas, Massachusetts, North Carolina, upstate New York, and Eggleston, Blacksburg, and Fairfax, Virginia, as well as the greater Princeton area, all there to honor John. Introducing Herb, I told about the tears that had sprung from John's eyes just two month before when the Rothschilds surprised him by showing up in his room at Georgetown University Hospital. I pointed out that one of the pictures on the slideshow showed the two men resuming the political discussions they'd start every time they met, except that last time when they did not argue.

Herb presided graciously while a remarkable number of friends, old and young, gave tributes to John. Earl Ramsey told of John's habit in graduate school of rehearsing his seminar papers while he walked around student housing late at night. Such perambulations ended when sorority girls reported him as a weirdly talking stalker. Hannah read a recollection from her best childhood friend, Brigid Vance, who recalled John's chauffeuring the girls and "occasionally offering his own observations on our conversations, often about British royalty." When they watched movies together at our house, Brigid felt very "grown-up" when John included her in discussions of the films. She remembered John's mouth-watering hamburgers, the best ever. (Actually I made the burgers and he grilled them, but I never minded that he got the credit.) Brigid thought John never fumbled for words. Johnny Waggener spoke of how he came from a Louisiana town where citizens were generally divided into the saved or damned. What a difference it made in his life, he said, through tears, to visit with us and hear John introduce uncertainty and irony into our dinner conversations. A former cantankerous colleague at LSU had written "The Ballad of Good John," which Michele and Matt read together. Another former LSU colleague sent her reflections on how when John was chair, he had reformed the workings of the English Department, making it a model of administrative efficiency and vision. Ann read a poem by Felicia Mitchell that begins "I don't think the soul leaves the body; / it has to be the other way around ..." The poem eased my conscience about having John cremated. It confirmed my sense that John's soul lives on, whatever was zipped into that mortuary bag.

I'd asked Weldon to read "Sailing to Byzantium." He began by complimenting David Lange on the eulogy, which expressed, he said, a Yeatsian sense of the complications of loving a life that we know will not last. Weldon explained that Yeats's *The Tower*, in which this poem appeared, was, he thought, the most important book of poetry in the twentieth century. (Later one of our older CWW friends said that this was the most educational memorial she'd ever attended.) Weldon said that I'd asked him to read this poem, which I'd first studied in his class, because I was reading it to John when he died. I wiped my eyes but did not break down. Nor did I cry when Bill read "Otherwise." Many others spoke, most of them eloquently, with nary a cliché.

Michael was splendid. He said he had first addressed us as Dr. Fischer and Dr. Reid, but I'd quickly put a stop to such formality and said to call us John and Panthea. He told about wanting to ask John for Hannah's hand in marriage, though he knew John would say it was not his to give. John had told Michael that the greatest gift he could give was the love and mutual admiration he and I shared. He also said that I could still surprise and delight him. Michael ended his tribute by saying that in Georgetown Hospital he had begun calling us Dad and Mom.

Then Hannah came to the microphone to read the poem she'd written after John's death about the bird that tried to get in her window and speak to her for John.

Ever since you died, Dad,
A bird, unremarkable in appearance,
Has been flying directly
At my window
And attaching himself

To the screen, where he stays
For a few beats of his wings,
His tail feathers so close
I can see each tufted barb.
And then, because he cannot stay,
Ass over teakettle,
The bird, a sparrow I think, flies off.
I long to open the window, but
Sparrows don't belong indoors.
Everything you have to say
Must now be said through glass.

She told of learning to ride a bike, when John told her to get back on the bike after she fell. He ran along beside her and she kept pedaling, not realizing that he'd let go. To the assembled friends that day she said, "What my dad taught me was that true courage comes not from fear but from love. You have to love and let go."

Then I rose to say that John Fischer was a truly great man. My point was that John's greatness rested in brilliance muted by modesty and generosity. I said he never used his brilliance to bully others less smart but to help them to better understanding. I quoted from several condolence notes I'd received, all thanking John for the astonishing help he'd given them. One friend, just this last spring when he was silently wasting away, said she remembered him for being "So full of life, charming, entertaining, erudite, witty, and thoroughly delightful company." Another friend recalled "John's belief in storytelling and its power to address the human condition—leavened with humor of course, always humor." She went on to say, "I believe that Jonathan Swift would have found a worthy peer in John Fischer!" (How pleased John would have been by that remark!) Another former colleague said that John was "the best balanced person I ever knew." I pointed out that John's greatness included "forgiveness toward those who took advantage of him," then ended, "He was my great love, my great lover, my inspiration. I am so proud to have lived within the aura of his love. God bless John's great spirit."

Then I returned the microphone to Herb, who spoke of the reconciliation between Achilles and Priam at the end of *The Iliad*. As Priam kisses the "hands of the man who killed my sons," Achilles's faith in the warrior ethos dissolves. Both men feel the redeeming power of love, as both men shed tears for the pain that love brings. Many of us in that auditorium loved John enough to weep again over his death; certainly Herb, Hannah, and I were sobbing, as were Michael, Johnny, and others. Then Herb used John's early achievement as an Eagle Scout as an emblem for his earnestness. The story reminded me of John's initial reluctance to take on Arch's huge *Word-Book* project and then his absolute dedication to doing it right.

Herb said of his one-time political campaign that he hadn't really expected to get to Congress but he hadn't wanted to go to jail either, so he'd asked John to be his treasurer. He said that the FEC had probably never before or since gotten such detailed meticulous records of a Congressional campaign as the ones John submitted on Herb's behalf. Herb went on to say several things that probably made some jaws drop. He said that John and his first wife were not very compatible; thus John became a philanderer. (I'm sure the woman who'd whispered about getting an education at this memorial had second thoughts after she heard that.) Herb explained that John played around with women and raced dirt bikes because he was unhappy. After he met me, though, Herb said John became a "happy man." I know that was true. But then Herb said that after Hannah was born and both John and Hannah were baptized by David Lange into the Christian faith, John became truly happy. (I'm sure our Jewish friends and family were not happy to hear that either, but it also was true.) Herb mentioned the various setbacks and sadnesses that John had endured, including the death of his younger brother and the loss of much of his scholarly work.

Many people unscheduled to talk stood to do so anyway. Jane told the story of when she was sitting by John at Ann and Rick's wedding celebration. She was concerned by how little of his excellent chicken dinner John was eating, so when he went off to the restroom, she stole it, encouraged all the while by food enthusiasts from Louisiana. When John returned, he looked for his missing entrée and said, "I've heard of free-range chickens, but this is ridiculous," sending Jane and her friends into peals of laughter.

Mickey Freundlich, John's first cousin, said that her name had been Maxine until John renamed her Mickey. She said she represented the remaining four out of the nine cousins (all four are women) who used to gather at their maternal grandparents' home in Surfside, Florida. She spoke of Mary Jane who'd vanished for sixty years and then reentered their lives unexpectedly. John had been amazed to hear her voice on the phone, which he recognized. And he'd been so eager, as I've said, to see the celluloid film from their childhood that Mary Jane sent. Mickey said that Mary, as she now prefers to be called, deeply regretted that though she'd spoken to John on the phone, she hadn't seen him even one more time after those many years. I know John regretted it too.

People said they could have listened to stories about John for hours, but I thought it was time to enjoy the terrific food and drink waiting for us outside the auditorium. We left the slideshow playing and people lingered, eating antipasto, smoked fish, fruit and cheese, baked Brie, and pizza. We sipped wine, ginger lemonade, and iced tea. People said many more dear things about John to me. Earl said he was touched, even awed, by the many friends from our entire lives that John and I kept in touch with and by the many who showed up at the memorials.

Late that evening, Stuart Mitchner emailed me a marvelous assessment of that memorial: "I can't imagine any memory exchange where the sense of the man being remembered was so clearly heartfelt and central to the life experiences of everyone speaking. Even with the nicest, truest remembrances, you [usually] get the feeling that you've heard it all before ... With these comments on John, you really felt that this was someone like the Jimmy Stewart character in *It's a Wonderful Life*. To subtract him from people's lives would have been unthinkable, against nature." But unlike Jimmy Stewart's character, John Fischer had, unthinkably, been subtracted from our lives, and we were all now diminished.

After the memorials, Michael drove back to DC. Later that evening, while little Reid slept upstairs, Reid, Louise, Hannah, and I sat in the living room, reflecting upon the day's events. Louise sat bolt upright on one of great-grandmother's love seats. She asked Reid to bring her a glass of water, and we saw her swallow a pill. Before long, Reid helped her up the stairs to the bed, where little Reid was then sleeping and where John had slept during those horrid nights before he awakened me needing to get to the ER.

On that night, after Reid went upstairs with Louise, Hannah came to sit beside me on the other love seat and hugged me. I asked her, "How can we keep from despair?" Then Reid reappeared, and he, Hannah, and I rehashed the events of the last two days. (I won't call it a post-mortem, because it was more a celebration of John's life than an inquiry into his death.) Maggie curled up on her pallet by the fireplace, though there was no fire in June. Clearly she, like us, needed companionship.

Sometime in this period, Maggie had experienced a personality change. Before then, she'd hidden from every visitor except Hannah and then in the winter of 2015 Leslie. The Thorntons had once stayed in our house for three days and had never seen her. Hinda and Norbert had had countless dinners with us and had never seen her. Even the maid hadn't seen her, except once when we retrieved her from her "hidey house" at the back of my closet to put her in her carrier box. "Never have I seen this cat," our maid had remarked. After John's death, though, Maggie seemed to give up on her isolationist, scaredy-cat ways. She wasn't exactly outgoing but she no longer hid from strangers. She mostly just ignored them.

When he was ready to go back to the motel, Reid roused Louise and little Reid and brought them down to the kitchen. Hannah recalls this as my craziest moment, which I don't even remember. Hannah says I warmed slices of tomato tarts to feed Louise and sat at the kitchen table trying to talk with her. It was as though I had switched off the critical part of my brain and was on autopilot, regressing into a Southern hostess when becoming a Princeton strangler would have been more appropriate. Hannah and I were overcome with grief, near despair, but I'd acted as if Louise were the one needing sympathy. But after the Reids and Louise left, I disintegrated again into sobs as Hannah and I spoke. Grief had made me crazy in yet another way. By then, I just wanted to sleep.

The next morning I received another email message from Stuart, who writes a column on literature, music, and the arts for the local *Town Topics*. In the column he was writing on Stravinsky, he wanted also to cover the remarkable memorials for John. He hoped to quote one of Swift's poems in John's honor, if I could find an appropriate one. I set about reading Swift and John on Swift and soon wrote Stuart that, to me, the most appropriate quotation would come from John's essay on "Cadenus and Vanessa." The finale to my correspondence with Stuart came on Wednesday, 17 June, when *Town Topics* published Stuart Mitchner's "Celebrating Stravinsky's Birthday" and "Remembering John Fischer." His inside title was "On Stravinsky's Birthday, 'Dance, Dance, Wherever You May be.'" Of the Chapel service, he wrote:

The surprise was "Lord of the Dance," a hymn by Sydney Carter. After a morning listening obsessively to *The Rite of Spring*, music written, after all, for dancers, how remarkable to be singing a hymn with a jaunty beat and a joyous chorus ("Dance, dance, wherever you may be"), a hymn in which we seemed to be singing along with Jesus ("I came down from heaven and I danced on the Earth / At Bethlehem I had my birth"). Most hymns are like stately pageants. Here, in the austere, spacious, stained-glass wonder of the chapel we were singing lines like "I danced in the moon and the stars and the sun" to a catchy, folky melody that I recognized from many hours listening to Aaron Copland's "Appalachian Spring"…

Stuart went on to cite Yeats's "Sailing to Byzantium," as "the poem John's wife Panthea had been reading to him as he died. Best known for his writing on the poetry of Jonathan Swift, John once observed in the context of Swift's long poem 'Cadenus and Vanessa' that 'a relationship that mingles love and books is possible and joyous.' He dedicated that essay, 'itself about books and love,' to Panthea."

17

CARRYING ON

The Mercer County Courthouse is in Trenton, as is the seat of New Jersey State government. Except for county and state offices, the city has a ghost-like feel. A manufacturing center that formerly claimed "Trenton Makes, The World Takes," Trenton failed to recover from the loss of industrial jobs in the 1970s. John and I had worried that Trenton was a city of mostly office buildings and slums. But on Monday, 15 June, Trenton's economic plight made for easy parking for me and the Reids. We went to the handsome enough Mercer County Courthouse to file John's will in the Probate Court.

John had done this chore just over a year before for his mother, who died shortly before her hundredth birthday, so the process had a disturbingly familiar feel to it. (Again, I wondered why John had given his mother such astonishingly good care while paying so little attention to himself.) Until a year ago, probate might not have been necessary, since we'd owned everything jointly until John inherited a modest $51,000 from his mother. Still, filing the will made official John's generous bequests to Hannah, Reid, and his sister-in-law, Gael. As we left the courthouse, I reflected that at least some of the chores I'd shouldered for the last month had been pleasurable: choosing the memorial music, arranging for the speakers, planning the food, resurrecting memories with old friends, even crying with them over the phone. These had been creative and often touching experiences. But I sensed that there would be nothing pleasurable about the chores awaiting me.

Since 5 June, I had had the envelope filled with certified death certificates. Now I'd have to send one to the long-term care insurers. They must have been delighted at John's early demise, since they'd pocketed nearly a decade of payments from him and owed nothing in return. I had to send another death certificate to our old employer, LSU, and another to the Teachers Retirement System of Louisiana. I'd need to fill out and sign more forms attesting to the death of my husband. I had no idea then how endless the forms would be, how many times I'd have to send certified death certificates (and perhaps order more of them), how many regulations I'd have to obey, how many pieces of certified mail I'd need to send with green slips testifying that they'd been delivered, how much dull work I'd need to do just to carry on.

When we finished at the courthouse, Louise didn't answer her phone, so Reid dropped me and Reid Jr. off at the house while he went to wake up Louise. Little Reid and I took a walk down our torn-up street, getting our shoes muddy. I showed him how to wash off the soles of his shoes at the outside spigot, which he had never done before. He went back to playing Minecraft on his tablet, as he had at the courthouse. (I worried about the values that game teaches, endorsing theft and property destruction, but maybe I was just clueless about some up-to-date healthy values it may endorse.)

After over an hour, Reid appeared with Louise. Little Reid announced to them that he wanted to come back to Princeton. He liked the boys from across the street, and, I hoped, he now liked me. I took the forms from the probate office and spread them on the dining room table. Though Reid closed the door, I could hear Louise in the kitchen fussing at him. Then she slammed the porch door and went out to their car to sit alone. Both Reids gathered the pots of flowering plants Marge had brought me for the party and put them in my car trunk, packing them in with the big bag of plastic bags I'd collected for recycling. The older Reid next returned Hinda and Norbert's cooler. All that time, Louise sat in the hot car, until the Reids, Hannah, and I got in, and we set out for Bon Appétit.

On the way, Louise was so irritable Hannah in the backseat shrugged her shoulders and spread her hands to silently ask, "What's wrong?" I shrugged back, and we listened. It had something to do with a Fourth of July trip to Disneyland, which she had insisted on but now claimed she hadn't. Little Reid tuned out his mother's griping by turning on a computer game until Hannah distracted him with questions he was glad to answer. At Bon Appétit, he ordered lasagna, a big cup of fruit pieces, and broccoli. Just a year ago he wouldn't touch a green vegetable, so there'd been progress. After Reid finished his lunch, then his son's, and then mine, he dropped Hannah and me off at home. Reid picked up the no-nut cookies I'd made and kept for him in the freezer. The smaller Reid broke off a long stalactite of blue wax from the candelabra to take home as a souvenir of Saturday night's party. Reid the elder told me that sometimes before bed the younger subsided into tears after seeing boys his age in happy families. Other times he woke up screaming after dreams of being abducted. *Poor darling,* I thought. John and I had concluded that unless my son asked us to intervene, we couldn't really do much to help. Now I wondered if I could do more for my grandson, either by having him visit me more often or by moving closer to him.

That afternoon, I made another trip to Trenton, this time taking Hannah to catch the Amtrak to DC. I always hated saying good-bye to her, but that moment of realizing I was truly bereft without John or Hannah or Reid was awful. Back in Princeton, I sat at the kitchen table and put Maggie on my lap. Brushing her as she purred, I repeated "groom the cat" with each stroke, making blue-gray fur float in clouds. Afterwards she stayed by me, but with John subtracted from our lives, not much seemed left for either of us girl cats.

Chores seemed to metastasize. That seems an extreme metaphor, but when I finished one chore only to have another sprout in its place, chores felt like spreading cancers. I needed to weed the yard, or to begin the process, but there were so many indoor chores it seemed smarter (and conveniently lazier) to do them first, before mucking about in the soil, as the English might say. I retreated to the living room, where I looked at the handsome quartz bookends on our shelves. From the backside, they look like regular old rocks. Their inside surfaces, though, are polished triangles, with one side pressed against books and the other displaying glittering patterns of purple polished quartz. At the corner where the two polished surfaces meet, however, are empty chasms, with jagged splinters of quartz jutting into them. I too felt empty, jagged, and pierced without John. After Earl had asked Hannah to watch over me lest I do myself in, I had assured him I would not. Still, feeling such emptiness, I thought I should not make guarantees.

People aggravated me, especially if they thought their visits would help. Some talked of what an exemplary man John was and then told me "you'll get over it." I wanted to run them out of my house. Some, like Tamara and her beau, counseled me that many people who have lost a spouse find another without being disloyal to the lost one. They seemed poised before long to start trying to set me up with a new mate, probably a wealthy Princeton alum. "Shut up!" I wanted to say. I want no other men in my life, except my son, grandson, and son-in-law.

My beautiful cousin Kan Dickey Reid Cox in her eighties had a beau, a guy whose family often drove him from Pennsylvania to see her in Kentucky. She partied with him but would not consider marrying him. "You know, Panthea," she once said, "at my age, if you marry a man your age, you'll just end up nursing him 'til he dies." But that was not my reasoning. I wanted no dates, no affairs, no nothing with any man. I did notice male handsomeness but preferred it at a distance. No doubt I'm shy, but the real reason I wanted no other man in my life was because I loved John too completely for anyone else to begin to take his place.

During the week after the memorials, whenever I went downstairs I was met with the heavy sweet smell of lilies. Huge bouquets sat on the dining room table and the kitchen counter. The ones in the kitchen were pale greenish white. The ones in the dining room were pink, with flecks of magenta and matching stripes in the center of each petal. I had also left the last of the memorial programs, with that beautiful picture of John, on the dining room table. When I went down one morning, the arrangement of lilies and various berries and greens had dribbled green ooze on the programs. Clearly I was incompetent, unable even to keep these paper mementoes safe. Like the programs, I felt like damaged goods—not only did I not feel like carrying on, I felt incapable of doing so. While John and I had made a fairly equitable split of chores and responsibilities, it seemed now that I couldn't keep up my side of the bargain, much less his too. I was overcome by a sense of worthlessness.

I expected to be sad, not to lose my mind. "Mind blowing" was not a cool cliché. Losing John felt like it literally blew my mind. One morning I got out of the shower and couldn't recall if I'd washed my feet. One time I was backing out of the driveway and meant to veer to the right but turned my wheels to the left. I began asking myself if my emotions were blown, along with my brain. I began to wonder if mine was a normal reaction to loss or if loss had precipitated senility in my aging brain. I'd never wanted to hear or see much about the world's horrors. Now my reaction was more vehement. I refused to see another refugee drowned or another militant right-wing government turning away refugees at borders. Nor could I bear to hear, much less see, more of massacres, beheadings, rapes, and the other horrid stories of human inhumanity. Like those quartz bookends, my feelings were raw, jagged, and exposed.

I also could not bear to see happy stories, and I wondered if my emotional range was constricted. Loving John and being protected by his love, I had been free to experience a range of emotions. Without him, I was not. I didn't know if that was permanent damage or just a defense, like a hedgehog putting up its quills. I figured that when I didn't need the quills, I might feel again. But that might take a long time, even if I weren't permanently damaged.

I did not read much in this period. I did look at the *New York Times Book Review*, the front and opinion pages on the weekends, but it was mostly to "look at." I couldn't bear the details. I wanted to reread Shakespeare's *Cymbeline* with the lyric "Fear No More the Heat o' the Sun" that Nora had sung so beautifully. But John's complete Shakespeare was too heavy to take to bed, admittedly a poor excuse. The real reason was that my brain was tired. I thought of going away by myself, to be alone with nature, perhaps to the beach, perhaps to the woods, in hopes of restoring and refreshing myself.

Reid emailed me to say that he was going to a conference in Harrisonburg, Virginia, on 21 June, just a week after the memorials. Reid had graduated from the University of Virginia and had gone to law school at Washington and Lee in Lexington, thanks, I'm glad to say, to funds my mother left us, which we allocated to him. He became based in Christiansburg with a law firm whose central location is in Richmond. This conference was of Virginia treasurers from municipalities all across Virginia. Reid's forte had become supervising property sales and enabling municipalities to claim back taxes, so this was an important event for him. He told me he'd bring the smaller Reid to the conference if he had a babysitter. Of course, Reid Jr. was no baby, but I thought joining them might be a chance to befriend the little one. Reid Sr. told me that the group was sponsoring a food drive. I had lots to contribute, including jars of catsup and pickle relish that John had liked and I didn't so much.

I decided that I would meet the Reids in Harrisonburg and then drive into the woods, specifically into the Shenandoah National Park, just over an hour from Harrisonburg. I hoped that Reid Jr. might accompany me. He'd never been away from his parents, but I hoped his fondness for Princeton might signal a new fondness for me and an end to old resentments. The past Christmas at the Statue of Liberty, he'd tolerated the guide's long lecture and didn't complain about missing the trip up to Lady Liberty's crown, though John was furious.

On 19 June, the fifth week after John's death, again I read "Sailing to Byzantium" and reached out to hold a hand no longer there. I printed out a copy of the poem to take with me on my trip. Again, I wanted to put off chores but couldn't avoid them—phone arrangements, more recycling, naming beneficiaries, and ordering framed prints of the obituaries and Stuart's column about the memorials. That Friday afternoon, workers in their orange-striped vests were cheerily arranging long boards by the street over the gaping hole left by our poor uprooted maple tree. The boards were to mark the boundaries for a sidewalk to cross our property when the concrete mixer arrived. The Municipality of Princeton handed out a flier saying that "access to your driveway will be prohibited for at least 72 hours." *Good timing*, I thought, *I'll be in Virginia*. Now I had only to occupy myself until it was time to leave.

Remembering Earl's instructions to watch out for me, in an email, Hannah quoted Oscar Wilde: "To lose one parent may be regarded as a misfortune, to lose both looks like carelessness." I suppose literary humor was intended as a caution, since completing even simple tasks had become challenging for me.

For his seventy-fourth birthday, I had gotten John new walking shoes, since the old ones deserved a trip to the trash. A year later, the old ones were still on the garage steps, with the new shoes on top of them. Spiders made cobwebs in both pairs. I couldn't bear to give away the new ones or even to throw away the old ones. I was stymied, unable to act. For me, after the grief, sadness, and despair came numbness and then avoidance. I stared at stacks of papers I should sort and mostly destroy, convinced that I didn't need whole file drawers full of John's mother's papers. Still, I couldn't systematically sort, file, and trash because I did not even want to look at those papers. Clutter became a reproach and a threat. I couldn't bear to look in, much less clear out, my own drawers and papers. It seemed that clutter might bury me beneath an avalanche. My tendency toward avoidance was partly fatigue, partly an inability to cope, and partly self-protection, a sort of armor I put on to ward off further wounds.

Also, I was still afflicted by simple incompetence. There was so much I really couldn't do without John. Once at a service station, I noted the sign "Check air pressure here. Free" I didn't know how to check air pressure, when to do it, or why. I didn't know how to light the lanterns we ordered to help us survive power outages. Once when I was walking, a man in front of me kept going slower. I feared he was planning to grab me and throw me into his car, but I wasn't sure I even remembered how to scream or to run. I could answer if my new phone rang in the car, thanks to Hannah's connecting it via Bluetooth, but I didn't know how to add Reid's number to the Bluetooth device. I am often dismissive of people who are incompetent in areas where I am competent, like map-reading and navigation, but now I hoped computer experts weren't so dismissive of me for my computer incompetence. I didn't know how to get NPR on our sound system. When I talked too long on the phone while drinking vodka, I sometimes didn't make it to the bathroom before peeing in my pants. This was not John's gut problem but it reminded me of Yeats's "tattered man on a stick." I wondered how many such incompetences, ineptitudes, and bodily humiliations I'd have to endure before dying myself.

Then one day, looking out the kitchen window, I saw an enormous white bird swooping across our backyard before settling on the level branch of an oak. As it folded its wings, I realized that only its underside was white; its outer feathers were gray. It had a blunt beak and seemed to stare at me, as I looked at it for a long time. I'd never seen such a bird before. After I checked my bird book, I thought it might be a harrier or a rare kite. When I got back to the window, however, the giant bird was gone. Sometimes I went to sleep picturing it, happily thinking that the bird came to me from John. I searched the sky every day, hoping it would return. It didn't.

Planning to leave on Saturday, 20 June, I called to make a reservation for Maggie at the Cats Only Inn. I shocked the proprietor with the news that John was dead. In the past, while John drove out there, I could let Maggie out of her carrier box to sit on my lap. When we'd turned into the Cats Only driveway, she'd always stood on her hind legs to see the bird feeders alive with goldfinches and other busy little birds. Then she'd purred, knowing where she was going, and we'd known she'd be happy left there with so many birds to entertain her. We had last traveled there through rows of freshly planted Jersey corn barely more than two months before, when we'd dropped off Maggie before setting out for the Georgetown hospital. Now in June, Maggie had to stay caged in her carrier so she couldn't try to dash under the accelerator pedal. Thinking that I'd never been on that lovely country road without John, I began weeping again. At the Inn, I wiped my tears and told the proprietor about Maggie's pulling out patches of her own hair. "It's stress," she said. I could hardly imagine a cat feeling as much stress as I did, but she did really seem to be in mourning.

On Saturday, though I was hardly a father, a Father's Day special got me a bargain on equipment from Verizon—maybe because the clerks preyed upon me, a grieving widow without any electronic expertise. While my old information was being copied into a new phone, I went to the grocery and bought a few supplies to have for Maggie and me when we returned. Too often, she lay on her pallet facing the wall. She didn't purr much. Nor did I, whatever the human equivalent of purring may be.

I delegated my chores for the week to C. J., making a long list for him. Hannah had given John's keys to C. J.'s parents back in April when we thought we were moving to Georgetown, and now C. J. brought them over. From the key case, I retrieved the note Hannah added after John's death. She thanked them for "being such great neighbors to my parents and now to my mom." She left business cards for herself and Reid and asked them to "keep this set of keys in case she gets locked out." I was both irritated and touched by her note. Were my children afraid I was in such bad shape I'd lock myself out? Apparently. Actually, our lock system wouldn't permit that. At least I thought it wouldn't. I had to wonder, "How bad off am I?"

If I were so bad off, I wondered what would happen to me next. Could I pull myself back together or was this a steady decline? I recalled that John's mother had started her decline into incompetence and then dementia when she was in her seventies. One early sign was losing her sense of geography. If, on the way to Rhode Island or the Adirondacks, she saw a Shoney's or a Ruby Tuesday's, she'd say, "I've been here before." I'd tell her that I knew she had not, and she'd pout. On one visit to Columbus, John had insisted on riding along with her for some appointment. His real purpose was observing her driving. She crept along and then stopped her car in the middle of the street. With other cars honking and then circling her, she'd asked, "Son, where am I going?" John took over the wheel and got her to her appointment. We'd conferred about how to prevent her from driving, but she would not hear of going into assisted living until she was almost ninety and broke her hip and wrist in a fall. After that she'd had no choice. Navigation was one of my minor talents, so I consoled myself that I wasn't on that slippery slope to dementia. I was instead on a slippery slope to long-term despair.

Carrying on was not easy in despair.

18

YOU ARE AUTHOR?

When John and I had first visited the Shenandoah National Park, we'd had charmingly rustic quarters, complete with a big fireplace and kindling supplied by housekeepers. Families of chipmunks scurried under our deck and deer meandered close by, unafraid. John and I had walked down to a waterfall. On the way back up, I remember John stopping from time to time to say, "I've got to get my puff back." Still, he seemed no more out of breath than me or most hikers. We'd also taken easier walks, toured the meadow, enjoyed the rustic grandeur of the Big Meadows Lodge, and made love. I recall his trying to call Aubrey Williams from the porch outside Big Meadow's Great Room, a futile attempt given the poor cell reception on the mountaintop back then. The place was so peaceful John said, "Let's stop here whenever we travel to Reid's house, savoring calm before the storm."

"That's what spending a night with Ann and Rick can do too," I'd reminded him. Since then, we'd done both, visiting Ann and Rick and also the Shenandoah National Park many times, glad of a respite, much in love with each other and Mother Nature too.

On Sunday, 21 July 2015, I was on my way to Shenandoah, via the Holiday Inn in Harrisonburg. There I parked as close to a shade tree as possible and got my rolling suitcase out of the trunk. I'd driven almost nonstop to arrive in midafternoon, but the hotel staff had not prepared for the influx of customers—rooms weren't cleaned, reservations weren't in order. I walked around the lobby for over an hour, suitcase in tow. Virginians wore Bermuda shorts, flip-flops, and tank tops. Though many swelled out of their tops, they were more comfortable than I in long pants, sneakers with socks, and a long-sleeve shirt. By the time Reid's room finally opened, I was exhausted. The senior Reid seemed delighted that I'd driven so far to see them. My challenge was to entertain the smaller one while his father was in meetings the next day.

The children's museum we visited in the morning was designed for younger kids and bored us both, and I hardly knew what to do with a kid who didn't like to read. Still, his ever-present electronic tablet kept him entertained while I wrote down a few things from the last few days for this memoir. After Reid Sr. left meetings that afternoon, I asked him to give me a demo on pumping gas, which I hadn't done in years. At the Frontier Culture Museum in Staunton, we saw something of how people of different backgrounds had lived in log cabins, timbered farm houses, or mud huts, sometimes with sheep and goats sharing the households. I thought though that the younger Reid was most interested in the no-nut fudge I bought him. That night, while his dad went to a banquet, little Reid and I went out to dinner and talked about the Shenandoah National Park. He was glad enough to eat a pasta dish with me, but I still couldn't tell whether he liked me. At least he wasn't afraid of me.

I had half hoped that little Reid would spend three days alone with me in the park so we could get to be pals. When we got there we checked into my "traditional" cabin. It was plain and un-air-conditioned, making it rustic in a cheap rather than charming fashion. Reid busied himself closing the windows, though that cut off cross ventilation. After lunch at the lodge, we went to the visitor center. He remembered the historical panorama from when John took the family there for Thanksgiving in 2009, but today he was uninterested in a ranger's talk on bees. We went back to the cabin, hot and tired, and he locked the door as soon as we entered. I lay on top of my bed and fell asleep, hearing as if from another world the rhythmic clicks of his fingers on his computer game.

On waking, I suggested to Reid that we take the short steep walk up to Blackrock Overlook to see the valley below us. Met by swarms of midges, however, we turned back to retrieve insect repellent. Then I proposed a more level walk, which Reid clearly didn't want to take. Instead, we went to the lodge's Great Room, which held a supply of old-fashioned, non-electronic games, and together we played Jenga, a building block game. The elder Reid appeared in time for us to dine together. While Reid Sr. finished his meal and part of his son's, I had only a crab cake appetizer, which was more than enough for me as my appetite still hadn't returned.

The Reids and I then debated whether the smaller one should stay on with me or not. I said it would be terrible to go home and sit in front of a TV with nothing else to do for three days before coming back with his dad to meet me, as planned, on Friday. His dad said he wouldn't have to sit watching TV because he was scheduled for Cub Scout camp. Little Reid said that he'd already missed two days and so couldn't go to camp. Then big Reid began moving his son's things into my room. The thought of staying in a rustic cabin with only his granny apparently persuaded the little guy to go to camp for the rest of the week.

I expressed regret that we wouldn't have some time alone together on the mountainside. I worried that he still didn't trust me and that the good feelings he'd voiced in Princeton had more to do with C. J. and his brother than with me. Privately though, my feelings were mixed and I admitted some relief over the smaller Reid's defection. He had showed himself decidedly uninterested in nature hikes or lectures. I had forgotten how to play chess. He didn't want to talk about books. It was an effort to get him to talk about anything. Or maybe it was just an effort to hear him because he mumbled and my hearing was worsening. I couldn't imagine what the two of us would have done for three whole days alone in the woods. I also found myself yearning for time alone to open up my laptop and get back to my writing.

I had given some thought to building a house in the country, maybe near Reid Jr.'s Blacksburg school, where I could take a bigger part in his upbringing. I'd always wanted to build a green home, and perhaps I could do so there. Of course, my first husband still lived in Blacksburg. Would he harass me? Threaten me? What defenses did I have? Reid told me that his father had had hip replacements, so he couldn't be very nimble on his feet. The days when he could grab a kid and run or chase me down should be over. Still I didn't want unwelcome encounters or care to arm myself with a fierce dog or a gun. And the younger Reid's reluctance to stay with me seemed to weigh against the option of moving nearer him. I felt half disappointed, half relieved.

After the Reids left for home in southwestern Virginia, I put on the no-skid socks from Georgetown University Hospital that John wore so hopefully when he walked the halls with nurses and me. My feet were warm, and I felt cozy in my traditional cabin, but I deeply missed John's loving arms around me here. The beautiful forest was a minor consolation. As a deer nibbled grass just outside my cabin window, I opened my laptop and began writing earnestly about our lovely life of forty seemingly invincible years, before the firm terrain beneath us turned into quicksand. This memoir had become a lifeline indeed, rescuing me from forgetting or sinking deeper into debilitating grief.

The question of how to carry on, what to do with myself, lurked behind my writing. A logical enterprise would be to finish John's work on the *Word-Book*, but I feared that I was incapable of doing it. Still,

I decided that, after I'd finished writing this memoir, I'd consult John's scholarly "will" and the notes I took when John outlined to Hannah and me the steps going forward on the challenging project he'd assumed as Arch was dying. From the lodge's Great Room the next morning, I emailed the head of circulation at Princeton University asking if there were any way I could keep the library books John had checked out, either by continuing his privileges by renewing his dues or by paying for new borrowing privileges for me. I suddenly realized that our joint bank account would soon be canceled, yet another problem I hadn't faced.

The next day, I walked alone up to the Blackrock Overlook. Just the previous summer, John had held my hand where the log steps were far apart or the rocks were precarious. Without him, I once fell on my knees and often grabbed a prominent boulder to steady myself. At the top, I marveled at how, without smog and pollution, the view goes on for over a hundred miles. I also recalled that on this very climb just a year before, John had shown nothing to suggest COPD or any wasting lung disease. We had both indeed seemed impervious to mortal weakness.

After I got back, I walked about a mile, halfway to the visitor center and back on mostly level ground, marveling at the thick lush ferns growing in the shadows and the friendly doe I passed on the way back. When I got to the lodge I called Reid Sr. He had gotten the small one to Cub Scouts that morning, despite resistance. Reid said he thought his son was really afraid of new situations and had a kind of PTSD from listening to his mother yelling at him. Suddenly it occurred to me that little Reid's closing my windows and locking the door came from deep fear. *Oh, dear,* I thought. *This is too sad.* Still, I didn't know what I could do to help him. I now was feeling guilty for being relieved that he'd chosen not to spend three days with me. John and I had always been able to entertain little Hannah with games and stories we'd make up. She would have loved exploring the woods and looking for animals. But my grandson seemed only to love his electronic tablet. I wondered if I spent more time with him, I could get through his shell and help him enjoy reading books, exploring nature, even getting to know me.

I returned to my cabin, weary and sad, and took up writing once again. Then one of the cleaning staff knocked on the door. I said I didn't need anything except new coffee-making supplies and trash emptying. As he busied himself around my room, I sat at my computer, so he asked, "You are author?" I told him I was. He was from Turkey. He asked me to write my name. As I did, I told him that he could find me on the internet. He was much impressed. I stayed in the cabin, revising some of the earlier bits of the memoir, feeling guilty about staying inside when all nature beckoned, as they say. After all, I could write at home, though there I would have to contend with street repairs, a constantly ringing telephone, endless mail, and a neurotic cat. In Shenandoah, I was truly on my own, a situation that helped me to concentrate on my writing and to meditate on how to live without my darling John.

Just after writing down those words, I set out for another hike, putting on for the first time heavy boots. I'd ordered them in 2001, before we moved to Princeton, and had imagined someone at L. L. Bean wondering why someone in Louisiana wanted such cold-weather boots. Back then, I'd been excited to think of wearing them in New Jersey winters, but the excessive snow of 2015 had dampened my enthusiasm. Now in June of 2015, the boots buttressed my walk to a trail that meets the Appalachian Trail behind an amphitheater. At a milepost, a family was looking at their map to find out how to get to Lewis Falls. I was about to show off my map-reading skills when a young woman wearing a huge backpack came along the trail and explained the signs better than I could have. The older woman in the family admired her walking sticks. "Yes," she said, "but I wish they had shock absorbers." Alas, I thought, I wish I had shock absorbers too. Then I recalled walking sticks I'd bought myself the past Christmas. Somehow during the traumas of winter and spring, I had completely forgotten about them though they would have been useful here, if I only knew how to walk with them properly.

I followed the family along the Appalachian Trail for a while. The forest was strangely silent, almost serene: ferns on both sides of the trail, green leaves dancing in the sunshine above, tiny mushrooms with pinkish centers below. The trail was rough, with boulders on it and loose rocks. Though it was a downhill climb, I had to grab a few rocks, lest I lose my footing. I needed to hold myself up straight, almost leaning backwards, but that's hard to do when you have to watch your feet, lest you stumble.

I recalled John's observation that going downhill means coming back up. The others had gotten ahead, so I called to them saying I was turning back. I would have liked to see the falls. I thought how good it would be to take this hike with the Reids, so big Reid could offer me a hand when needed, as my dear John used to do. Even though I hadn't gone all the way down to the falls, I had a hot uphill climb on the trail back before I emerged near the amphitheater. My sense of direction took me toward the lodge, without calculating that now I was on asphalt roads, built for cars but hard on pedestrians. The midges had made no appearance in the forest, but outside the forest they attacked. Just after the scabs from those mosquito bites I'd gotten a month before healed, I had new bites on my scalp, calling for anti-itch gook in my hair. I was so tired, my right side threatened to collapse, my left to slip out of its hip joint. But instead of falling, I returned to my little cabin and indulged in fudge and bourbon, hoping John's spirit approved. I remembered him saying gently, as I'd asked him to, "Straighten up, Panthea."

After a day of eating cheese cubes, left over from the memorial at the Arts Council, with a Kind bar, I was glad to dine in the lodge, but first I bought a pocket guide to "Familiar Plants and Animals" in Shenandoah.

Then I placed calls and checked email. To my delight and terror, the head of circulation at the Firestone Library said that they would make arrangements for me to continue to use John's library books. That meant that I had committed myself to finishing the enormous scholarly project that both Arch and John had died before finishing. *Well,* I thought, *I'm so ignorant, I've got reason to be terrified. If it kills me too, it will be death in their honor.*

The lodge's Great Room was crowded with folks playing checkers, chess, and countless old-fashioned games, while other folks searched for internet connections to the outside world. In the dining room, a pleasant hum of chatter extended from table to table. I noted different sorts of people, dressed as they pleased, though not much racial diversity. I ate the special of pan-seared salmon with blackberry sauce, which would have been even better if the chef had had the confidence to take the salmon out of the searing-pan earlier.

Walking back to my humble cabin, I thought that after that day's walking I should be standing taller and straighter. Instead, I found myself listing further to one side. Clearly my posture problem wasn't going to be solved by one day's exertions any more than by John's exhortations to straighten up. Back at the desk, I set about writing once again. John would not have liked to see me writing into the night, but what else could I do? My stiff fingers ached from so much typing but I could not quit. I wondered if I had become a maniac author; certainly I was an obsessive one.

I hoped that rewriting my diary-like log and the notes in our Smithsonian calendar and then adding my reflections on those experiences might help restore my sense of worth and competence. Something told me that if I could get my "groove" back, as the saying goes, perhaps I would have a publishable memoir, of use to others as well as myself. I considered and then addressed myself to the first writing chore, getting rid of the present tense. I couldn't say "today" or "now," as I had when these had been diary entries, but rather "on that day" or "back then." Distance between having an experience and recording it also allowed me to objectify the story, even my own state of mind. Thus I could say that I forgot or suppressed certain memories. Looking back, I could ask why I did so. I could also say that my brain improved its focus as I taxed it to write details I'd forgotten, as I had the story of the three children who shoveled snow for us and whose mother repaid us with a cake. And I had simply suppressed an absolutely crucial story—that John had "crashed" after his bronchoscopy. Writing about the endless snow resurrected memories, good and bad. In fact, writing helped me suture back together broken bits of myself, making me feel less fractured, less worthless, potentially in command of myself and my life once again.

I pondered again the question of whether my current obsessive writing was an analogue for my absorption long ago in meeting some deadline rather than noting John's ashen color or, more recently, in writing the hitchhiker story rather than in trying to cure John's sickness. Up in the Virginia mountains, I needed to write what happened to us both, whatever the conclusion. I wanted to understand how I guided myself rightly and wrongly. And I needed to publish this memoir at least as a warning against deference to careless medical practice.

I am no expert; still our experience suggests a few cautionary tales. First, be on your guard against doctors who do not talk to you. Hannah was able to speak personally to the head of pulmonology at Georgetown, yet Dr. G. never called John at home or even had his nurse do so. The GI doctor did call once after the esophagus stretch, but only then, as if to confirm the results he expected. Also, be suspicious of doctors who do little more than order tests, since ordering them seems to absolve the doctors of further responsibility. But I think the main warning sign of poor medical practice must be when a doctor offers one hypothesis and sticks to it, despite contradictory evidence, refusing to consider other possibilities. When John had his first swallowing test, the radiologist stopped the test, saying that John had pneumonia—yet the GI doctor ignored that conclusion because it didn't fit his diagnosis. And it still burns me up that on 14 April, when John could hardly breathe or walk, his pulmonologist just ordered another swallowing test, instead of exploring other options! So the major warning sign I offer is that when a doctor will not reconsider his or her hypothesis, it is time to find another MD and another opinion, and right away.

On Thursday, 24 June, I went to the visitor center, hoping to find out about the waterfall that John and I had climbed down to and up from on our first visit to Shenandoah. Identifying Dark Hollow Falls was easy. We had embarked on the hike because it was only a short one-and-a-quarter mile round trip; the walk, however, was "very steep." Being several years older, with a poor back and no companion, I decided it would be unwise to walk down to the falls alone. Instead, I walked a trail called The Story of the Forest. Since there was no guide to tell that story, however, I had to infer it from the flora. I saw white and red oak, something my pocket guide called eastern white pine, which has fluffy needles, and another tree that seemed to be black birch. There was a flower called fly poison and a plant with cascading little blooms, which looked rather like a miniature fireworks display. Much visited by bumble bees, it turned out to be milkweed, the only plant monarch butterflies live off.

Though it had seemed cold as I set off, I was definitely warm enough on my return to relish a long drink at the water fountain in front of the visitor center. Back in my abode, I ate my leftovers of salmon dinner and cheese, with some wine, and continued to contemplate the loss of my beloved. I dreamed that night that I was visiting with Virginia Woolf's crowd, particularly the Stracheys, when Lady Strachey (mother of the revolutionary biographer Lytton Strachey) was about to put one of her houses on sale. In my dream, John drove me there. Of course, it was nearly a century after such a thing might have happened. And why the Stracheys? I had no idea, except that they were, more or less, of the William Morris Arts and Crafts period. Maybe my dream had to do with house-hunting. But the real point, I concluded, was that John had driven me there in my dream. *Oh, my darling,* I thought, *you did enable my writing on Woolf and the Bloomsbury Group. I hope I was so enabling for you.* When I woke, of course John, who'd been alive in my dream, was not with me anymore. My sense of a jagged emptiness inside still lingered, but drowning myself or taking enough pills to finish me off would only leave more grief and horror for Reid and Hannah. That would be unfair, hardly a loving legacy from their mother.

Hannah, by the way, thought me nuts to save the tidbits from the reception or my dinners, spending little money on meals, even while spending a good bit on this trip, my treat to myself and the chillun. "Well," I said to Hannah from the lodge where I could get cell phone reception, "my mother lived through the Depression, so I learned from her." I doubt that made any sense to Hannah, who lacks my scruples about wasting food. John did not think my parsimoniousness out of the ordinary, though he could tire of leftovers.

My endless authoring would be another matter. Since, as I've said, John and I wrote "side by side," or at least simultaneously, that remark may seem inexplicable. But John knew when to quit. I didn't anymore. After John had his bourbon in the evening, he would be game for watching the news, taking a walk, relishing a good dinner at home or out, reading a book or magazine, watching a movie or more television, or making love. This pattern had replenished wells of energy and creativity for us both. Without John, though, I mostly just wanted to write. Mother Nature and my subject matter colluded to replenish my creativity. The beauty of the forest calmed me, as did memories of our happiness together. Even memories that made me weep inspired me to make such memories live on for a prospective reader. Still, I realized I couldn't write so obsessively forever, lest I use up my inspiration. Also, I sensed that a "writing life" would become a dull one if all I did was write.

After the next night's dinner in the lodge, I walked nearby, coming close to a number of deer in the evening fog. A woman held a St. Bernard in tow and kept him quiet while a doe passed nearby. After it wandered off, I told the animal, "Good dog!" On Friday, 26 June, I took the forest ranger's guided morning walk through Big Meadows, which is reportedly the highest wetland meadow on Earth. In 1936, FDR dedicated the Shenandoah National Park here with 10,000 or more people listening to his talk. On the trail, we heard about different stages of meadow conservation over the years, from mowing everything, to burning everything, to building gliding runways, to monitoring conservation and renewal. We saw huckleberry plants, milkweed with chrysalises for monarch butterflies, and fly poison flowers, so named because when people smash up the petals in a bowl of milk, any fly that settles in the bowl dies. We also saw an insect called froghopper, which can accelerate using over 400 G's of gravity propulsion. (For comparison, a rollercoaster uses 3 G's.) John had enjoyed a similar foray that we'd taken together some years back. I found that recording what I learned, even of plants and bugs, had a healing effect on me. As FDR said in 1936, the Park could provide not just recreation but a re-creation of the country and the spirit.

After returning to the visitor center, I listened for a while to a talk on the peregrine falcon, probably the fastest creature on (or above) Earth. After I got back to my cabin, the Turkish man appeared, though I'd been gone two hours with a "service please" sign on my door. Clearly he had waited to see me. He got a few things I named, then asked, "You want vacuum?" Given my habit of eating cheese and crumbly crackers in my room, I said I did. He plugged the cleaner into an electric outlet, heretofore cleverly disguised as part of the knot in the knotty pine wall. I'd originally thought there were too few outlets and had had to choose which electronic device to charge when. After he left, I started writing again, proving myself, I hope, the author he thought I was, even if John would not approve of my spending so much time tapping at the keyboard.

To my distress, however, at about 12:15 I realized that it was Friday, six weeks after my dear John's death. I closed the drapes (these were hardly "draperies"), pulled out the page on which I'd printed "Sailing to Byzantium," and lay on the bed. I read it maybe three times out loud, weeping at the end over "what is past, or passing, or to come."

I had reserved more commodious rooms for my chillun, who were scheduled to join me on Friday evening. I hoped that by then the little guy would be more interested in nature walks and that the rest of us would be capable of taking them. Hannah and Michael arrived as planned about six and checked into their "preferred" room, which had a big bathroom, a television, and air-conditioning, not needed that evening. The Reids arrived about eight, checking into the room next to Hannah and Michael. Louise did not come. She has no interest in the out-of-doors—or maybe she was too afraid of Lyme disease to venture near deer—or possibly she was afraid of me.

At dinner together that night, I ordered river trout, which the chef must have known more about than seared salmon and tuna steaks. I ate heartily, for a change. We all toasted John, Hannah remarking how unfortunate that he wasn't here to celebrate two landmark Supreme Court decisions. Since I hadn't been paying attention to the news, I had to ask what they were. "Equal rights for gay marriages in all fifty states. And the Affordable Care Act is finally law."

"Hallelujah!" I exclaimed, sorry again that John couldn't shout "Hallelujah!" with me. My ignorance of such groundbreaking decisions proved the downside of being isolated, of concentrating on writing about my own emotional state to the exclusion of the world.

Little Reid told us about Cub Scout camp, which he seemed to have enjoyed mightily. The boys had built a rope bridge. Michael asked him cleverly pointed questions, getting him to acknowledge that the bridge-making and other activities all went better when the boys worked together. Apparently, it didn't matter much that he'd missed the first two days of camp. He seemed less afraid and more willing to joke with us now. We laughed about his troubling the waitstaff for glass after glass of water and for straws. Though we needed to conserve water and straws were not recyclable, the staff brought him whatever he wanted.

I again dreamt about John in the night, something about our going away together. I woke during a storm to find my cabin almost icy. For the first time, I opened a closet door and was relieved to find a folded blanket stored on a shelf. I put it on the bed, still folded, glad of the double warmth, and went back to bed wearing John's socks from Georgetown. I still left a crack in the windows so I could breathe fresh, albeit very cold, air.

Saturday morning was wet and cold. I'd heard that ranger programs go on, rain or snow, and are only cancelled in really dangerous weather like lightning. In the amphitheater, someone wiped off the benches with towels, and we five sat shivering in a steady drizzle. Big Reid gave up his jacket so his son wouldn't be too cold while we listened to a presentation on birds of prey. The ranger passed around an owl skull and owl feathers, explaining how cleverly designed the owl is for its main job—diving, killing, and eating small creatures. The ranger cautioned us that we should not throw out of our cars even biodegradable stuff like apple cores. Mice will scurry to eat them, then raptors will dive to catch the mice. Their eyes can spot a mouse from far above the Earth. Once they focus on the mouse, however, they see little else, like cars, which often kill them. So a better phrase than "tunnel vision" seems to be "raptor vision."

After we'd sat for about thirty minutes in the cold drizzle, the ranger invited her audience over to her truck and opened its back lid. We could hear her saying sweetly, "Step up now." When she turned around, an adorable screech owl was perched on her glove, still under the truck's lid, since owls do not like rain. She told us that the pointy ear-like extrusions on top of owls' heads are not ears but instead are there to make the bird look taller and fiercer. This one's eyes had been injured in an encounter with a building, and so he could no longer hunt. Now he's well cared for as a demo bird. Despite the cold rain, Reid Jr. was fascinated. "He looks mean but he's sweet," he said. Reid also loved getting closer and closer to deer until he could take really good pictures of them. Hannah took one of him photographing a deer. Flattened perspective made it seem he was in touching range of the doe. We all tried a walk to the spot where salamanders live, but my gut rebelled, and so we quit. It was too cold and wet to climb down to Dark Hollow Falls. I decided I'd make it next time.

On Sunday after breakfast, we gathered at the visitor center for a last look over the great meadow. "Mom," Hannah asked, "can you tell us about it?" Perhaps it was my old schoolteacher self getting back in gear, but I enjoyed walking the meadow with my chillun and telling them what I'd learned. It felt really good to know something that was entirely new to me and them. Back at the center, I saw the ranger who'd given the tour on Friday and confirmed the astonishing story of the bug that propels itself at 400 G's. We said our goodbyes in time for Hannah and Michael to get to a ranger program on bears further north on the Skyline Drive. Little Reid gave me a perfunctory hug, leaving six or so inches between us. "That's not a real hug!" I protested, and so he squeezed me tight, for a moment at least. I was going to Charlottesville that night for a brief visit with Pat Spacks. I'd told her I'd get there about 4 p.m. Not wanting to arrive early, I used my extra time to buy her a gift of coasters with maps showing major spots in the Shenandoah Park, then I drove back toward the lodge.

Fortunately, everyone drives slowly in the Park. I came to a quick stop because there was a deer standing in the middle of the road. I had to search for the horn, which I'd probably never used before, until I found it and tooted softly at the deer. She moved only a step or two. Cars coming in the other direction stopped too. It seemed a standoff until a spotted fawn scampered out of a ditch on one side of the road and mother and child scurried off on the other side. I stopped in the lodge to call Ann and reminisce about John and the memorials, thanking her again for the poem about the body leaving the soul. Then I set off on the one-hour-plus drive to Charlottesville. This beautiful university town, located halfway between Hannah and Reid, was one of the places John and I had contemplated moving to. Passing the world-class medical center there, I regretted that we had not made that move. Now all I could do was to author this book of love and regret.

19

THE BODY
LEAVING THE SOUL

Pat Spacks owns a spacious condo in a lovely older building. From her windows she has views of two churches, one synagogue, and the Blue Ridge Mountains beyond. She is just a block or so from Charlottesville's downtown pedestrian mall, with its many shops and entertainments. This was the sort of place I'd thought John would have loved. At least he wouldn't have had to mow a lawn or shovel snow. Though Pat's condo has an elevator, it also has eight or so intimidating steps up to the first floor. I'd packed efficiently with minimal stuff in a tote bag, plus a purse, a bottle of wine from the party at home, and the coasters, which were heavier than anything. I'd given her such short notice that she didn't have time to prepare a gourmet dinner, but still she served a perfect assortment of foods, cold and warm. She had been deeply upset over John's death, so I'd sent her a copy of the Chapel program, which she too pronounced beautiful.

Neither of us felt up to more talk of grief just then, so I spoke some to her about this memoir and writing's usefulness to me. She'd just completed an essay on poems about mourning and so was understanding and interested. Then I brought up the issue of whether I could finish John's work for him. She thought it sounded doable, if I stuck mostly to what John had almost finished. She cautioned me, however, against trying to follow Arch's plan of offering notes on every word in the book, a "sinkhole" for me, she said. She reminded me that I could now be the author in charge of Swift's *Word-Book*. I could shape it as it seemed right to me, while also respecting Arch's and John's wishes. Her words comforted me into a sound sleep.

Pat is an early riser, so it was easy for her to wake me at six a.m. and easy for me to get on the road by eight. I avoided most beltways and traveled up state roads to Frederick, Maryland, around Baltimore, to my GPS's apparent indignation. I suspect they program those voices to sound irritated when telling you to make a U-turn and go back to the closest approach to the freeway. When I got onto I-95, I swear my GPS voice relaxed. Driving along, avoiding eighteen-wheelers, I meditated further on the poem by Felicia Mitchell that Ann read at the memorial. Could John's soul hover about me, like "a dragonfly over water"?

When I finally drove into Princeton, I wept. Everything in this beautiful town reminded me of John, except the sidewalk now completed in front of our house. Some of the ugly mud hole where the maple tree used to stretch its roots was still there, though. I arrived in time to pick up Maggie. She seemed glad to see me, and I got a lesson on how to poke a thyroid pill down her throat. John had smushed them up with a catnip treat in a little mortar and pestle we'd bought from wood-craftsmen in Argentina. A pill poker looked easier, until I tried it.

Wednesday, the first of July, I went back to a strenuous Pilates lesson. Janell had only met John twice, but she had come to the memorial at the Arts Council. "What a remarkable man!" she said. I wondered if I'd managed to stand up straight during my presentation, and she replied,

"Yes. And you were beautiful." I worked extra hard on the frog stretches, comforted by her kind words.

Later I drove into downtown Princeton, finding a handy parking spot on Nassau Street, a rare bit of luck in busy Princeton. I first went to the Firestone Library, where I paid for a year's extension of John's borrowing privileges. "Let's just hope I can finish his work," I said to the librarian, before bursting into tears. Then I stopped in the quiet Chapel, asking for John's blessing, God's too. Afterward I went to the religious offices, where $235 was saved from the memorial in the Chapel, with the understanding that undesignated donations would go to Oxfam. The only way to deal with the cash was to put it in my local bank account, from which I wrote a check to Oxfam. Other contributions were independently made to the local Center for Family, Community and Social Justice, founded by our neighbors Hinda and Norbert, and to Doctors Without Borders, all in memory of John Irwin Fischer. Hermann and Erika Real sent a cash gift of 100 euros, which I could not deposit directly. At the downtown bank, I had the cash changed into dollars to be sent to Doctors Without Borders. Even in the impersonal bank on Nassau Street, such dealings left me in tears. I had thought I was no longer vulnerable to sieges of uncontrolled weeping, so my tears in the library and bank seemed irrational. I guessed that I was more vulnerable when I wasn't on guard. I could speak with friends about losing John, but when I had to tell a stranger, "My husband died," I fell apart.

After I spent time downtown dealing with the donations, I came home to write the usual monthly checks. Then I settled down to deal with long forms of major annuities and IRAs and their transfers to me, while I named Hannah and Reid my beneficiaries. Annuity forms include intimidating warnings that "All elections are irrevocable," meaning that whatever choices I made were permanent. Belatedly, it occurred to me that John should have left more money to Hannah and

Reid rather than to me. I was lucky enough to have a paid-for house, to be financially secure with both our pensions now paid to me, and to have no desire to go on the sorts of extravagant tours that suck up many a widow's resources.

On 2 July, I woke, wondering if I should begin my morning by writing or by attending to chores. The chores won, barely. I cut up John's credit cards and called American Express to cancel his name on our account. I needed to call our dental insurance to let them know there was only one of us. I needed to get ownership of our car and house transferred to my name alone, but I postponed those tasks. I packaged up the annuity and IRA forms with five certified copies of the death certificate. At that rate, I feared that I'd run out. Simple photocopies would not do, only certified copies would. Who knew it was so complicated to be a survivor?

I had to mail the package to our financial advisor in Baton Rouge. He was so impressed by Stuart's article on Stravinsky and "Remembering John Fischer" that he'd distributed it around his firm. With all those forms and death certificates sent to him, I included a memorial service program, not too damaged by green ooze from that bouquet of lilies.

Despite all that work, I was still overwhelmed with tedious chores. I seemed to have lost the online link to the funeral "urn" that Hannah had chosen, a handsome cherry box. I needed to order it and have it sent to the funeral home. The police truck came back across the street. Colin told me that the road construction company pays off-duty cops time-and-a-half to sit there all day, doing nothing except keeping strangers off our street. I wondered if the cop could bring a book to read. Or was he sentenced to solitary confinement in a cop car just watching for intruding traffic? Belatedly, I realized that he could text as much as he pleased. The advantage of texting is that the texter need never learn how to spell and punctuate English.

Hannah sent me her account, a painful log or diary of sorts, of John's last month. We are both authors, highly aware that writing, even memoir writing, is a considered undertaking. Memoirs emerge from authentic memories and deep emotions, but the memoirist polishes sentences, eliminates repetition and irrelevancies, chooses better verbs, searches for specific details. Sometimes, though, oversight can interfere with honest emotions. And weaving her log into my narrative was not simple. I had to avoid telling the same story twice and had to choose between dramatic versions of events, clarifying whose words I was using. It was a pleasure and also a cautionary tale.

I found that Hannah's memories were better than mine. After John's bronchoscopy, I had omitted the resident's calling us back to the operating room because John had crashed. I had not mentioned the medical staff's asking us about intubation. I had said nothing about John's shaking his head no, reminding all that he emphatically did not want to be kept alive artificially. I forgot that he'd said he wanted "no code" tattooed on his chest. Perhaps I had intentionally forgotten such painful stories, but they remained branded into Hannah's consciousness and, after reading her accounts, were permanently burned into mine. Her log strengthened my memoir, as I hoped mine would enhance hers.

I wrote obsessively almost all that Friday, taking time out only to mail the seemingly endless forms with the death certificates and to rediscover, with a clue from Hannah, the website where I ordered the cremation box to be sent to the funeral home, with a note about whose ashes it should contain. Then I returned to write the scene of John's death and the scene when the funeral guys took his body away in that zippered red rubber bag. Weeping again, I feared that writing and weeping would be forever connected for me.

During my revision process, I realized that, in addition to telling my own story, my book might provide useful aids to others. After

all, we want to read about someone else's grief not to wallow in grief
but to understand and also to learn. Thus, I added an appendix with
information about ways to find better medical care if you need it;
resources for advice, counsel, and guidance in coping with grief; and
a list of grieving memoirs and of novels treating death (all known by or
recommended to me), which might divert, engage, poignantly touch, or
sometimes even delight a reader trying to heal after a loss.

I can't recall when I bought Tess Gallagher's love poems written after
the death of Raymond Carver. Surely I did not suspect that I too would
lose my beloved, but when I looked back at *Moon Crossing Bridge* after
John's death, I found Gallagher's passionate grief burning through those
poems, which I read and reread because her loss so completely resonated
with mine. As a poet, Gallagher had no obligation to characterize Carver
or herself; her assignment as poet was to convey the intensity of their
love and her loss.

Prose memoirs have further obligations. In *The Light of the World*,
Elizabeth Alexander too touches me with her genuine grief. She offers
a lively sense of her husband, Ficre Ghebreyesus, an Eritrean whom she
met in New Haven, and she conveys Ficre's vitality as a chef, painter,
host, father, and lover. She presents her own delight in him and their
histories so enthusiastically, we understand her devastation after the
terrible shock of his unexpected death.

Joyce Carol Oates's *A Widow's Story: A Memoir* also conveys
a powerful sense of the lost one. She says that Raymond Smith was
"an editor of living things." That wonderful phrase encompasses his
great patience, his gardening, his care with manuscripts as editor of the
Ontario Review, his sense of responsibility, and his love for her. Oates's
disbelief and anguish over his death reifies my sense of horror over John's
death. Both deaths were unnecessary, inexplicable. Because Oates sets
up Ray Smith's character so beautifully, we readers suffer and empathize

with her agony. More personally, the widow's trip to the surrogate court in Trenton was all too familiar. The power of her memoir lies, however, not so much in circumstances familiar to me, but in Oates's eloquence, which touches us all.

Joan Didion is of course a great and accomplished writer, but I found her stories of loss in *The Year of Magical Thinking* and *Blue Nights* less gripping than those of Alexander and Oates because her accounts were much more egocentric. By definition a memoir is egocentric, but, as I've said, a grieving memoir must also be other-centric. Didion seems too busy name-dropping and too absorbed in herself to offer a full sense of her lost husband or daughter. Though Didion writes of her seemingly endless grief, to me her memoir feels hollow because we don't know these people well enough to grieve with her. Also, I suspect that Didion has little desire to grow beyond her grief.

Hannah told me that Helen Macdonald's *H Is for Hawk* was helpful to her because Macdonald too had lost her beloved father and transferred her grief into training a hawk. Macdonald is a poet, and I'd read rave reviews of her poetic prose, but I could imagine no consolation in having a hawk swoop onto my shoulder. (An unfortunate incident when I was a small child exploring a chicken coop full of angry flapping hens gave me a lifelong phobia of flapping wings, and my cousin claims a feather in a doorway would keep me from entering a room.) Given Hannah's recommendation, however, I steeled myself to read *H Is for Hawk*. Despite Macdonald's testimony about her hand and face being raw from the blows of the hawk's wings, I read to the end. Macdonald's father was a news photographer and also a falconer, vocations that help Macdonald see clearly and transcend her grief. I wish, however, that Macdonald had written more about her lost father and less about the writer T. H. White, who had also trained a hawk. Here too, I crave more personal revelations behind her grief.

A curious book that seems to challenge what I've said about grieving memoirs is Julian Barnes's *Levels of Life*. Only in the third part of this rather quirky book does he turn to the loss of his wife of thirty years, but he is so far from writing biography that he doesn't even share her name with us readers. We barely know more about Barnes's lost wife than a fine phrase about her "radiant curiosity." I yearn for details, examples of that curiosity. Yet he successfully captures us (or at least me) in his philosophical and personal meditation on grief. When Barnes says he has no emotions left "to lend," his words echo the reactions all these writers have to loss—certainly they resonate with me, in my avoidance of intensities, painful or even pleasant ones.

Though not a believer, Barnes is a moralist. He thinks of love as John did, as moral, as "a call to seriousness and truth." He continues to live because he believes that when he dies his wife will also be truly dead. Like John, I am a believer, though a somewhat agnostic one. Barnes's thoughts have prompted me to reread and contemplate his reactions to death of his beloved. As I indicated in my preface, I think that love and loss are intimately connected. Barnes says it too: "every love story is a potential grief story." I think he would agree with me that the depth of the love is reflected in the depth of the grief. No biographer, Barnes succeeds as autobiographer. He writes a serious and engaging meditation on his own grief.

Prolonging grief after some time (maybe more than a year but for Barnes it lasted nearly four years) seems a bit like drawing out a topic of conversation after you have already exhausted it, as well as your friends' capacity for listening. I came to realize that we have to go through and beyond our grief, as Barnes does on his last pages, without any diminution of love for the lost one. Maybe long-drawn-out grief is simply selfish. Maybe that's why, in my own healing process, I do not care to reread Didion, but will reread Alexander, Oates, and Barnes.

The selfishness of grief is a vexed topic. Great writer though he is, Julian Barnes feels he is less interesting without his wife. Certainly I know I am less interesting without John. I'm not given to witty repartee. People, I suspect, invited us to dinner for the pleasure of John's conversation (though perhaps I carried my weight in the dishes I brought to potluck dinners). It is selfish to want our loved ones back so that, as part of a pair, we are more interesting. And it is selfish to perpetuate grief to try and evoke sympathy.

This consideration of other grief memoirs, their successes and failures, brings me, as I write, to examine myself and this book. I wonder if I have been truly honest, if I have adequately laid myself bare, and if I have been truthful about my failures of competence, memory, and empathy. On the question of honesty, after Hannah told me that she was memorizing Puck's speech at the end of *Midsummer Night's Dream* while Hurricane Andrew raged, I invented a lovely scene when she and John recite the "Epilogue" together. The problem was that that didn't happen. I sent it to Hannah, who said it was a charming fiction. Reluctantly, I removed it. Even an honest memoirist can't (and shouldn't) tell everything. (It would have been extraneous and simply nasty, for example, to tell more about my first marriage.) During my initial writing, I was not quite ready to expose myself. I finally came to do so in the last chapter, as readers will see, when my children's reaction to an early version of this book suggested that I had been inconsiderate of their feelings.

It was easy to confess my memory failures, which worry me greatly as a forecast of diminished brain power. It was less easy to delete my characteristic snide remarks, often about political enthusiasts who seemed dumb or others who seemed willfully ignorant. I had and have little patience for those incapable of understanding the depth of my love and loss. Still, I cut out some wicked remarks, while being, I hope, still honest and a bit sassy, at times.

I have praised the memoirs by Alexander and Oates for succeeding so strongly as biography, giving us a sense of the lost one, as well as a sense of the writer and her loss. Sometimes in this book, I fear I forgot so much that I let John slip away from me. Though I have lost much of his wisdom, I have tried to convey something of his uniqueness. His ways with money were his and no one else's; ditto for his unbelievably conscientious research, his generous ability to forgive, and also his great ability to love. I had to make that biography palpable so that readers would both appreciate John and understand me, as well as my great love and my terrible grief.

Another Friday went by without reading "Sailing to Byzantium" aloud. I forgot it, but I did not forget John. In the night, I had another sexy dream in which I longed for John and went looking for him. He was alone in an empty space under a sheet, where I joined him, making love. On Saturday morning, I read "Sailing to Byzantium" aloud several times as atonement to his ever-present spirit for skipping it the day before.

I expected the financial forms to arrive in Baton Rouge on Monday; they did not, nor did they arrive Tuesday or Wednesday. John would never have put such important documents in the mail without getting a tracking number, a registered signature, a certified green form establishing their arrival, so he would have been tearing his hair out over this delivery failure. I began to fear that I'd betrayed him by careless over-confidence in the US mail.

In our backyard, sunlight glinted on the new bamboo shoots that replaced the dead brown leaves destroyed by winter cold. I gave up poking thyroid pills down Maggie's throat. I couldn't risk her distrust, so I started again mashing them in her food, as John had done, in hopes she would still get enough medication. I rediscovered Stilton cheese and fed Maggie crumbs. She began to eat again, especially if she got a morsel of cheese with her ocean fish paté. I started talking aloud to keep her company. Then I began talking to myself, instructions, sometimes reflections, and often accusations like *you idiot* or *have you lost your mind?* Somehow, rudely accusing myself of losing my mind was a kind of assurance that I hadn't lost it, not yet anyway.

CWW friends recommended a different veterinarian. She looked at Maggie's blood work and concluded that Maggie had inflammatory bowel disease, which the previous vet had failed to diagnose. That part sounded vaguely familiar, a doctor not responding to the evidence. The new vet prescribed, believe it or not, Prednisolone! She ordered five milligrams of prednisone a day and five milligrams of thyroid twice a day, both in soft tuna chews, which were easy to smash into Maggie's food. I thought of the difference a good doctor can make and reflected on the irony that I seemed to have found a better doc for Maggie than I'd had for John. Again I regretted not having tried harder to find him better care sooner.

On Tuesday, 7 July, at Hannah's insistence, I went back to the Princeton hospital to collect the records of the bronchoscopy and blood work. Dr. Barton wrote that he had performed "a bronchoalveolar lavage to rule out an untreated infection." John's albumin was low, the alpha 1 and 2 were high. The check for tuberculosis was inconclusive due to "low lymphocyte count." His "Neutro" and "Neutr Abs" were quite high, while his lymph counts were very low. His glucose level was very low, and his white blood count was high. I didn't pretend to understand those medical terms, but they certainly sounded unhealthy. I thought of asking Dr. Barton for more information, but he'd already avoided saying much. I imagined that Hannah was right when she speculated that bringing in Dr. Barton as a "consultant" and then choosing him to do surgery was somewhat audacious. I doubted he'd now want to reopen the case and examine the mistakes made by John's regular doctors. By then, neither did I. It was too late.

After getting the records, I went up to the floor where my dear John spent his days from 3 to 14 May. Carrying a little notebook, I walked the halls I'd walked so many times before, renewing my memory of which paintings were where and of how the colors coordinated. I'd been there only a couple of minutes when a woman asked if she could help me. I said that I was just refreshing my memory of this place where my husband spent almost half of May. "How is he now?" she asked.

"I'm sorry to say he's dead. I'm writing a memoir about him." After I'd walked around taking more notes, the woman came up to me again and asked me to leave, lest I "disturb the patients." I was being quiet and unobtrusive and didn't think I was disturbing anyone, but I realized this woman was trying to protect the hospital so I left.

Finally, I got word on Thursday that the financial forms had arrived in Baton Rouge, six days after I mailed them. Whew! Mailing yet another copy of the death certificate, I switched our joint dental insurance coverage to a single policy for me. I feared that our dentist, who seemed to love John, hadn't been told that John died. Maybe the insurance company would inform him. Street workers in yellow vests with orange stripes began watering the pitiful earth they'd dumped around the new sidewalk. I suppose they planted grass seed when I wasn't looking. Our front yard should look smoothed, a proper suburban lawn, but that soil didn't promise much.

I reflected on my ineptness. I had scratched our car. I didn't know how to switch my new smartphone from the vibrating to the ringing mode. Hannah sent me a link to the recording of the Arts Council memorial but I couldn't play it. But I could read "Sailing to Byzantium" at the appointed hour, eight weeks after John died. Finally, I got news that the cremation box had arrived. The funeral director assured me that not just any old ashes but only John's would be placed in it and delivered to me.

At noon I went to Marge's house where she had prepared a quiche and salad for me and two other widowed women. Before we sat down to lunch, Marge showed us a former aquarium, where she'd brought in chrysalises from her garden. One had just opened and a swallowtail butterfly had sprung out, flexing its wings on a little branch. I told the story about being asked to leave the hospital. Lynn said, "It must have been the combination of the word 'dead' and your notebook. She thought you were preparing to sue."

I suspected Lynn was right. The woman had been acting protectively, as though my taking notes on artwork might have given me evidence for suing the hospital. Besides, if the medical records did contain damning evidence, as I suspected, John would not have wanted me to file suit. "What's done is done," he might have said. Or "What's dead is dead." Besides, I was too exhausted for a drawn-out legal battle. Against the Goliath hospital would be only me, little David without a slingshot. Any good a suit might have achieved, either for me or for other patients, would have been outweighed by the stress and strife of reliving those painful months in a drawn-out and likely quite expensive legal battle. Instead I chose to put my energy and efforts elsewhere, to try and infuse my life with more positive actions to honor the four decades of love I'd shared with John.

Before we left, Marge encouraged the newborn butterfly to alight on her arm and took it outside. First it fell on the walkway. She picked it up again on her hand, encouraging it to fly away. It flapped its wings and then soared into her rows of tomato plants. I wanted to tell John about this butterfly's apparently happy flight away from us before remembering that I could not. Hannah told me she is always thinking about what she must ask her dad. She wanted to know what he would think about the crisis in Greece, Hillary's deleted email, people taking Donald Trump seriously, the vagaries of the stock market. I wanted and want to know if John's soul is content without his body.

On 30 July 2015 I played some of the music John and I had loved. I started dancing slowly to a Randy Newman Louisiana song, but then came Pete Seeger's "Michael, Row the Boat Ashore." Words about getting to the other side shredded my emotional carapace. I quit dancing, turned off the sound, and began wailing, maybe howling. Again, I wondered how I could live without John. I thought again about getting to the other side by drowning myself, no easy matter. It took Virginia Woolf two attempts and stones in her pockets to accomplish the deed. I am too cowardly for suicide. And, as I have said, that would be a terrible maternal legacy for my chillun. I love them too much to give them that "present." So I knew I must carry on.

Three months after John's death, in August of 2015, Hannah went to a conference of parliamentary librarians in Cape Town, and Michael joined her after the conference. They spent a day or so in Cape Town, seeing Robben Island and other sites, then they flew to a camp named Dulini. I loved the pictures Hannah took, including a favorite of a leopard cleaning the face of her young cub with her tongue. Hannah said the trip had helped her survive her father's death. Getting completely away was useful, seeing wild animals was energizing, and in the wilderness she could sometimes feel John's spirit. I envied her the experience.

The next time I turned on our sound system, I heard Kristina Olsen's "I Cannot Live Without You." It was of no particular relevance that she shares a birthday with John, except that I felt an affinity between the two of them. We used to sing along with her, thinking neither of us wanted to leave the other. One of Olsen's lines was: "When I close my eyes, we are dancing all around the room." That happened to me in the early mornings, when I felt John's presence holding me. But John was not holding me. He had died.

Finally, someone from the funeral home brought John back to me—or that was the way they phrased it. After I had purchased the inlaid cherry box of Hannah's choosing, I'd had it sent to the New Jersey funeral home with repeated instructions that this box was only for John Irwin Fischer's ashes. When it was finally delivered to my house, I asked, "How do I know that these are John's ashes?" The messenger said that his brother, the funeral director, went with every body as it was cremated, collected the ashes, and sealed them until the bereaved supplied an urn for them. Then I asked, "Is John's DNA in these ashes?" He said he doubted it, explaining that the body tissue is vaporized in the cremation process. The "ashes" are the remains of bones that won't vaporize. They've been through so much heat they are like coarse sand, hardly keeping the character of the deceased. Paleontologists have found traces of the DNA of a Neanderthal, but John's DNA was gone. I wondered it I'd made another mistake by having him cremated.

I picked up the cherry box, surprised at how heavy it was, unsure whether the heaviness came from the box or from John. I imagined myself falling backwards on the stairs, with the heavy box on top of me springing open and spreading John's ashes over my dead body. Instead, I carefully carried the box upstairs, holding onto the banister. I moved aside his LSU watch to place the box on the center of his dresser. *Listen,* I said to John in the box. *If a dinosaur's DNA can survive in some bit of rocks for millions of years, your DNA better be in this box near me!* But then I rethought that private remark. I cared about his soul, which was not in that box. *It's okay if it isn't, dear.*

When I gave a small dinner party for two other couples, I seated them on either side of me at one end of the table. At the other end, I put papers and files for the *Word-Book* in John's armchair to keep anyone else from sitting in his place. His work felt sacred to me. I did not want it violated—though of course, if I took it up for him, I would violate it in ways more radical than moving it so someone could sit on his chair.

The obligation to deal with the *Word-Book* and John's scholarly legacy nagged at me. Typical of John's conscientiousness was that all those bags and files that we loaded into the car whenever we'd traveled contained all of Arch Elias's files, electronic and in print, almost endless copies of records from the British Library, Sotheby's, Christie's, Dictionaries of National Biography in Ireland and England, letters to Arch and John about handwriting and provenance, John's own exhaustive notes, and much more. I feared, however, that John's own compositions on the *Word-Book* were only on a zip drive connected to his almost thirty-year-old Toshiba, which, I feared, could not be turned off, lest it self-destruct. I was terrified even of touching it. Finally, I thought to call our computer guy. He copied all the *Word-Book* files safely onto my computer, where I could work on them with impunity. The question remained, however, whether I wanted to work on them. I fretted and walked, wept and read, and then, with great trepidation, I decided to have a go at it.

I've remarked that John and I always critiqued each other's writing, but my critiques had been largely stylistic, while I remained nearly oblivious to the detailed ins and outs of early-eighteenth-century literary, political, and theological intrigues. By the fall of 2015, I'd realized that I must not sully all the painstaking work that Arch and John did by introducing blunders, so I applied myself to learning more about Swift's life, work, and times. Of course, in his scholarly "will," John spoke of an eighteenth-century scholar as his successor. I am no such a scholar, but I am a fair writer, stylist, and editor. So as a tribute to Arch and especially to my beloved John, I set out to finish the *Word-Book* myself.

As Pat Spacks had suggested, I could excuse myself from tracking down every use of every word before the early eighteenth century, Arch's scheme now probably being outdated by the internet. After extensive reading in histories and biographies, I began doing some fairly tedious copyediting of Arch's and John's writings. I deleted repetitions, added subtitles, separated sections, highlighted headings, moved paragraphs, and corrected the typos that even great scholars like Arch and John occasionally make. This "donkey work" (to use Virginia Woolf's phrase) could seem a violation of their work, but instead I intended it as an enhancement, a further polishing of an almost perfect stone. At least it began taking my mind off grief and afforded me a more intimate acquaintance with Arch's and John's work.

Arch had passed on photocopies of the *Word-Book*'s pages on which he'd made detailed mark-ups of the additions and corrections that Jonathan Swift had made to Esther Johnson's pages. No doubt Arch was planning to write about Swift's corrections. John's essays on the *Word-Book* offered new background and biographical information. It occurred to me, however, that John had not taken a hard look at Arch's mark-ups. As I transcribed Arch's work, I realized that Esther Johnson must have spent many months copying her book from Swift's looseleaf list. She wrote the entire book in a precise hand: rounding each letter, lining up margins and definitions, allotting a limited number of definitions to a page, and interrupting their flow for letter headings alone: "AB," "AC," "AD," and so on.

In one of his essays, John had disagreed with Arch about dating the *Word-Book*. Arch dated it about 1713, but, given Esther's still-young handwriting, John argued that Esther Johnson began her transcription from the list of hard words that Swift had made for her in 1710. She was then twenty-nine and Swift forty-three. Swift was in England from 1710 to 1713, writing for the Tory government (even drafting one of the Queen's speeches) and composing biting satires on human pretensions. He wrote letters to Esther Johnson and her companion (addressing them as "MD" or "My Dears"), mixing tales of high political intrigue with charming expressions of affection for the two women, often couched in baby talk. He also began an intense flirtation with the woman he called Vanessa and by 1712 wrote (or started) the poem "Cadenus and Vanessa."

Synthesizing that history with the times suggested by John (1710) and Arch (1713), I figured out that Esther Johnson probably bought a small blank book after Swift left for England at summer's end in 1710. Then she ordered and transcribed into her little book the list of "hard words" that Swift had written for her edification. On Swift's reappearance in Ireland in 1713, for his installation as Dean of St. Patrick's Cathedral in Dublin, Esther Johnson had at last many opportunities to present him with the *Word-Book*, perhaps as a present.

In Princeton, 302 years later, in the fall of 2015, as I continued my work and the winter returned, I started to put the green flannel sheets back on our bed. I could find only one of them. I searched the closet shelves, trying to think where the other sheet might be. With my brain still working slowly, I finally recalled asking Hannah to put the sheet on the hospital bed after we brought John home to die. The undertakers must have wrapped him in it when they took him away. I am glad his poor cold body was covered in something warm and soft inside that stiff rubber bag. And I am glad his soul wasn't in that bag.

There is consolation in thinking that the body leaves the soul, not the other way around. That means that John's spirit must still be intact and not far away. As we pledged at our official wedding, we are together as long as love shall last.

20

HEALING:
A TALE IN SLOW MOTION

The Farbrengen Synagogue meets in the Washington Ethical Society building near Silver Spring, Maryland, across DC from Capitol Hill. For Hannah and Michael, the innovative service is worth the drive. In a big open room, people make a circle around the Torah in their midst. Members, who seemed exceptionally bright to John and me when we once attended, take turns leading the service. Congregants have time to voice their concerns, whether global or personal. One woman, who often sits shoeless and cross-legged on the floor, responded to Hannah's anguish over not knowing why John died. She told Hannah that her father had had an "old-fashioned death." People just used to get sick and lose strength until pneumonia finished them off, with no one ever understanding what really killed them. Likewise, John's illness and death remained a mystery. Certainly he had emphysema or COPD, but so do many people who live on for years. Those diseases did not explain John's sudden, drastic wasting away. At the synagogue, Hannah had voiced her outrage: "How could a pulmonologist miss pneumonia?" Thinking of it as "old-fashioned" confirmed Hannah's sense that John's death had been "an outrage in this age of medical sophistication!" Knowing that, of course, did not bring him back or help her or me to heal.

In August, I opened a letter from Dr. G. announcing his retirement and replacement. It was addressed to John. You'd think a doctor's office would remove the names of the deceased from their mailing lists. The GI doctor who warned us against going South had also retired. Each was younger than John and me, and neither looked old, from my perspective at least.

The guilt I felt and still feel over not doing enough, not noticing enough, not talking enough, is real. Certainly I did not use my imagination to explore other options soon enough. I was too numb or dumb or both, but I cannot go back and do what I didn't do last spring. As I said earlier, alarm bells should go off when doctors just keep offering the same hypotheses despite declining health. I hope I've alerted readers to the importance of seeking alternate medical opinions when one course of treatment isn't working and there is no improvement to or even a worsening of one's health. I also hope that I've recovered mental flexibility myself after a loss that nearly destroyed my mind and life. I have tried.

Grief will never vanish, but it may subside. Deborah Rothschild wrote me that Herb felt an intense period of anguish after John died. Then, "When Herb's moods began to lighten, I noticed that he had put a framed picture of John on a shelf above his desk where he displays pictures of his family. I don't know if Herb thinks of John as a brother or not, but when Herb put John's picture on that shelf, John became part of the Rothschild clan."

John had been part of my life for forty years. Without him, I am slightly different from "Mrs. John Fischer," but only in minor ways. I am less fastidious about neatness than John was. (Believing that his soul is hovering nearby, I sometimes hope it's not too near until I scrub the kitchen counters.) I need visual harmony. I don't like noise, and that includes most television. I find reading in the evenings consoling, whether or not the book has anything to do with grieving. I finished *Gilead* again while Maggie sat on my lap or curled up by the gas fire, which I ignited most nights. I am more an environmentalist than John was, while he was a more political animal than I, but my true values turned out to be John's. So my crucible of selfhood mostly revealed how much I am like John. No wonder we were so close.

A friend wrote to me that "the worst thing about grief is how it isolates the griever." I had to ponder that comment. Certainly the very presence of friends and family does prevent isolation and distract one from grief. But many grievers fear they have little to talk about beyond their loss, nothing to share. Perhaps that's the point of the advice I quoted earlier about talking with a living human being every day, especially a stranger. With them, the bereaved must resume normal modes of interaction. I found it gratifying to interact with neighbors, the plumber, the new vet, C. J., and the man at the deli who used to joke with John about which of us would get the bigger half of our sandwich, even though chatting with him brought me once again near tears. I was grateful for others' concern, but I didn't mind isolation, and often even craved aloneness. Maybe I sensed that whatever well-wishers said, they couldn't really feel my pain. Hannah did, or rather she felt her own similar pain, so I welcomed talking to her anytime. Visits from Bill and Ilse Goldfarb and Leslie Mitchner were consoling and diverting but I still treasured my time alone. Maybe that was a hangover from being an only child. Or maybe it was a manifestation of writing: I had to think through Swift's *Word-Book* and this memoir, and people broke my concentration.

I began to describe myself as a hermit. I didn't go to fundraising events. I didn't renew season theatre tickets. I preferred to stay home and read or write. I did go to services at Princeton University Chapel where architecture, music, and rituals again and again made tears seep from my eyes. I reread the Gospel of Matthew, for the first time in over sixty years. The story of the Crucifixion brought me to tears, as if I did not already know how Jesus's life had ended. Sometimes I entertained friends, but I couldn't honestly say if cooking and entertaining made me happy or if I just felt obligated to return invitations. I could say that I loved talking to my chillun, especially Hannah, who shared the emotions of the horrid spring of 2015 so completely with me.

Earlier I said that the genre of memoir-writing requires a happy ending, a resolution. For a long time, I couldn't imagine one for me. More probable than healing was drinking too much, falling down the basement stairs, and dying of a concussion. That would certainly be a dramatic ending for me and this memoir, closing both off together. Such a fall probably wouldn't kill me, though, but would instead leave me in an incapacitated or disabled state. I know there are better ways to heal.

Hospice programs across the country offer bereavement services, including counseling and support groups with others who have experienced a similar loss. The Princeton hospice program sends out a list of "What we need during grief." It names time, rest, relaxation, small pleasures, security, hope and caring, goals (even small ones), and permission to backslide. That very sensible list replicates what I had discovered on my own. A clear implication of all that I have written is that the love and considerateness of family and friends, as well as their willingness to leave me alone when I wished, helped me survive the early days of grieving. And even the chores that simply had to get done were survival aids. Necessary routines kept me from asking questions like: Why am I cleaning up after the cat? Why am I cutting up John's credit cards? Why am I eating three times (if not three full meals) a day? Why am I flossing my teeth or washing my face or putting in eye drops? Such questions were diversions from constant rumination upon the important one: Why did John die?

When my routines became more complicated, I often backslid. I thought I could not cope with two checkbooks, one from our joint account and a new one in my name alone, and a confusion of checks written on each. "I can't handle that now," was my reaction to the stacks of forms I had to fill out and submit. I reacted the same way to the news, not wanting to hear or to read about droughts, fires, refugees, kidnappings, massacres, murders, beheadings, and the other afflictions that beset this Earth. Though I couldn't handle news of disasters, I also couldn't bear Cialis ads featuring happy, sexually active middle-aged people. Without John, I seemed to have lost desire. When or if it returns, I can pleasure myself, but I will never invite another man into my bed.

Planning the dinner party and the two memorials forced me, with great help from Hannah, to mastermind events. Afterwards, I was left with the nitty-gritty details of death's aftermath. Signing the probate and financial forms, cancelling accounts, writing thank-you letters, paying bills, mailing copies of the awful death certificate, all kept me busy, though they were hardly satisfying activities.

The turnaround for me began in Shenandoah. Being completely alone until my chillun showed up that Friday evening was revelatory. I could write as I wanted, when I wanted. I could be alone with nature. I could and did learn many new things: the history, the terrain, the animals, the plants, even the bugs—all were objects of curiosity. And I reveled in the sheer beauty of the place.

There seem to be several secrets to recovery from loss, given my experience. One is keeping busy, which at first is not a matter of choice for a bereaved person. Another is accepting the concern of family and friends, of people who care about you. If you need but lack such people, you can join a group like those that hospice programs organize. Even virtual groups or communities on Facebook seem to help. Make new friends, without scaring them off by your neediness. Another is faith in a Supreme Being or at least in the survival of the soul and the conviction that life does have meaning, despite the fact that it ends. The fourth seems to be having a project—organizing the memorials was my first attention-absorbing project, followed by the *Word-Book* and this memoir. Helping others can rescue you from despondency. Ann and I once had lunch with a beautiful, talented woman who seemed depressed. After she left, I asked what was wrong. Ann said the woman does no good deeds and is not involved in any issues larger than herself, while Ann's efforts to improve the lives of indigent children (among many other things) have kept her a most lively person.

The fifth secret is, I think, learning something new. I've considered really ambitious projects, like building a green home or going to architecture school, but at my age I am too weary for such undertakings. Simpler endeavors are more reasonable and preferable because they do not risk exhaustion and failure. One might sign up to read stories to elementary school children or to tutor older ones; one might become a master gardener, enroll in adult classes, take pottery lessons, learn to dance, join HistoriCorps, support a kids' ball team, go on Road Scholar trips, volunteer at a soup kitchen, whatever. I signed up for Learning Ally, designed for reading to the blind and dyslexic, but checking others' recordings of poorly written textbooks bored me. I haven't yet found another satisfying way to give that has engaged me as much as when I was writing, but I will. The point is that a new and relatively captivating activity, one that bestows pride, can help overcome grief.

But everyday continuities also matter. I could hardly bear to think of Maggie dying, at least not soon. From the new vet, she got fluid injections, with B-12, encouraging her appetite and general well-being. She ate apparently yummy new brands of cat food. It pleased me to see her stretch her long pink tongue into the edges of her bowl to lick up every last bit of din-din. As I was trying to conclude these chapters, she appeared in my study every afternoon to curl up in a basket by my desk. Like Maggie, I mostly recovered my appetite; at least I was no longer the incredible shrinking granny.

Recovery is external too. I found that lighting the lanterns we bought in case of power outages was an uncomplicated matter of turning a switch. I watched pedestrians strolling along our street, thanks to the new sidewalk. I too walked, sometimes practicing with my walking sticks. The scratch I put on our car almost faded away. The dogwood branch that Michael pasted together remained sealed. Like it, I partially mended, though, as with John's death, my healing was in slow motion.

For Labor Day, I drove to DC and Reid drove from Blacksburg with Louise and the younger Reid to meet us. They stayed in a motel near the Mall, while I stayed with Hannah and Michael. At night, I took my time mounting the fifteen steps to their second floor and thought about John's last visit in his daughter's home. Tears pooled in my eyes as I recalled the evening when John was released from Georgetown Hospital and refused to sleep downstairs on the sofa but insisted on sleeping with me on the sofa bed upstairs. I don't know how many times he got up to use the half bath downstairs. I suppose he didn't want to monopolize the full bath upstairs. Climbing up the fifteen steep stairs to sleep beside me must have been arduous and painful, but John of course did not complain. I wondered if he stopped on every step to catch his breath. I wonder if the pain brought him tears or fear. He didn't mention it. *My darling John.* Hannah said it occurred to her later that John had been surprised to be released from Georgetown and had thought, *Okay, if I'm recovered, let's see what I can do.* He was testing his strength on those stairs.

Hannah, the younger Reid, and I saw an IMAX film at the Air and Space Museum. My reaction was not very scientific, but I keeping thinking that, with all those galaxies swirling about after the Big Bang in an apparently empty universe, there is plenty of room for souls too to swirl about, including John's. Hannah gave us all her personal tour of the capital, short on history, long on gossip about current Congressional leaders, but very entertaining. We also went to an open house in a development in Alexandria of condos, apartments, houses, shops, and parks. We wandered the neighborhood, which had many advantages, like a penthouse with a view of the capital and a free shuttle to take residents to the closest Metro station. Both Hannah and Reid encouraged me to think of moving there, where life would be simplified and Hannah would be close. I was tempted.

Back in Princeton in November I got a call from Stuart Mitchner. He was writing a column on Swift's birthday, 30 November, when Swift would have been 348 years old. Stuart wanted to borrow a few of John's books—not the priceless ones but rather college paperbacks. Stuart said he'd pick them up after a trip to the grocery, so I asked him if he would also pick up eight bananas for me, because Reid the younger and his dad would be up for Thanksgiving and wanted to make banana bread with me. In the 26 November *Town Topics*, Stuart described our exchange as "a bunch of Chiquitas for a handful of Swift." Stuart called me "our friend and neighbor Panthea Reid whose Swiftian husband John Fischer died in May." After I showed him Arch's photocopy of the *Word-Book*, Stuart wrote: "Now here we are on Mt. Lucas Road in the luminous autumn of 2015, a week short of Swift's birthday, and I'm looking over Panthea's shoulder at the actual handwriting of the woman to whom Swift may have been 'secretly married'..." Stuart and I agreed that Esther Johnson's handwriting was beautiful.

Going back to the *Word-Book*, I realized that Swift had taken the lovely book Esther had labored to produce and settled down with ink and pen to correct where she'd misspelled, misidentified, or omitted words. He did not seem the jovial, charming guy who had written lovingly to "My Dears," but instead a harsh taskmaster. The corrections he squeezed between lines and page bindings destroyed the symmetry Esther had labored to achieve. I of course agreed with Arch and John about the reasons for the *Word-Book*'s importance, but I came up with another reason. I began to suspect that Swift's corrections cooled Esther's relationship with him. If Esther felt she had sacrificed her life for him while rumors suggested he was dallying with another woman, his disregard for the *Word-Book*'s artistry seemed only to have confirmed her fears that, to him, she was still a girl to be taught, not a woman to be loved.

Esther Johnson may have demanded that he reward her lifelong devotion by marrying her. Their possible marriage has been the subject of debate for three centuries, but John Fischer found evidence that might substantiate the claim that Swift did marry Esther in 1716, though Swift insisted that it be a marriage in name only, as he did not cohabit or even remain alone with Esther Johnson. In 1719, when she was nearing forty, Swift began addressing Esther as "Stella" in a series of poems, often birthday celebrations. By that time, she was no longer his pupil. She had developed a wicked sense of humor and could vent her anger at Swift himself, as he says in "To Stella Who collected and transcribed his Poems." There he notes that her "Spirits kindle to a Flame, / Mov'd with the lightest Touch of Blame." The implication is that he felt free to blame (or correct) her but thought her resultant anger inappropriate. He never publicly acknowledged a marriage, but, near death, she apparently did. That was part of the story John told in one of his introductory essays to the *Word-Book*.

At Thanksgiving 2015, Hannah and Michael and both Reids came to visit. The smaller one did make banana bread, adding so many chocolate chips that it became a yummy chocolate-banana cake, a chunk of which

I saved for Stuart. Hannah brought arts and crafts equipment for Reid to make turkey placetags, and we had a wonderful feast, half homemade, half brought in from McCaffrey's. On the Saturday after Thanksgiving (27 November, actually the thirty-ninth anniversary of my and John's official wedding), Reid drove us to the Wheaton Arts and Cultural Center to see a glass-blowing demonstration, which intrigued Reid Jr. until he learned that he was too young to try glass-blowing himself. Still, the demonstration showed him new ways of being and doing. He was no longer the frightened kid who locked doors and windows out of fear of being abducted. I saw and felt his growing self-confidence.

At Thanksgiving, I turned on our sound system, quietly retreating to be alone during "Amazing Grace," the first time I had heard it since the memorial service. Later, I listened to "Fever" and Johnny Cash's "I Walk the Line." It reminded me of what Herb said at the memorial about John's playing around with other women—until, that is, he met me. Of course John had downloaded that song because he had indeed been faithful since I became his. Then when I heard Johnny Cash's "Wayfaring Stranger" with the lines about going over Jordan to see his father and then his mother, I broke down once again. I want to go there to see my dear John, however disembodied his soul is and mine will be.

Unlike Esther Johnson, I have no reproaches to level at my beloved. In the "Stella" poems, Swift repeatedly had to assure Esther that she had not wasted her life and that she was an ideal woman, except for her temper. After she died before reaching age forty-seven, Swift wrote about her as the most perfect of women. He gave the *Word-Book* to their most sophisticated literary friend, where it descended through family and friends over centuries until Arch Elias bought it at Sotheby's. After writing about her perfections, Swift destroyed every scrap of writing in his possession that Esther Johnson had produced by herself.

John was deeply, deeply distressed when he realized that there was no other explanation for the complete absence of letters from Esther Johnson to Swift. The point John developed was that Swift had indeed been a Pygmalion, "rearing and instructing" (Swift's words) a young woman to become an ideally accomplished "human Creature," as Swift described her after her death. Her letters might have revealed a less accomplished creature. I expanded John's Pygmalion reference, saying that "Swift did not love Esther Johnson (or kiss the statue of Galatea) deeply enough to accept her growth into a complicated, flawed, perhaps independent, perhaps sexual, woman, certainly not someone else's wife. Instead, he transformed a lively, handsome young woman into an elegantly carved statue." I signed my comments "[PR]." I hope John's spirit is pleased that I did not violate his work but instead brought it to a logical conclusion. John had been a great scholarly help to me, and at last, I was a scholarly help to him. In working on this project, I had added a chapter to the love story of John Fischer and Panthea Reid. I also began to free myself from the numbness that had crippled my brain.

In December, after I sent Jonathan's and Esther's, Arch's and John's *Word-Book* off to the University of Delaware Press (for the first but not the last time), I began another marathon drive to Blacksburg where Reid the younger had a cello recital and Ann had no less than five parties for her seventieth birthday. After Blacksburg, Hannah wanted me to visit her in DC. Driving along I-81 by myself, I passed many places, memorable to John and me. I drove over the James River, which meanders by Randolph College, which I attended too briefly when it was Randolph–Macon Women's College. On the James, below Charlottesville, John and I had spent our last Thanksgiving in the old river town of Scottsville, about halfway between Hannah and Reid. I had tried to convince John that we should move there.

As I remembered that missed chance, I saw other mementos of the past, including the little brick restaurant on a hill near Natural Bridge

where I had bought a hand-crocheted toy for Ann's first grandchild.
There were no customers there in December of 2015. As I sped along
I-81, even The Pink Cadillac Diner brought back memories. On our
one stop there, John's pork chop sandwich was terrible, but it had been
fun to see Elvis memorabilia with pictures of teenagers like ourselves in
the 1950s.

Saddest were the exits to places where I had schemed to move,
Scottsville, Virginia, and also Shepherdstown, West Virginia, barely
more than an hour from DC with taxes at a quarter of what we
paid in Princeton. This charming little town had figured in both the
Revolutionary and the Civil Wars. We could have bought a 1775 house
or an 1845 one, but we instead almost chose a 2005 house on a golf
course, with bedrooms, kitchen, dining room, and studies all on the first
floor so I could avoid steps. As John began coughing in 2015, however,
we couldn't move anywhere. Between wheezes, John had said, "Thank
goodness you didn't park me out on a golf course."

I wondered why passing the Martinsburg exit, near Harpers Ferry
and Shepherdstown, made me so miss John. The grocery in Princeton,
where he and I shopped every Tuesday for fourteen years, does not
often remind me of him, yet Shepherdstown did. And sometimes so did
Blacksburg. After John had realized that it was not always so cold as that
first time we picked up Reid, we had visited a realtor and had talked of
maybe moving there, but Tech's collection of eighteenth-century books
could not rival Princeton's or the University of Virginia's. All such places
signified possibilities we did not fulfill, opportunities I thought that
might have made things otherwise. Such thoughts, I later realized, were
magical thinking.

At the cello recital, I was up in a top balcony. I could see that Reid
pulled the bow across the strings just as the other kids did, so I assumed
he did as well as they in this huge Blacksburg strings initiative. Reid the

younger's problem, though, was that his mother couldn't be counted on to get him to lessons or doctors' appointments on time, so his dad, in addition to his busy lawyering schedule, dropped the younger off at school, took him to cello, Scouts, doctors and all other appointments, and also cooked dinner for the three of them. *He could use help,* I thought.

At her birthday parties, Ann sported a winter tan, a cascade of blond-gray hair, and gorgeous clothes. Many people touted to me the virtues of Blacksburg, said to be one of the country's best retirement spots. I had a great time seeing friends, mostly Ann's family. We even danced one night in the barn Rick built. One morning Ann's sister Jane, with whom I stayed, sat beside me at her kitchen counter. Each of the four Goette sisters is beautiful, each in her own way. Jane is thin and wiry and has straight silver hair to match. Jane very earnestly asked me if I remembered when John knew he was dying. I told her about the scholarly "will" John had written in early March. That recollection, of course, resurrected my guilt.

I next drove to DC to visit Hannah and Michael. When Hannah was only about ten, John and I had taken her to see *Pericles* performed by the Royal Shakespeare Company. She remembered it as the first Shakespeare play that she'd understood. In December 2015, she and I went to the Folger Library to attend a performance of *Pericles* by the Oregon Shakespeare Company. However improbable, we both wept at the end when the lost wife and daughter reappear, wanting for ourselves the reappearance of our lost husband and father. In the morning, Hannah produced a mix of caffeinated and decaf coffee, saying, "I keep them for you guys," without pausing to correct herself and say "you." She listed all the advantages of life in DC and urged me to move there or to Alexandria.

Both my children now thought Princeton was too saturated with sadness for me to live on there. Reid began checking real estate listings near him and sent me a video of a huge house he'd visited with his son. "What would I do with that much house?" I replied.

"We'd share it," he announced.

The younger Reid told his mother, "You can't yell at me any more 'cause Dad and I are leaving you to move to Blacksburg and live with Granny."

I told Herbert Rothschild about possibly sharing a house with the Reids, but not with Louise. He thought it a dreadful idea. Hannah and Ann thought it might be a good plan, but I could imagine Louise showing up at my house and accusing me of stealing her baby. I was at a loss, trying to think what to do.

I almost ignored Christmas, skipping my usual yearly catch-up letter to friends and family, not making my cranberry-orange-date relish, not having a turkey dinner. I only attended the candlelight service, reminded that just the year before we'd taken the chillun to it and entertained them with such invincible energy. Ten days into the New Year the weather was as mild as the previous 10 January had been fierce. The little snow we had melted before I needed to hire C. J. to shovel it. As I was doing an early revision of this book on 15 January 2016, I noted again how it seemed natural to weep and write, write and weep.

Eight months after John's death, I read "Sailing to Byzantium" in the morning. In the evening, I checked my email and found a message from Reid. After a basketball game and a lunch at a fast-food place where teammates congregated, Reid Jr. said, "It makes me sad to see them with their families." I thought then that perhaps I should move to Blacksburg after all, to help make a more balanced family. That project should keep me occupied and distracted from grief for some time, as finishing John's scholarly work promised to continue doing. Hannah conceded that her nephew was needier than she, so soon the possibility of moving to Blacksburg became a more appealing option, though forty-two years ago, Blacksburg was the very place I could not wait to escape.

Of course, few of the bereaved have a project to finish for their lost one or a grandchild in need of some rescuing. But each of us has something. Assuming a project that the beloved cared for can help restore your closeness and help you heal, as it did me. And an altruistic project helps heal better than does a selfish one. Here Ann Goette is a model. Not only are she and Rick Claus sponsoring a foundation for the education of underprivileged kids, but she also personally began a concerted effort to clean up the New River. She credits my dear John with the slogan: "ReNew the New."

I felt that I probably should see my obligations, as the Reverend Ames says in *Gilead*, as a Grace, an opportunity to do better and perhaps save my soul.

21

INTO BLACKSBURG
AND OUT TO AFRICA

On Sunday, 17 January 2016, the Gothic Princeton University Chapel "rocked" with music, social awareness, and promise. For Martin Luther King Jr. Day, the music included arrangements of "We Shall Overcome" and "Lift Every Voice and Sing." Our preacher was an African American woman who spoke on manmade states of emergency like poverty, racism, and war, and, most particularly then, water pollution in Flint, Michigan. When the congregation wished each other peace, I recalled that at the peace blessing, John always kissed me, decorously, on the mouth. I missed that kiss, but I nevertheless felt his presence. The sermon seemed one he would have approved, as he too believed that we individually cannot stop the brutalities that seem unleashed on our world, though joining together we can help. I reminded myself that we do have ways of reading, thinking, and acting that can help humanity resist the darker forces of hatred and untruth.

In the next days, I finished an early version of the previous chapters and sent them to Wild River Books. Afterwards, I found Maggie in my study, curled in her basket, expecting me to come up and write. She seemed to reproach me for not being at my desk. In early February, I left her at the Cats Only Inn again and I drove back down to Blacksburg in time for Reid's forty-seventh birthday. The huge house had been sold. *Good riddance,* I thought, but I couldn't rid myself of worries about my grandson. No longer "little Reid," he was thin and handsome, with clear blue eyes that reminded me of my father's. He had sprouted, it seemed, half a foot and was almost as tall as I. My worries were not about his appearance, or his cello playing, or his skills in reading and math. I worried about his emotional state, his fears, his need for friends, and his longing for an attentive mother. Maybe a grandmother would do.

I called the realtor whom John and I had once consulted. We hadn't so much intended then to move to Blacksburg as to get information in case we ever did. We'd liked the realtor's forthrightness and her English accent. She'd spent barely thirty minutes with us and never expected to hear from us again. Six years later, she heard from me. We waited until Reid picked up his son, then the realtor took the three of us to four houses. With the fourth, I felt such excitement it reminded me of meeting John forty-two years before when he'd asked if I could run in the rain. I first saw the mountainside house on Monday, the first of February. I bought it on Saturday, 6 February 2016. I suppose I became a realtor's dream story.

Here's part of the note I sent to friends:

My new house looks modest and plain from the front (like a box with slanted opened lids) but inside it is spectacular—it has fifteen big windows all across the back looking over woods and a valley and mountains beyond. The Reids were with me for several explorations; the younger one even discovered an elevator. Then Hannah and Michael joined us. Her main comment was, "Oh, wow!" She and I agree that this is a house John would have approved and loved to live in. I shall enjoy it even without him but with our great, great memories intact, along with my deep love for him.

Hannah and I also agreed that the house is rather like John: it is modest and unprepossessing on the outside but awesome inside, as John was up close.

I was confident of John's approval of the house but not of my financial arrangements, but they worked out splendidly. I had a quick sale in Princeton, even a short "bidding war," followed by extremely harried packing up. I didn't have time to dig up the volunteer cedar tree, but the Goldfarbs assured me it would have been an invasive plant in Virginia, so I broke that promise to John, with at least a good rationalization. In the daytime, I revised John's edition of Swift's *Word-Book* after a reader's critique finally arrived. In the evenings, after cocktail hour, I packed boxes and more boxes, feeling as if I had an overseer's lash at my back. I, however, was the overseer, as I had made myself take on these troubles. In the midst all my work, I kept in contact with the mover, realtors, Hannah, and Reid over my schedule.

The schedule was doubly complicated because Hannah was engineering a miraculous safari for the two of us to take together! Having so enjoyed the safari she and Michael had been on, she decided she wanted to go on another one with me. In preparation, she sent me information about checking the website of the Centers for Disease Control. I found that yellow fever was not a danger where we were going, but I would need medication against hepatitis A and malaria. To simplify matters, I went back to the old clinic, where my records were kept, glad that I only needed to see a nurse, not one of the doctors. I kept huge lists of dealings to be concluded before leaving, as well as a long list of what I must load in the car for the move.

My furniture was loaded on 12 April. Maggie and I spent four nights in motels, the last three in Blacksburg. She began throwing up, but

I got her to a Blacksburg veterinarian early on 16 April. The furniture was to show up at my new home by 9:30 that morning, but the movers only arrived about noon. Meanwhile, thanks to an injection, Maggie stopped vomiting and got her curiosity back. While she explored our empty house, I unpacked the stuff I'd brought in the car, including her "hidey house," which I put in my closet. After the movers came, Maggie retreated to it for the rest of that day. I began unpacking seemingly endless boxes, including the one from McCaffery's that had contained our 2014 Christmas dinner. It was silly to be sentimental over a cardboard box, but I remembered how John had looked so quizzically at me when I'd suggested saving it for packing. He knew I was thinking of a move. He'd never have suspected this one. Nor would I.

The movers and I worked until after ten p.m. when they quit. One said, "Don't know nothing about antiques." They left ancient bookcases and cabinets unassembled, my dresser mirrors unattached. The shelving for the beautiful secretary remained stacked on the floor. And they "fixed" the broken leg of that ancient marble-top table with glue that oozed out in ugly white clumps. When Maggie came out of hiding, she seemed intimidated by the large space but settled down when she found familiar pallets. Once she followed me into the elevator but scurried out when I started to shut the doors on us. I enlisted the help of the Reids with some unpacking. After three weeks of living in the chaos of unopened boxes and unfound essential items, I hired a cat-sitter and readied myself, remarkably enough, for a safari.

Hannah had made all plans herself, bless her, and instructed me to get a suitcase without wheels or a frame, since luggage is casually thrown into small planes and truck beds on safari, so I'd bought a backpack before moving. Hearing that southern Africa in May is hot at midday and cold at night, I filled it with cool and warm clothes. I packed my canvas briefcase with binoculars and writing materials but could barely carry both. Before I departed on 8 May, I explained to the pet-sitter that Maggie prefers an unmade bed. The sitter would feed Maggie in the mornings, and Reid would do so in late afternoons, after he left his office and was on the way to pick up the younger Reid from after-school care. Reid took me to the bus stop in Christiansburg and Hannah and Michael met me in DC. I had a day and a half at their place, which I spent mostly reading about safaris and African wildlife. When I picked up the *Washington Post*, I found another Africa-centered article: Robert Mugabe stopped a parade to kneel down before a billboard picture of himself. My pet-sitter e-mailed me: "I've never seen a cat who liked to burrow under the covers like Maggie does. She's so cute!"

On Tuesday, 10 May, Hannah ordered an Uber to take us to National Airport, where we sped through the check-in process. Our only problem was bags. Hannah had a duffle bag of clothes and medicine and a huge carry-on filled with camera equipment, including two large rented lenses. Hannah insisted on carrying my backpack too, since harnessing myself into it threatened to keel me over. "I'm not going to let my mother have a heart attack on my watch," she proclaimed. My only request, which was hers too, was that on the anniversary of John's death, we not be rushing through some airport but could be alone, at peace, close to nature and, we hoped, to John's spirit.

We flew coach to Atlanta and there boarded a first-class flight to Johannesburg. (Hannah had cleverly traded points on different charge cards for first-class tickets). Wearing my new sunglasses, I was astonished to find beds angled on either side of the aisles in our cabin, with some people stretched out on them. I sat (or fell) on the floor in the middle of mine. "Oh, Mom," Hannah cried, but the man behind me in a safari jacket hopped up to say in a Southern accent, "Can I help you?" He held my elbow as I was pulling myself up. I removed my sunglasses to discover that my space was not a bed but an expandable seat and a footrest with a gap between them.

We were served champagne before the plane took off, then cocktails, then an elegant three-course dinner with wine. Once Hannah leaned over the low wall between our seats and giggled: "What would Dad have thought?" After dinner, I began reading British journalist Tim Butchner's *Blood River*, which I had recently downloaded on my Kindle, a gift from Hannah. I found Butchner's history of Livingstone's and Stanley's explorations fascinating. Soon a steward pulled out my seat and made it into the bed I'd first thought it was. While I awaited my turn in the restroom, I could see, through a screen-like curtain, the economy class passengers in the cabin behind us in cramped upright seats, like those John and I had endured on all our international flights. Like Hannah, I wondered if John would disapprove of this privilege or say that his hard work had rightfully bought our upgrades. Thinking he'd say the latter, I slept soundly, as I never had in economy class.

In Johannesburg the next day, we were met by a porter with a sign saying "Fischer." He wheeled our luggage across a parking lot to an elegant airport hotel. Hannah had a good supply of South African rand, from which she paid bills and tips. The next morning we were driven to Federal Air, which seemed some distance away but was actually just around the airport on its other side. The waiting lounge offered free snacks and a lush tropical patio encircling a fountain, with airport emergency gear just over a fence. The kind Southern man from the plane, now also sporting a safari hat, and his wife greeted us like old friends. Hannah and I waved to them as we boarded a small plane that flew us onto Sir Richard Branson's private landing strip in the Sabi Sands, above which he owns what seems like a whole mountain, or at least its top. On landing, Hannah was excited to see Fred, head ranger, who'd taken Michael and her on animal rides the year before.

Fred drove us to Dulini, where staff members met us with warm lemongrass-scented hand towels and then escorted us along a wooden walkway to our cabin. Beneath its thatched roof, it was elegant, with a sitting area, a large two-bed bedroom, and a bath containing both a fancy tub with a handheld shower and a glassed-in shower stall looking out over the African bush. Out our back doors, patio furniture sat by a round dipping pool with a running motor and a path to an outdoor stone shower. We freshened up and walked back to where other guests were lunching on the lawn. At our table for two, a staff member brought us little round rolls with cups of butter and took our orders. Hannah pointed to monkeys frolicking at the edge of the lawn's dining area. "They're vervets." On the closest one, I could see his clown-like black and white markings. "What a cute fellow," I remarked, whereupon he sprinted across the grass, grabbed my roll, and was gone. A staff member appeared with a slingshot, and the monkey scrambled into a tree where he sat, it seemed, laughing at us. Hannah had a luckier visitor, an African monarch butterfly, which settled on her butter. "Maybe Dad's spirit is in the butterfly," she hoped aloud. As we ate delicately broiled trout on good china, we watched impala, baboons, monkeys, and the majestic curved-horned kudu parade beyond the edges of the lawn. "What a mix of the wild and the tame," I could imagine John saying, were he only with us.

After a nap and then high tea at 4:30, we assembled for our first animal ride. As we left camp, I saw a huge bag of twigs hanging from a tall tree. Fred said several families of birds called buffalo weavers built it and raised their young communally inside. Fred operates in partnership with Martin, a tracker, who sat on a seat up on the far left edge of the Land Rover. When they saw tracks, they leaned out of the Rover or stopped and walked to determine which way the creature had gone. "Patience, chaps," Fred would call back to us tourists in our safari hats and sunglasses sitting in the Rover. Swinging back onto their seats, Martin would point the way and Fred would charge our vehicle through bushes. Once we encountered a leopard that had left the carcass of an impala to a hyena since, Fred said, she didn't want to get so wounded in a fight with the hyena she couldn't care for her cub. Her behavior reminded me of how John had sold his motorcycle after Hannah was born, since he didn't want her to grow up with a father maimed or killed in some motorcycle accident.

On my first night, memories of chores that awaited me at home interrupted my sleep. My iPhone lacked John's password, which I didn't know, so my phone couldn't send messages or access pictures and tunes he purchased. Verizon wouldn't let me transfer John's account to my name. The screen on my car's dashboard said ENTER CODE; "What code?" I'd asked. My new house was full of stacked boxes that I couldn't unpack because the movers had left all those shelves out of the bookcases and cabinets, making boxes inaccessible, including whichever one contained my coffee maker. I feared a further hassle over Swift's *Word-Book*, as the press director had mentioned changes without telling me what they were. Reid the younger still hadn't warmed much to my presence. I realized, though, that on safari I was so out of touch with my life back home that it was useless to fret about unsolvable problems. A better way of conquering jet lag should have been reading, but in *Blood River* I had finished stories of the famous explorers and was into tales of flagrant exploitation first by the Belgians and other colonial powers, then by native leaders after independence. Such grisly tales made my personal troubles seem minor and irrelevant, but that hardly helped me sleep.

Hannah had prepared me for the safari schedule, which involves animal rides twice a day. That means being awakened at 5:30 and served coffee and a nibble of food before embarking on the first ride. In the bush, about 10:30, there'd be a stop for coffee, usually made in a French press by the ranger, which in Dulini Fred would spike with amaretto if we chose. We'd return for brunch, then lunch at 1:30 or 2, then have time alone for writing or napping. At 4:30, guests would gather for tea and a late ride, on which we'd stop for "sun-downers," usually gin and tonics. On all these animal rides, especially the morning ones, the guides and our fellow tourists all made discreet trips into the bush. Everyone except me, that is. I guess I was just too prudish to pull down my pants in the wilderness.

Dinner, after our return from the second ride, was about 9:30. At Dulini, it was served à la carte in an outdoor pavilion with chandeliers hanging from beams beneath a thatched roof, a fire in a huge stone fireplace, and animals lurking just outside the secure ring of light. One evening the Dulini staff held a boma, a traditional outdoor cookout, with chanting in African languages and swaying to drum beats. I rose and danced with one of the rangers. Thereafter he amused Hannah by calling me his dancing partner.

On animal rides, we passed many termite mounds, odd structures looking like porous miniature mud volcanoes. A huge one was now inhabited by several hyena families. "How cool is it to watch baby hyenas play?" Fred asked. It was not so cool to learn that little hyenas are born with sharp teeth and sometimes kill each other in what's called "siblingicide." Fred claimed that hyenas are not quite from either the cat or dog family and they seem sexually ambiguous too, since female genitals resemble male ones. Fred claimed that their status as hermaphrodites got them condemned to hell long ago by the Roman Catholic Church. Nevertheless, Fred insisted that hyenas make good mothers. He confessed, "I love all animals except baboons. They'll break into your room, tear everything apart, and eat whatever they can find, including soap and medicine, which they treat like candy."

Once he cautioned a guest to lock his door. "Oh," the man asked, "does the staff steal?"

"No," said Fred, "but baboons will if they can." He shared the tale about how once baboons had created a medical crisis by stealing a man's diabetes medications, requiring more to be air-lifted in. And wealthy patrons seemed more inclined toward stealing than the staff. Each cabin at Dulini had a carving of the armored pangolin (an ant-eater) in it. I remarked on the skill and artistry these carvings show, and the manager disclosed that one was missing, apparently taken by guests.

Fred entertained us with stories about occasional offensive guests who exhibit their wealth by arriving with servants. Typically, such people call expert ranger Fred just "the driver." One ordered her maid to go to the breakfast bar for her. Another ordered his servant to get out of the Rover and arouse a sleeping lion. Fred stopped him, saying, "You could get the man killed!" Privately, I asked Fred about the nationality of such offenders. He said, "American."

Perhaps because I asked such questions, Fred told Hannah her mother was "tough as nails." I meanwhile felt less tough than a rusted paper clip and just as useless. I feared I was catching cold, so I skipped an afternoon game drive. I thought to soak in that elegant big tub, but I was so tired I turned the water on without thinking about the hose balanced atop the tap handle. When water rushed through it, the hose went dancing about like a wild snake, spraying water over everything, especially me. *Oh John*, I said to myself, *how we would laugh if you saw me in soaking wet jeans. You'd probably say, 'Take 'em off.' We'd both strip, and you'd rub me dry with one of these fleecy towels, then we'd crawl behind the mosquito nets into bed, naked together.* Instead, alas, I used the fleecy towels to dry the floor and put my wet clothes in the laundry bag. (At each camp, the staff did our laundry, quite well, as compensation for our bringing only a duffle bag or backpack of clothes.) I showered alone in the glass stall, unworried about monkeys and baboons seeing me naked, even if they laughed.

One night we were joined at dinner by Dulini's owner. He was buying and remaking other camps, even eliminating cabins because, he said, in larger camps guests remain anonymous to each other and to the staff. His camps each now have only six cabins, housing twelve people, just right for two touring vehicles. I thought to ask a John-like question: "Won't that make it even more expensive to stay in your camps?"

"Not really," he replied. "Happier people are more likely to return and recommend us to others, so we're always full." Like the rangers, he expressed contempt for camps that cater to tourists who care little for the infinite varieties of animals, plants, and landscapes but only want to see the "big five," a holdover from days when hunters bragged of killing buffalo, rhinoceros, elephants, leopards, and lions.

Driving to a partly dried-up lake one morning, Fred exclaimed, "See the hippo!" I could see no such thing, until Hannah explained that the two bulbs on the water's surface were hippo's eyes. They spend most of their time in the water, though they can't swim and so just walk on lake bottoms. Once when Martin had to miss a day, his substitute pointed out tracks. "That's a hyena, not a lion," Fred corrected. "Look for paw prints as large as the palm of your hand." Each ranger goes through a rigorous training program, book-learning about flora and fauna and field-practice in identifying and tracking. The final test is being left alone without radio or phone and getting out alive. Then the trainee must take a map and trace for the authorities where he's been. (There seem to be no female rangers, yet.)

When Hannah remarked on the butterflies, Fred groaned a bit saying that he can't identify all 252 African species, just local ones, like the African monarch. Hannah and I thought that if her father had been with us, we would have surprised him with a book on African butterflies. We laughed to think that he would have kept it handy looking for species unimagined in Princeton, New Jersey. He also would have been delighted to see guides follow animal tracks in the sand, over wet grasses, and through broken branches. Their painstaking, tedious searches were a bit like, as John used to say to Hannah, kissing frogs.

One afternoon, through a radio system, Fred heard that a leopard and cub had been spotted. "That's the pair you saw last year," he told Hannah as we sped to them. A few of her 2016 photos lack clarity because she was weeping to remember the mother sweetly licking its cub back in 2015. Now he was an overgrown rambunctious kitten. Mama cat matched him in rough play, readying him for hunting alone.

On the morning of 14 May, before our game watch, Hannah read "Sailing to Byzantium" to me and to John's spirit. Dulini was gracious and understanding enough to invite Hannah and me to a private dinner that night at the lodge, a grand room complete with rough poles under a thatched roof, huge chandeliers, a robust fire crackling in a stone fireplace, seven-foot-tall bookcases filled with books on Africa, candles shaped like kudu horns in hurricane lanterns, carvings of pangolins, and native-embroidered sofa pillows. It looked rather like a hunting lodge, without hunting trophies. For dinner, we both ordered ostrich, which I'd never had before. We were told that the giant birds are raised humanely, and their red meat tasted better than steak. Still, I doubt I'll ever eat ostrich again. Over dinner we recalled the year before, when we'd agreed to have John brought home from the Princeton hospital to die.

Hannah considered how she'd gotten a nurse to continue his antibiotics during John's first weekend in the Princeton hospital, against the presiding doctors' instructions. A year later she feared her meddling had deceived the absent docs into thinking that her father had gotten stronger over that weekend. I recalled that I had gotten a CT scan from a new doctor while John got none from the regular docs. That, I told Hannah again, was an early signal that I missed. It should have warned me to pull John out of those doctors' care.

We reflected that there are worse ways to lose a loved one: The violence in our society takes its victims senselessly and tragically without warning. Terrible diseases ravish the lives of millions with slow or quick fatalities. Inexplicable circumstances and unexpected attacks are almost impossible to cope with. I know of two different women who have come home to find their supposedly healthy husbands dead in their beds. I had to admit that that shock might have been worse than mine, which had seemed unbearable, though drawn out over four months. Hannah reminded me that we were blessed to have had those four months with John. Though we did not know or admit that he was dying, we were with him until the last. As we rehashed our guilt and grief, the fire subsided into a feverish glow. We said to each other that we had tried to do right but each feared that we'd done wrong, or at least not enough right.

On 15 May during our morning game watch, only half a dozen or so elephants were to be found. When we walked over to the lodge at 1:25 for lunch, Fred was waiting for us, saying he had something to show the two of us. We climbed into the Rover, and he drove us down to a sandy river bank where at least seventy elephants had appeared since morning. We saw the smaller ones get down on their knees and slide down the banks like country kids playing in a mud hole. Fred paused for Hannah to take some astonishing pictures of little ones cavorting in the water and of young males trying swordplay with their newish tusks. Then Fred drove on up the riverbed instead of back to camp. At a distance we saw a white truck. When we approached, two staffers emerged and welcomed us. On the far side of the truck they'd set up pillows stacked on a canvas blanket over smoothed sand. There was a cooler holding sauvignon blanc and champagne. Napkins covered glasses, silverware, and dishes of avocado and pea salad, roasted chicken, and vanilla mousse with chocolate shavings.

"This is amazing," Hannah said. "How elegant!"

"How kind of you and of Dulini," I said.

They made courteous bows and said, "Our pleasure." As he departed with the staff members, Fred explained that he'd left his Rover's radio on, in case we needed to report an invasion of curious elephants or of hungry hyenas in search of roasted chicken.

I poured us each a glass of the crisp wine, and Hannah and I settled against the pillows to keep minutes of silence in honor of John. "It's still hard to believe that it happened at all, just a year ago," I said.

"True," Hannah agreed. She cut into her chicken and gazed at the river banks above us. "Yum! I think Dad would have loved this feast."

The cold chicken was crisp outside and tender inside. The peas too were crisp, while the avocado was soft and tender. We chatted as we ate. "Weren't there scenes like this of elegant meals on the desert sands in *Lawrence of Arabia*?" Hannah asked. I didn't remember, but I did know that this scene was splendid.

"I only recall one good holiday when I was growing up," Hannah remarked.

"Well, when we did have holidays, other than an offshoot of some scholarly trip, John felt obligated to take them with his family. We organized them, paid for most everything, and did all the work."

"Yeah," Hannah said. "Then they complained about how uptight you two were."

"True, but I'm sorry for the way they ended."

In the summer of 2006, Jeff Fischer had been diagnosed with acute myeloid leukemia and confined to Mount Sinai Hospital in New York City. John took the train to New York at least three times a week to be with his brother until he died. He also gave his mother indefatigable care, spending hours just to visit her at least twice a week over the course of ten years. When he took her for doctors' appointments, each excursion lasted about four hours, and she was not an easy passenger. All those exertions, not to mention the time-consuming efforts he made protecting her finances, tired him. Hannah and I agreed that the incredible sadness and exhaustion of tending to others must have depleted John's stamina. We lamented that he'd always been less mindful of himself than of others.

"But we did have one great family holiday, just the three of us, when you guys weren't working and we biked in France!" Hannah recalled.

That had been in 1991, when I arranged for an easy ferry and train trip from London to the Loire Valley. A travel company supplied the bicycles and some transportation, and we biked around the beautiful countryside in the day, only needing to show up at the next hotel in time for an excellent French dinner before setting off in the mornings for a leisurely ride to our next destination. Though the Loire runs through almost flat country, I was slow pumping my bike up little inclines. On the first day, John and Hannah looked back at me and sang the "Anvil Chorus," "dum, dum, ta-dum," in time to my labored pedaling. Then they apologized for teasing me so. Afterwards, I walked my bike up hills, and John got off his and walked with me. Anyway, it was a beautiful treat, just the three of us alone, without responsibilities for anyone else.

"Remember that I reminded him of it just before the bronchoscopy?" she asked. I had forgotten that.

"What do you think he'd like best about here?" Hannah asked me.

"Our being together," I replied, "in far-away Africa where there is plenty of room for his spirit to find us. Butterflies too." They flitted about us, blurs of yellow and orange, blue and black.

We finished off the wine with the mousse, leaving the champagne untouched, and ended our grand picnic, elephants safely in the distance, feeling great compassion for John, that wonderfully giving man. I was glad to talk openly with Hannah about our love. I used the word "inspired," explaining that he inspired my confidence both intellectually and physically.

"Right, Mom. I remember when he said, 'Jump, Hannah, jump. I'll catch you.' Where were we?"

"I think over some hilly crevice in Cornwall after I checked out Virginia Woolf's beloved Talland House."

"I was terrified, but I did it because Dad told me he'd catch me. And he did."

"He gave me courage too."

Then we shared our mutual regrets over John's final months. "Oh, my darling," I said out loud, looking into the crystal blue sky. It seemed strange to have gone a third of the way around the world to commune with John's spirit, but we did feel him with us.

At dinner that evening a new guest arrived. Saying that his wife was too tired to join the party, he sat on my right, rather too close. When someone looked at the menu and asked what part of a lamb was its shank, he stood and pulled up his shorts, tapping his thigh. "This," he said, "is a shank." His name was Siegfried; he lived for three months at a time, alternately, in Johannesburg and the Austrian Alps, "a very romantic set-up," he said confidentially to me. He mostly made pronouncements, often while touching my arm, such as, "When the poor man can't eat, the rich man can't sleep." That was not a liberal protest against economic inequality, but a justification for living in walled compounds in Johannesburg's middle- and upper-class enclaves.

Were John there, he might have said, "You, sir, ruin your own sleep." Siegfried impressed a waiter by speaking some Zulu. "I have a gardener," was his explanation. If John were there, he might have asked, "Does your gardener eat?" I moved my wine glass and my chair to my left away from him and his repeated pats on my arm. He responded with pats on my shoulder. John would have interrupted dinner by saying, "You racist son of a bitch, keep your hand off my wife!" As I scooted away from Siegfried, I felt John's presence with me, powerfully, urging me to keep my distance.

Despite him, I hated to leave Dulini. Our travel agents had arranged for us to be taken next to the Zambian border. At a hot, crowded customs office, a uniformed woman informed us that the fee for entering Zambia was $50 apiece. "It says $20 on the web," Hannah volunteered.

"The fee is $50," the woman insisted. We paid the $100 and walked across the border where a different driver was waiting to take us to the Zimbabwe border. Customs there was seriously intimidating, with soldiers brandishing AK-47s. We did not quarrel about paying another $100. On a bus, I started to tell Hannah of the corruption and exploitation that characterize the rule of Robert Mugabe, according to *Blood River*, but thought better of it then.

We arrived at Livingstone and were driven to the beautiful 1904 Victoria Falls Hotel. After those scary customs offices, I suggested we take a peaceful river cruise. On it, among other tourists, I could talk about corruption in the Congo and Zimbabwe. Tim Butchner says that in the twentieth century, after locals expelled the colonial powers, the outside world overlooked the "corruption and venality" of native dictators. In Zimbabwe, for example, dictator "Robert Mugabe was allowed to run his country and its people into the ground because Western powers gullibly accepted [him]... as the only leader able to guarantee stability and an end to civil strife."

"Good thing you didn't read that aloud in Zimbabwe," Hannah remarked.

We got back to the hotel in time to walk toward the gigantic falls, one of the seven natural wonders of the world. We had to pass through a well-patrolled gate and pay another stiff entrance fee. Then a man in uniform appeared to serve as our guide. We spent more money hiring him, not realizing that we had any choice. When we discovered that all paths toward the falls are well marked, we let him go and lost our money. Hannah used her phone to take a few photos of the spectacular falls, not wanting to let the towering cascades of water endanger her fancy Nikon, as the extortion we'd experienced had sullied our sense of the grandeur of the falls. As we walked back, past another guy offering to guide us to the hotel, we giggled to imagine John scowling, "Does every son of a bitch here have his hand out for a payout?" At Dulini, as in our two later camps, there had been no tipping until, on leaving, we were provided envelopes with suggestions for appropriate tips (in dollars and South African rand) for the staff in general and the ranger in particular. I'm sure Hannah was most liberal with gifts from us for everyone, especially Fred.

The next morning we had to awaken at 5:30 again, not for a game ride but for a bus. I looked at the grand portraits of English royalty and all the historic maps and pictures and thought more time in the hotel would have been a pleasure, except that it served as a reminder of English exploitation and the resultant corruption and incompetence. On our bus we were at first glad to sit near an American woman working in Dubai, which she described as a great country where women are well treated. She said everything is kept so perfect that any fender-bender must be fixed by the next day. "But what if you are too poor to get to a garage so soon?" I asked.

"There is no poverty in Dubai," she replied.

"What about workers who repair the cars and who cook, serve, clean, and build Dubai? Are they wealthy?" Hannah chimed in.

"I doubt it, but they stay in compounds run by the government and are bussed in and out. They are mostly invisible." Later, Hannah and I remarked that this woman was worse than Siegfried. At least he knew his gardener and could speak some Zulu. If we ran into the American again, we vowed to channel John's outrage at her obliviousness to unseen workers. We did run into the couple we'd met in Atlanta another time or two, but we never saw the Dubai apologist again, perhaps because we were on our way to eco-tourist sites and she was not.

Our bus took us to catch a plane to Botswana, a flat landlocked country northwest of South Africa. There customs procedures were only a perfunctory check of our passports and a step through a tray of dirty water, to prevent our importing hoof and mouth disease. We were flown in a small plane belonging to Wilderness Safaris into the Kalahari Delta. As she taxied slowly along the runway after landing on the air strip, our pilot announced a treat for her passengers—a den of wild dogs just beside the runway. As she slowed the plane, the photographers on board craned over each other for views of the spotted dogs. I suppose wild dogs are a menace to ranchers; Wilderness Safaris, however, promotes the balance of nature, and these dogs are appreciated as an endangered species.

At the airstrip, we were ushered into a really small plane. Hannah sat by the pilot, I behind him, our bags thrown in the back of the single prop plane. We were in the air less than ten minutes when we began the descent onto another sandy airstrip. Near landing, the pilot suddenly lifted the plane's nose and banked upwards. Behind him, I shuddered, assuming that we'd just missed a nosedive into the sand. Hannah looked back, saw my terrified look, and marched the fingers of her right hand over her left arm. That made no sense to me. As we circled for another descent I braced for a crash, telling John's spirit I'd soon be joining him. Later, standing on firm soil, Hannah confided that the pilot had aborted his first descent because a kudu had wandered onto the runway.

We were motored to Little Vumbura, a water camp in the northern Okavango Delta. In our family cabin there, Hannah looked out of her bathroom window to see an elephant looking in. On our first evening at Little Vumbura, Russell, a ranger for Wilderness Safaris, gave a slide lecture on Botswana's history, geography, and efforts to save its wildlife. He told how the designated tribal king Seretse Khama had studied at Oxford. There he met and married an English woman, creating outrage in England and in apartheid South Africa, whose governments forced the couple's separation. After they were reunited, Khama became the first president of Botswana. Unlike other post-colonial African leaders, he was chosen in a free democratic election, and he saw that tribal leaders would share the poor country's wealth. Luckily, diamonds were discovered there, so Botswana did not remain desperately poor. It now enjoys the highest human development index in sub-Saharan Africa.

Botswana's aggressive defense against poachers has resulted in a staggering amount of secure wildlife. On our first day at Little Vumbura, we saw huge numbers of zebras, giraffes, and cape buffalo, all being groomed by yellow-billed oxpeckers, who eat ticks and other parasites off the huge animals. Butterflies were everywhere. One is even called the flag butterfly because the central black stripe across its blue wings seems to mimic the Botswana flag. The next evening Russell gave a talk on the poaching of rhinoceroses for their horns, said in Asia to be an aphrodisiac, though horns grow from material rather like toenails. Animals, including predators, maintain the balance of nature until something unnatural, like human beings with rifles or AK-47s, intervenes. While elephants have long been preyed upon for tusks made into delicate ivory carvings, the market in rhino horns is newer and even deadlier. Destroying the rhino population to appease the appetites of men who feel sexually inadequate is tragic, as Russell said and John would have agreed, had he only been there.

At Little Vumbura, meals were less formal than at Dulini, informal enough so that an elephant had recently approached an outdoor brunch table and used his trunk to scoop the fruit off a tray into its mouth. On a game ride, we watched a cheetah, another endangered animal, chew the side of an impala she'd killed. We were close enough to hear her teeth crunching the carcass's bones. We saw brightly feathered bee-eaters and sun-catchers, as well as the soberly colored African fish eagle, which looks like our bald eagle. Our ranger Nas repeatedly told us to duck as we passed acacia bushes. He said red-billed buffalo weavers line their nests with the sharp acacia thorns to ward off snakes trying to steal eggs.

Botswana's views stretch from horizon to horizon. Shepherd trees have had their leaves and branches trimmed by giraffes. They leave a neat line of vegetation above which their teeth can't reach, so the silhouettes of these trees look like giant umbrellas. On a sun-downer by a pool of water, a very unhappy bird, whose name Hannah recorded as a blacksmith lapwing plover, made horrible squawks to keep us away from the nest she'd built in the sand. We watched the sun painting the sky and water a color like paprika. An impala crossed the other side of the water, its silhouette, like those of the umbrella-shaped trees, upside down and black in the red reflecting pool.

I thought our ranger Nas was good at picking up animal signals, but Hannah was less impressed. Still he was good on flora, explaining how the shiny-barked baobab tree can grow to legendary size and the "sausage tree" grows big sausage-looking gourds, which baboons love, giraffes nibble, but elephants mostly disregard for tree bark. When I asked about a lovely scent that followed us everywhere, Nas paused the Rover to pull green sprigs from a nearby bush. "Wild sage," he explained. As Nas drove through clear delta water, I asked rhetorically, "Who knew that Land Rovers could swim?" and Nas said that the water is cleaned by papyrus and other reeds. On our last day, we were taken in a flat-bottomed canoe called a mokoro, propelled by a man who stood in the rear, poling us through the water like an English punter on Cambridge's River Cam.

Driving us to the airport, Nas said he'd just heard of a lion sighting. We had thirty minutes to make the plane, and the lion was ten minutes away. Hannah said, "Let's do it!" so he drove at race-car speed, leaving me to wonder if his name was derived from Nascar. We found the lion licking her cub, who licked her back. We spent ten minutes there, Hannah taking multiple photos that revealed what gentle tenderness a fierce lioness can muster as a mother. Then we took another ten minutes to get to the air strip. We were more winded than the Rover but on time, though our departure was delayed by giraffes on the runway. Hannah had written a rather critical evaluation of Nas, but after that race to see the pair of lions I saw her give Nas a tip, despite regulations.

We were flown, by the woman pilot we'd met earlier, southeast to where palm trees grow in grassy floodplains. The Chitabe Camp features platforms and cabins built high against expected floods. At one point, the platform leading to our cabin had been repaired with fresh wood because an elephant nibbling greens on one side had crashed through the elevated walkway to get to enticing greens on the other side. Cabins on stilts boasted sliding-glass doors and ironwood floors, doors, and window frames, all beneath heavy canvas tops. Once we heard a crash like a fallen tree branch. It turned out to be only a two-foot-long gourd, weighing about twenty-five pounds, dropping from a sausage tree onto our roof. Another afternoon, the whole cabin shook to wild hooting noises, and we realized that baboons were using our roof as a trampoline. Fearing they would rip the canvas open, I recalled Fred's cautions and asked Hannah to sound the emergency alarm. Male staff members came running. Baboons, we were told, fear men and not women. At any rate, we escaped having a troop of baboons cavorting in our beds.

In Chitabe, our ranger was an older man named Phenley, pronounced "Finley." I sat behind him on our game rides, the better to hear him. He spoke, however, in such a soft voice, I was often unsure whether he was speaking English or his native Setswana. Either my hearing was terrible or no one spoke clearly or both. The guides and staffers spoke British English with an African accent, which was hard to decipher even when I caught their words. One pointed out a "goliath crane," which

I thought was a "guttural crane." The rangers spoke softly, so as not to disturb wildlife. They talked on radios to other rangers in a mix of, for me, indecipherable, native tongues. When I'd say, "Pardon?" a ranger would repeat himself, still unclearly, or point to a microphone he was whispering into. Still, I couldn't hear all that I should have. Sometimes it was just as well. I wished I hadn't heard Siegfried or that apologist for Dubai so clearly. And on our rides in Chitabe, a young wife from Ohio could not utter a sentence without "like," as in "I, like, am so excited," or "My in-laws, like, travel all the time." I'd rather not have heard her or the German couple who bragged about going on 200 game drives and had challenged Nas about who was first to spot giraffes across an open plain. It was easy to tune out others' speech, though I sometimes suspected that my aural laziness really signaled mental laziness.

At Chitabe too, the staff sang African tunes. They called us to hear the evening menu with an ear-piercing shriek made with the tongue vibrating against the roof of the mouth. Out on a drive, we saw large birds called red-billed and yellow-billed hornbills who hop along branches like toucans. Phenley pointed out varieties of cranes and noted that Canada geese are the meanest. We saw clouds of small-grass yellow butterflies following baboons and other creatures.

One day, we watched a long parade of baboons loping out of the bush toward an arena where elephants had rolled about in the mud and destroyed the vegetation. The dried mud looked like a concrete playground, which is how the baboons took it. They swung from dead tree branches, leaped from mound to mound, chased each other around fallen trunks and into tunnels, and hopped on each other's backs. Large males watched and then set out after sometimes unwilling females. We saw a willing one, her genitals swollen red and pink, pause for a giant male to pump himself into her. A troop of impalas followed the baboons. Phenley told us the two species often stay together for mutual protection. I mentioned Fred's dislike of baboons, but Phenley said they are good mothers and besides, very amusing.

One day a leopard was taking her siesta in a tree. Land Rovers gathered beneath her, like trucks filled with paparazzi. Phenley finally said, "It's time for coffee," so we left the spectacle. After coffee, we returned to find that the leopard had only turned around on her branch, while paparazzi still waited below in hopes of sensational photographs they might place in *National Geographic*.

One feature of our time at Chitabe was what Hannah called our acquaintance with two sister lions. We first saw them with their muzzles bloody from devouring a warthog. When the older one had had enough, she lay down to rest. Soon the other began scratching grasses into a depression—her motions reminding me of Maggie in her litter box—where she dragged the warthog's carcass. There was little breeze that day, so two male lions, snoozing in the shade a quarter of a mile away, did not know the girls' secret. After a while, though, the males set off around a herd of cape buffalo, trying to find the females but unwilling to tackle fifty or more big horned beasts. Later that afternoon, as breezes picked up, we saw nine or ten buzzards lined up in trees taking turns on the poorly hidden carcass of the warthog.

On another day, Phenley found the female lions at rough play; then the older one settled down to tracking another warthog. Her sister was stationed nearby, but when the first one set off at dazzling speed after the runt-like hog running with its bare tail straight up, the younger sister missed the signal. The warthog—an animal so ugly it's cute—got away. On our last morning, the sisters were prowling along logs, which made a primitive bridge in a swamp near our camp. The younger one playfully jumped her sister, who no longer felt frisky. She was probably pregnant and hungry after not eating since the warthog two days before. By the time we left, the sister lions had yet to catch another dinner, and the elder one was clearly exasperated with her mischievous little sister.

Hannah posted a wonderful account of our travels online. (Visit the website www.dcfocused.com/2016/06 and search for the name "Hannah Fischer" on the site.) The last of Hannah's safari photos is one of Phenley with the two of us. Truly, she is my beautiful daughter!

While we waited at the tiny airport for a Wilderness Safaris plane, I wondered how long before I'd see a true bathroom. For the first time since we'd arrived, I retreated into the bushes to relieve myself, thinking my morning rides would have been more comfortable if I'd not been too prudish to do so earlier. When the plane arrived, it flew us to Maun. In an airport building about the size of a gas station at home, we waited with, it seemed, hundreds of others. The peripatetic Southern couple we'd met on the Atlanta plane reappeared here too. We wondered if they were trailing us or vice versa. But we were leaving Africa; they were not. Our bags were checked by the Wilderness staff into Dulles. Though we were flying home, it seemed strange to leave Africa, where our adventures had brought us close to nature, to each other, and to John's spirit.

OUT OF AFRICA,
FOR HANNAH AND ME

Virgin Airline's lounge for first-class passengers in Johannesburg's airport is elegant. Sofas and chairs are gathered in arrangements to make everything from napping to interviewing comfortable and private. A tile mural of Sir Richard Branson and his many accomplishments adorns one wall. The waitstaff was solicitous and efficient. I took a shower in a tile-enclosed bathroom, scolding myself for not stashing a change of underwear in my briefcase. Then I drank a glass of sauvignon blanc while Hannah showered. *What privilege,* I thought. I'd never even known before that such lounges offered amenities like showers, so welcome before long flights.

While we waited for our departure, Hannah and I considered what we had learned on our safari. She said she had absorbed the animals' ability just to do what they do without trying to control what they couldn't. She applied that lesson to several career choices but also to her guilt over not preventing John's death. She told me that one morning at Chitabe, she had awakened sobbing. "In my dream I told Dad if he'd just come back, you wouldn't move and we'd put the Princeton house back together, if only he'd come back." Our wide-awake selves knew that such plans were a fantasy. We had seen his corpse zipped into that red body bag. Hannah had approved of my move. Something lethal had caused John to waste away. We'll never know exactly what it was, but no one (not even Dr. Barton, who signed the death certificate) could stop its deadly progress. "I guess it was meant to be, at least sometime, if not precisely on May 15, 2015," Hannah concluded.

I had put aside worries about chores that awaited me at home, but I had invented new worries. I still feared that my forgetfulness meant I was losing my mind. Names had slipped away as soon as they entered my hearing. A few days after we left Dulini, I couldn't recall its name. I had had nothing with which to associate names like Dki, Dizzra, or Busi, but I should have recalled names like Witness and Name. I even forgot the so spectacular experience of Nas's racing us to see the mother lion and cub before our plane boarding, but fortunately, Hannah's photos brought it back to me. Hannah suggested that I've been drinking more since John's death and that drinking causes forgetfulness, but it occurred to me that my brain also simply was tired.

After all, in the spring of 2016 alone, I redid Jonathan Swift's *Word-Book*, according to a reader's suggestions that had only arrived that January. I sent the revised manuscript off to the University of Delaware Press and put it out of my mind. I decided to sell our house, packed and donated boxes of books to two different libraries, and gave John's shoes and clothes to three different charities. (I could not, however, part with his tuxedo, leather jacket, academic gown, rain jacket, and barn coat, all "very John" things, which I am glad I kept.) Meanwhile, I packed eighty-three boxes for my move, numbering them and listing their contents. I organized the storage of some furniture and the rearrangement of the rest according to realtors' standards of simplicity to make an appealing show for the market. I contracted for house improvements. I sold one house, bought another, and moved to Virginia. In the new house, I tried to unpack my boxes but couldn't find the list of their contents. I also had to tally everything that the movers had misplaced or damaged. Then I headed on safari. Maybe, I thought, my brain would heal by not asking so much of it. Or maybe all those doings were just an excuse. I wondered if it's better for the mind to relax, to enjoy scenery passively, and to fall asleep, or if it's better to try to make the brain remember names, places, and facts. I concluded that it's good both to ask nothing and also to begin to nudge the brain into getting back on the job.

After our showers in Johannesburg, while we awaited our plane to Dulles, Hannah and I wondered what would have happened had we ever tried to take John on a safari. He would have started with objections: "My gut won't let me go game-watching at six in the morning," or, "Our budget won't permit it." If he could somehow have gotten over or around such objections, Hannah and I thought he would have loved a safari. The beauty of the wildlife, including amazing butterflies like the "flag" one, would have stunned him, as would the golden glow on the long grass we saw every morning.

"He'd have loved the beautiful African bush," Hannah said.

"Maybe we overuse that word," I pointed out. "You could say it's not even pretty—just pale sand, the color of cantaloupes, straggly bushes in all shades of green, burrowed out pig-holes, built-up termite mounds, dried-up water holes." I was being a provocateur.

Hannah frowned at me over her cappuccino. "Don't forget those grand trees looking like live oaks that were everywhere, and in Botswana even palm trees! And how about the amazing birds, the sun-catchers and rollers with their yellow, turquoise, and lavender feathers? Dad would have marveled at them."

"Sure, but what about standing skeletons of trees everywhere, killed by elephants stripping off bark for dinner?" I put my legs up on the seat beside me.

"But that's their nature. And being so close to elephants, zebras, lions, leopards, and the rest is majestic, literally awe-inspiring! I loved it!"

I brought my feet back to the floor, leaned forward, and smiled at my daughter. "The pervasive quiet, with only birdsong, a far-off elephant's trumpeting, a rumble from stampeding cape buffalos, a lion's growl—it is astonishing. You're right. It's so mystical that even a Land Rover's engine chugging sounds good in the bush."

We both knew that John would have appreciated the respect for nature here, except when our Rovers sometimes crashed over bushes and fledging palm trees on the trail of lions or leopards. He would have marveled to see displays of both orange sunrises and pink moon-settings at once. Land Rovers' two-lane tracks made for easier walks for lions and other creatures than rough terrain. Other than tire tracks and sequestered camps, the African bush looked much as it must have millions of years ago, except that there are fewer lions, leopards, rhinos, cheetahs, and other creatures, thanks to hunters and poachers. (In the June 2016 *Smithsonian*, Joshua Hammer writes that between 2010 and 2012, poachers killed 100,000 elephants across Africa. This was a sad follow-up on the article Hannah had read to John in his last days.)

We considered that sometimes John might have been bored, as I was during that wait at Chitabe when the leopard would not leave her perch on a tree branch. But John would have gotten out his butterfly book or some other book while we waited. He never would have let himself be bored. He would have regretted his ignorance, not knowing enough about history, animals, or current politics. As we passed through Zimbabwe, John would have hated not being able to ask people about their cruel, corrupt, and apparently now senile leader, and would have been appalled that Mugabe still ruled (and ravaged) the land and the people. The corruption of the dictators in their palaces and the poverty of the people in their mud huts would have upset John, as it did Hannah and me. But John would have been livid, feeling, like Swift, "savage indignation." He certainly would not have been bored.

John would have approved the leveling effect of safaris themselves. Presumably everyone on safari has money, and in fact, newlyweds sometimes asked for safari funds as wedding gifts. Nevertheless, when one can carry only a duffle bag, would ruin expensive shoes, shouldn't wear make-up or jewelry, and cannot access spas, no one can tell how wealthy anyone else is, with fancy cameras being the only clues. Furthermore, servants are treated with dignity and respect. Rangers, trackers, and staff members visit and often dine with guests. The camps' astonishing luxury comes from humble natural materials: thatching, stone, rough plaster, polished concrete, ironwood, often handmade glass and hand-sewn mosquito nets. John would have appreciated the professional skills of the rangers and their knowledge of nature and of the mechanically temperamental Land Rovers. If a ranger had had to open the bonnet (hood) of a Rover, I bet John would have been beside him, examining the engine, commenting on its quirks, speculating on its efficiency.

On our flight home, just as elegant as the flight over, I began reading another book. *West with the Night* includes wonderful descriptions of Africa and is a landmark story of a woman pilot, Beryl Markham, there in the 1920s and 1930s. However, Markham appalled me with her casual attitude toward the destruction of animals. She seemed delighted to herd elephants with her plane into the bull's-eye focus of animal hunters. While I was reading about her, Hannah was watching the movie featured by Virgin Atlantic, *The Big Short*, the premise of which is that only a very few guys (maybe three) predicted the 2008 fall in the stock market and profited from it. "Wrong," Hannah reminded me, leaning over the divide between our beds. "My dad predicted it!" John, however, did not play the market and wouldn't have wanted to profit on others' disasters.

We flew into Dulles, but our bags remained in South Africa, thanks to confusion about transfers. Looking for them made me miss both evening Amtrak trains from DC to southwest Virginia. Back at Hannah and Michael's for the night, I read a text message from the pet-sitter about Maggie, who'd had a near death-experience while I was gone. Tunneling under the covers, Maggie had managed to burrow inside the duvet, knocking it into a heap on the floor. Neither Reid nor the sitter could find her. Finally, when the sitter poked at the piled-up duvet something moved. She found the duvet's opening, and Maggie had escaped, drank a bowl full of water, and rushed to her litter box. I was relieved to learn that Maggie was safe and had gotten back her gumption.

Early Wednesday morning, 25 May, Hannah and Michael dropped me off at Union Station, where I caught a Megabus that traveled, with one quick break, south to Christiansburg. Riding along through the Shenandoah Valley, I reflected again on its beauty. Nature did wonders with high green mountains, fertile valleys, and rushing streams and rivers, but humans had uprooted forests to grow tobacco and then wheat, rye, corn, soybeans, and other crops. Neat fences corralled herds of docile cows and a few horses. The landscape was dotted with old chimney-heated farmhouses and electric-heated red brick ranch houses, old sagging and new erect barns, tractors, silos, barbed-wire fences, telephone poles, and billboards, some with flashing neon lights. Along interstate I-81, even on hardscrabble farms, everything seemed, after Africa, controlled. This landscape was tamed in a way Africa had not been.

Reid met me in Christiansburg and drove me the twelve or so minutes to my new home, where Maggie seemed recovered from her near-death experience and was very glad to sit in my lap and purr. My backpack wasn't delivered for six more days. "Thank goodness I gave you extra malaria pills," Hannah remarked on the phone.

"You did?" I asked. She said they were in my key-case. I found and took them for the seven post-travel days prescribed after visits to third-world countries. We both escaped malaria and all other illnesses. It even seemed silly that I'd thought of catching a cold while abroad.

I'm isolating here two sentences I wrote just after coming home:

In Africa and back in my new home, physical aloneness was essential to my healing. I think it should be for others, though, as I've admitted, I carry an only-child hangover that makes me less sociable than most.

When I wrote these lines, I had in mind the solitude one feels far away from city life, daily hassles, and everything that interferes with confronting loss. But somehow those sentences didn't read the way I meant them. They sounded perverse. Anyone reading about our safari could remind me that I was *not* physically alone in Africa. I'll return to these lines later.

After my return from safari, the missing list of boxes appeared where I had cleverly stashed and then absently forgotten it. I continued to be overwhelmed by technology, undone by numbers, particularly codes and pins. I could not use the gizmos on my phone—iTunes, the photos, even the news app—without being asked for John's password, which I didn't know. It seems that Congress had passed an electronic privacy act that requires a court order for me to access John's account. In the chaos after his death, I did find the piece of paper on which he had recorded his passwords and answers to trick questions, like the name of his best friend in elementary school. Unfortunately, I don't know where I hid that piece of paper. In this I remind myself of what's said in *The Sound and the Fury* about Jason Compson: "You fools a man whut so smart he cant even keep up wid hisself." Sometimes I seem to have been too clever to keep up with myself, but maybe even losing and forgetting important papers has been salubrious, as I have learned to let go. I did not leave my troubles behind, but I did distance myself from them. Amazingly enough, forgetting hassles while in Africa and then back in my new home has played some part in coming to peace with my loss, accepting my sadness, and, I think, moving on.

A joyous aspect of moving on was befriending my grandson. I picked him up after various camps and brought him to my new house. He took swimming lessons at the Blacksburg Community Center where I also took back exercises at roughly the same time. Together, we went to our classes and did grocery shopping afterwards. He began tennis lessons in the valley below me. After school started, he began taking the school bus to my house a couple of days a week. After tennis lessons, he helped me toss my garbage and recycle bags at the county dump, and then we'd go back to my place, where I often made dinner for my two Reids. The younger would open up with a smile and some real conversation now and then, but his homework kept him almost as distracted as his computer tablet. I do not know how this will turn out, but I'm delighted to say that Reid has transferred to a small private school that encourages academic curiosity—although an unexpected fallout of so much grandmothering is that I need to brush up on old science and learn a lot of new science, which is considerably more complicated and abstruse than the theory of condensation. I am delighted to offer in my home a haven of calm and stability where the Reids know they are loved and welcomed.

I am pleased to live on a Virginia mountainside, where a deer just scooted by my study window, her fawn skipping behind her; where endangered bluebirds live and peck in the mulch; where cabbage butterflies and hummingbirds flit in crepe myrtle bushes; where raptors (red-tailed hawks, perhaps peregrine falcons or kites, I haven't learned yet) soar above. For some time, an energetic green spider built her web anew outside my front window every day. Now a red-bellied woodpecker hangs on the brick wall outside my study's window, a berry in its mouth. I would not want to live where a monkey can steal my lunch, a baboon can play on my roof, mosquitoes can infect me with malaria, snakes can poison me, or lions can pounce on me if I step away from a truck. Still, I am so very, very grateful to have been in the wild of the safari with Hannah and what I feel was John's spirit.

After feeling so simpatico with that big bird sporting white under-feathers in Princeton, I was gratified to read an article in the *Roanoke Times* about migrating creatures. It featured a picture of a sharp-shinned hawk (not in my bird book) with such white under-feathers that it seemed to be the very bird that visited me in Princeton. Maybe it will find me again; after all, my new home is on a road called Falcon Ridge. (It's so aptly named I sometimes see a shadow gliding over my house and think it's an airplane, but it turns out to be a falcon or hawk.)

I'd been hoping for another sign from John when I saw out my study window a huge gray bird floating onto a tree above my house. I rushed out and called, "John?" (Here I was glad to live isolated enough so no one could gossip about the nutty widow calling into the treetops for her lost husband.) After a few minutes, the bird reemerged from a leafy tulip poplar tree to fly back over my roof and pause in trees down the slope behind the house. The resident birds were in an uproar, sounding alarms to each other against the intruder. After a few minutes, it took the hint and glided away on huge extended wings. I rushed to check my bird book. It might be a gyrfalcon, but they are Arctic birds. It was much bigger than a peregrine falcon or a goshawk. Possibly it was a rough-tailed hawk, but I decided it was a golden eagle, another migratory traveler through here. It does seem that I am visited by very large birds, as Hannah was visited by a smaller one. I do hope John has sent them and keeps sending them. *Thank you, my darling.*

Healing has been slow, but it has happened: sometimes I seem less healed, sometimes more, depending on the circumstances of the day. Like other writers of the grief memoirs I have endorsed, I have rejected suicide, but I also know that I do not want to remain grief-obsessed. The better way to honor John Fischer is by living well instead of dying or remaining morose.

I hesitate to set up my experience as a model to follow. Few people are lucky enough to enjoy an escape like mine, thanks to my retirement funds and a daughter smart enough to arrange an elaborate safari trip. Nevertheless, my experience does suggest that escaping the distractions of everyday life and finding peace is essential to dealing with grief and recovering from loss.

Almost everyone has options. There are lunch breaks and times after work when you can take a walk; family members or hired helpers can babysit children or parents and take over chores. National and state parks offer chances to be alone with nature, which is grounding and restorative. Randolph College in Lynchburg, Virginia, invites people to walk its labyrinth, but you must leave distractions like cell phones behind so you can "quiet your mind." Absorption in music, art, literature, meditation, prayer, and nature can help you distance yourself from grief. Counselors from faith and hospice groups offer valuable consolation and advice. Friends can help you pull your life back together, as you would and will for them.

I've heard stories, however, about people quarrelling with the widow or widower over funeral plans, questioning a decision for or against cremation, protesting the terms of the will, and interrogating the rights of the executor. A widow seems especially vulnerable to having her expenses questioned. Even her wardrobe can be subjected to intense scrutiny over such trivial matters as whether she should have worn all black or bought a new outfit. Your only option, as I see it, is to do what feels right with the time and money you have. You should ignore such quarrels and walk away from anyone who tries to start them.

Getting a break from duties is necessary, I think. If you can afford it, hire a maid and/or a yard worker and stay away while they're working. If you hope for a family holiday as a respite from grief, reconsider being the host or hostess. If you would end up planning, babysitting, cooking, overseeing, paying bills, cleaning up, and quarreling about it all, you've had no respite. For some people, sports are a useful distraction. I personally can't imagine finding peace on a golf course or in a stadium full of cheering fans, but that's just me. If it works for you, that's great. The point is to distance yourself from grief so you can achieve peace.

I recommend simple calming tricks, like walking, biking, baking bread—whatever calms and distracts you. I take walks. I drink wine. I nap. I eat chocolate (sometimes in that order). For resting, I wear the sleeping mask that that Georgetown University Hospital nurse gave me. I repeat the Lord's Prayer and pray for (and contribute to) those millions less fortunate than I am. I take back-strengthening exercise classes (cheap at recreation centers almost everywhere). I've promised to get a hearing aid (and I will do so when I finish this book). Alone, I talk out loud. However nutty that may sound, it has helped me better know and understand what I'm about. If nothing else, it should prevent me at least from losing my voice. I have declared myself a technological dummy. Maybe my children can fix the things that I can't, or maybe I can hire someone to do so, but I'm not going to drive myself crazy trying to set up cable television in my house or to make my radio work or rescue John's apps from the iCloud, whatever that is.

My ability to let go of hassles had serendipitous results. Names like Dulini no longer eluded me. Though I did not recall Hannah's putting those malaria pills in my key-case, I began paying better attention and so not forgetting so much. I still could not (and can't) multitask, however. The state of New Jersey, for example, wrote to say that I owed over $2,000 in back taxes for 2015. That was one of the complications I could not handle while I was concentrating on this memoir. When I took a break from writing, though, I gathered the records and called Trenton. It turned out that some of our taxes had been paid under John's social security name, some under mine. Combining our payments meant discovering that New Jersey owed me a refund of $65. I had to be calm and centered before I could pursue the tax issue (and save nearly $2,000). I'm not always so centered, but I may be getting my memory back, thanks to not overloading it.

Here I want to return to those lines I penned earlier about physical aloneness: In Africa, I was with my beautiful daughter every day and night. How could I ever have described my experience as "physical aloneness" when she guided me every step of the way? And why didn't I include, in my first draft, more details of all Reid's help to me? My children were the wizards who made the magic work. As I planted myself before my computer and my front windows to revise my manuscript, staring out at turning leaves above my house, I turned this memoir into a record that, I think, would (will!) please John. I acknowledge with gratitude how much our children charmed the demons away from me.

Several times, on our trip and later, Hannah remarked how rare it is for a mother-and-daughter duo to get along so well on an extended trip. There were many good reasons, the first being that our shared love for John and our grief over his loss formed a tight bond between us. We did not carp at each other. She included me in the alliance of witty and wise social critics she and her father had long ago established between them. She and I together included John's soul into our alliance of nature lovers. Hannah and I dream of each other and of John. Neither of us was physically alone in the bush, thank God.

Nor am I truly alone in Virginia. At home on my mountainside, I am usually by myself, but I am not alone. The elder Reid helps me with heavy lifting and tall-man duties, as I help him with grandmothering his son. He put together my new furniture for the deck; he set up my DVD player; he brought mattresses in on his back; he stopped a leaky faucet and bought me garden hoses; and he fed Maggie once a day while I was gone. He has been a great help, a generous person, and is a considerate, beautiful son!

In an earlier draft of this book, I told several stories without calculating that they might hurt my children's feelings. My writing and rewriting were aimed at turning my private jottings into a memoir about John and me. Hannah suggests, however, that I failed to consider how she and Reid would react to the publication of some of my private observations about their lives. I took her point, as John might have said. In the process of revision, I have I hope rendered a more balanced and compassionate story.

Hannah has been enormously helpful to my writing since I began my biography of Tillie Olsen and she earned a graduate degree in information sciences. She has researched answers to my obscure questions and replied even to my nuisance questions, but I wonder if I have thanked her adequately. Since she was a child, Hannah attended many speeches her father and I gave, both close to home and in far-flung spots. She has recently given several on her GIS (geographic information system) work, mapping and clarifying the meaning of geographical data for the CRS, but I have not heard them. In Africa, I wonder if I let my desire to ask smart questions supersede my appreciation of Hannah's genuine knowledge. Similarly, I haven't yet credited Reid's enormous legal assistance. With complicated papers, he often says, "Just send them to me," and it is with grateful relief that I do. After Africa, I wonder if my ego outweighed my honesty, as I pictured myself as a lone pioneer, a seventy-five-year-old woman who didn't need assistance from either of her children, even as I was so dependent on it. As I revised my memoir, I came to realize that I may have felt alone, but I never truly *had been* alone.

Parents naturally accept the kindnesses of their grown children as rightful payback, often overdue, and fail to give them credit. Now that I think about it, though, I find that each of my children has been extraordinarily kind to me, while I find something worse than ordinary in me. It's related to my sense of exclusivity. I always credited John, but it was part of my ego to discredit his family, his colleagues, or anyone who quarreled with him. I made a cocoon for the two of us. Hannah was mostly inside it with us, and sometimes Reid too. I saw us (usually the three or four of us, but always the two of us) set against an unappreciative world: his parents who sent Jeff to MIT and bought him a Corvair, while telling John that there was no money even for sending him away to college; all the people who'd enjoyed our hospitality and spilled wine on our carpets, and then voted against John for reelection; the preacher who'd preached a sermon about John's reelection loss; the scholar who cut John out of the massive Swift edition. And then there were the doctors in the winter of 2015, who hadn't worked hard enough to find the actual cause of John's wasting away. For years, I have knitted my cocoon closer, squeezing such people out, deservedly. In the summer of 2016, thinking only of me and my lost love, however, I may have done something comparable to my children in an earlier draft of this memoir. I had put John and me, true lovers, in that cocoon, alienating my precious children.

I said earlier that writing this memoir has been a lifeline for me. I mean that it helped me concentrate and focus my mind once again, but I now realize it has been a lifeline in another way. Writing a memoir is an act of egoism, but as I've brought this one to its close, I think it has also rescued me from egoism. I did not walk alone in Africa, nor have I lived alone in Virginia. I thank both my children for being such great helps to me, and I am deeply sorry to have written my first draft without sensitivity to their feelings. This memoir, in other words, has put me back in touch with John's generosity, one of the many reasons I so loved him. As Yeats wrote of Swift, John too "served Human liberty" and human kindness. I must try better to imitate John, if I "dare."

After I returned from Africa, I received a personal copy of the 2016 *Swift Studies*. Here John's former reputation as something of a wild man reoccurred in a tribute by Hermann Real, German Swiftian and organizer of the Münster symposia. Hermann wrote: "Before I had even met him, John was known to me as a volcano who would read his papers at scholarly conferences with a panache bordering on bravura." Soon Hermann found out that "John's passion did not stop him from being a most kind and warm-hearted, tolerant and understanding, encouraging, charitable, and honest human being. Although he loved to argue, he would always do so with respect and politeness towards his opponents ..." Hermann said he "will continue to count my friendship with John one of the greatest blessings in my life."

In mine too.

After another reader's report from Delaware asked for further changes, I yet again revised Swift's and John's *Word-Book*. My Virginia handyman and picture-hanger turned out to be a good photographer, who made photos of some pages from the *Word-Book* that illustrate Swift's harsh, I think, revisions of Esther Johnson's vocabulary. I sent the much-revised manuscript off to Delaware early in August. I understood that the press board would meet in early November 2016. Instead, they met in late October.

It was with great excitement that I learned the news that Jonathan Swift's *Word-Book*, edited by Arch Elias and John Fischer, has been accepted by the University of Delaware Press! After all my writing and weeping over this memoir, I surprised myself by bursting into more tears over news about the *Word-Book*. I must have been afraid that my efforts would not do justice to the valiant work of Jonathan Swift, Esther Johnson, Arch Elias, and John Fischer. Now I am so grateful to have had the chance to bring their efforts into print. I hope their spirits are pleased. Perhaps the press can produce the book or at least a formal announcement about it in time for celebrations of Swift's 350th birthday in the summer of 2017 in Dublin and Münster. I am most eager for people to read and see Jonathan Swift's vocabulary, Esther's copy with his revisions, and Arch's and John's brilliant essays about the *Word-Book*.

I still read to John and talk to him, as Hannah does. And Reid thinks about him as a guide and model. But each of us has finally learned to live without him. After over a year of weeping every time I had to say that my husband died, I have gotten through—not over—my grief (though I still sometimes fight back tears, as Hannah does). Sometimes I sing my version of that old "Darling Clementine" tune: "Oh my darling, Oh my darling, Oh my darling, dearest John: You are lost, but not to me, dear, oh my darling precious John." He is not lost, nor is Hannah, nor are the Reids.

But Maggie is lost, at least to us now. British Blue cats are affectionate, not cuddly. But after I returned from safari, she wanted to cuddle with me, especially after I got in bed and she could hop up using her stool and sleep beside me. An old cat, however, her thyroid problems worsened and her hindquarters weakened. Once she fell trying to make the jump onto my bed. After that, she spent the nights on her pallet by the glass door onto the deck where small birds play in the morning. The vet prescribed more prednisone, which did no more good for Maggie than it had for John. The vet also prescribed injections of Epogen for anemia (a drug rumored to be the blood enhancer that got Lance Armstrong through so many Tours de France). I patted Maggie while Reid injected her, once breaking a needle on her bony frame. Maggie got so infirm she would no longer eat salmon off my plate, baby food, half-and-half, or even the Cat-Cal that had revived her the year before. Her innards were breaking down. Two or three times, when I came into my study to work on this book, I smelled something bad, which turned out to be cat poop. I dreamed that the injections of Epogen had so revived her she got up and played, while Reid the younger dreamt that she pooped on my book.

Maggie seemed to be dying, but I didn't want to put our dear old companion down, not yet anyway. On 27 July, I came home from my back exercise class to find that Maggie's sphincter muscle had given way. She'd spread poop on the floor by the dining room table. I spent an hour cleaning up after her. For the rest of the day, she lay in the sunshine, but would not look out at the birds. Nor would she eat cream or any treats that I offered. That night I put her on a pallet with a green flannel pillowcase over it. I carried her on it to sit on my lap and watch the Democratic National Convention. When we got up, her bladder seemed to let go. I took her, still on the pallet, to her water bowl, near her litter box, and cleaned up again. In the night, when I got up to check, she was in the same position as when I'd left her. In the morning, I patted her and told her what a beautiful cat she was and how much the Daddy-Cat and I had loved her. Her jaw opened, making clicking noises. When they stopped, her jaw and eyes stayed open. She was still.

I'd prearranged for landscapers to dig a grave, but I kept thinking I saw her little chest rise and fall. Though I'd seen her die, I couldn't bury her yet. I picked up the younger Reid from camp. On her pallet, Maggie was by then as stiff as a plank, her jaw and eyes still open. Reid the elder soon arrived and carried her out for a little funeral. I read "The Maggie Rap," with its lines like: "Doves cooing? What is that? / Just the purring of our Maggie cat." Hannah by phone read a recently written poem about a dying cat. We all thanked John's spirit for his care of our dear MagnifiCat. Reid lowered her, pallet and all, into the hole, and covered it with dirt and stones. The next day, landscapers planted a weeping redbud on top of her. It will be beauteous in the spring, unless the deer kill it by nibbling off its tender leaves. (I wish they'd go on a dandelion diet.) I'd told Maggie she couldn't die on me too, but at least she waited a year before doing so.

The sun seems to have sped up its journey south, as has the moon. In July, a big wild cherry tree out my study's side window had one orange leaf, then it had as many orange as green ones, and now it is leafless, though leaves on other trees are just beginning to turn orange, red, and gold. When I sit on my deck overlooking the valley in still warmish evenings, I often call, *Where are you, my love?* I want John with me to watch the movements of the sun and moon. They are slowly abandoning northern climes, leaving us colder and colder. I once started to explain these movements to my grandson, but he actually understands them without my help. Maybe John is thinking, *As I said years ago, Blacksburg is too cold for us.* I have reminded John's spirit that my upcoming winters in Blacksburg can't be as cold for as long as winter in Princeton was in January 2015.

When the weather further cools, I won't use another green flannel sheet and pillowcases. After one was cremated with John and another buried with Maggie, I'd better tell my children to wrap me in the last of them before I'm zipped into another big red plastic bag.

Feeling a bit lonely, I began to think of finding another British Blue cat. Somehow, an old football cheer came back to me: "I want another one, just like the other one." These cats are very distinctive, so I thought maybe it would be possible to get something like a replica cat. But there could be no true replica of Maggie.

And there can be no filling my essential lack, my loneliness without John.

But I have my son, who survived the upheavals in his early life to become a wise counselor and a most gentle, loving son and father.

There is no Jewish Christian who looks and behaves like John Fischer. But I have Hannah Fischer, a Christian Jew, who is so much like her father.

I hope I have reached closure, at last, with both children, after I have apologized for earlier disregarding their feelings. They are most definitely now inside my cocoon.

That is the happy ending a memoir seems to require.

John was unafraid of death. He did believe, though, that how he died mattered. He knew Revelations 14:13: "Blessed are the dead which die in the Lord." John did so die and thus must be so blessed. I'm not so good a believer or person as John, but few are. John's legacy will live in his fastidious scholarship on the world's greatest satirist, however flawed were Swift's relations with women. John's legacy lives on in the love and respect so many people have expressed among themselves, in notes to me, in public tributes, in continuing remembrances, in Hannah's poems and recollections, in my body and soul's memory of John's undying love and astonishing generosity, in my regrets for my selfishness and my vows to dare to be, like John, more generous, and in my slow healing after the loss of my true love.

When I look at the sky, especially at night, I know John's soul was not in that zipped-up bag the undertakers took away or in the cherry box that sits on his dresser. I believe his soul accompanied me to Africa and remains not far away, beyond the body's travails, wandering freely but occasionally hovering nearby, awaiting my spirit's arrival.

ACKNOWLEDGMENTS

First of all, as this book testifies on every page, my greatest debt is to John Irwin Fischer. My heartfelt thanks go to Hannah Fischer for sharing memories of her father's late days, including his sojourns in two hospitals. Her recollections are written so poignantly that I cannot reread them without weeping. I am deeply grateful to both my children, Reid Broughton and Hannah Fischer, for being my ballast and stabilizers in very difficult times.

I deeply appreciate Wild River Books for venturing to publish this memoir. My thanks go to Joy Stocke and Kimberly Nagy, Founders, and Raquel Pidal, Managing Editor. I especially want to thank Raquel for her supportive and wise comments and her willingness to make even last-minute changes for me. Tim Ogline too deserves thanks for his book design and especially for the lovely cover to this book.

For permission to reprint lines from the poem "Revelation at Philpott Lake," I thank the poet Felicia Mitchell. Her reflections on the body and the soul became a motif and theme, reflected in this book's title. I thank Stuart Mitchner for permission to quote from his treatments in Princeton's *Town Topics* of the two memorial services for John in Princeton University Chapel and the Arts Council of Princeton on 14 June and for covering Jonathan Swift's birthday and writing again about John in November 2015.

I especially thank Trammell Maury for assisting me with a thorough and most helpful list of resources for the bereaved, which forms the bulk of my appendix. I also thank the many people who supported me in hard times. And I am especially grateful to those who sent me their memories of John. I mention some of them by name; others I mention only as "a friend" or perhaps a "former colleague." Whether or not I use your name, I want each of you also to know that you have my deepest thanks for your help and also for respecting, missing, and loving John, my dear lost love.

EPILOGUE
AND APPENDIX

While writing this memoir, I often heard complaints (and sometimes horror stories) about inept medical care. One woman told me her husband died because his physician was in the early stages of Alzheimer's disease, but his colleagues allowed him to continue practicing even though he was unable to conceptualize the care her husband needed. Another told me that her husband had gone to a very good hospital about three hours from home for a simple knee operation. When he developed post-anesthesia delirium, however, local hospitals would not treat him because he had gone to a distant hospital. While his delirium intensified, she called hospital after hospital. Finally, she found a hospital about forty minutes from home that would admit him. EMS took him there. He died about nine hours after arriving. Such unnecessary deaths are tragic. They are also infuriating because they should not have happened.

From family, old friends, and members of my new exercise group, I have received helpful recommendations of sites to consult, services to use, and books to read, some of which I list below.

My son, Reid Broughton, tells me that he frequently has clients appear in his law office with a will and other documents but without any notion of what to do with them. He recommends checking certain sites. Each state's bar association should have a guide on what to do in case of a death. In Virginia, it's: http://www.vba.org/?page=guide_estates.

A national site for finding out about proper procedures is: http://www.americanbar.org/groups/real_property_trust_estate/ resources/estate_planning/guidelines_for_individual_executors_ trustees.html

In the process of writing my memoir and working to overcome my own devastation, I began assembling the following appendix. In doing so, I encountered an unexpected schism in the "American Way of Grief." I quote from Ruth Davis Konigsberg's *The Truth about Grief: The Myth of Its Five Stages and the New Science of Loss*. Konigsberg finds a distressingly unscientific approach to grief in what she calls the "industry" of grief counseling. The programmatic reliance on Elisabeth Kübler-Ross's model of "stages" of grief seems destructive to Konigsberg. She faults the grief "industry" for not encouraging resilience after loss. She cites the many books by Alan Wolfelt as examples of that industry. Such vexed and complicated issues are outside the scope of this memoir, but I raise them here as a caution to readers, who can make up their own minds after reading and investigating for themselves.

Investigating is complicated, however, when there is really too much information available. The parish nurse at my new church in Blacksburg found that Barnes & Noble lists over 1,000 titles on death and dying. Obviously, that's more titles than any one person can check through. Partly to make a compassable list here and partly to avoid seeming to proselytize, I have not listed books associated with any particular belief system. As I say in my acknowledgments, I am most grateful to Trammell Maury, my Randolph–Macon Woman's College class secretary, who has compiled for me a list of reliable sources. Trammell worked for ten years as librarian for the National Institute on Aging's Alzheimer's Disease Education and Referral (ADEAR) Center as a contractor. From that position, she says she found these organizations and resources to be "reliable and very useful to a wide range of issues related to aging, caregiving, and end-of-life care." My thanks to Trammell for this amazingly thorough and helpful list of online resources, both for medical care and for counseling.

ONLINE RESOURCES

American Geriatrics Society sponsors the **Health in Aging website:** www.healthinaging.org

Online information for health topics A-Z, including: finding healthcare professionals; medications: making your wishes known; and local community support resources.

Caring.com

https://www.caring.com/questions/find-a-grief-counselor

Caring.com is the leading online destination for those seeking information and support as they care for aging parents, spouses, and other loved ones. Its mission: to help the helpers. They equip family caregivers to make better decisions, save time and money, and feel less alone—and less stressed—as they face the many challenges of caregiving, by providing information, resources, and email newsletters.

Evaluating Health Information on the Internet

Provided by the National Institutes of Health and the National Library of Medicine is MedlinePlus: https://medlineplus.gov/evaluatinghealthinformation.html

This site provides many resources on finding current, unbiased research on health information.

Family Caregiver Alliance
https://www.caregiver.org/

FCA CareJourney is a secure online solution for quality information, support, and resources for family caregivers of adults with chronic physical or cognitive conditions such as Alzheimer's, stroke, Parkinson's, and other illnesses.

Healthfinder.gov
https://healthfinder.gov

A Federal Government website managed by the US Department of Health and Human Services, sponsored by the National Health Information Center, it is designed to help users find services, doctors, and specialists.

National Health Information Center
www.health.gov/nhic

The National Health Information Center (NHIC) is sponsored by the Office of Disease Prevention and Health Promotion (ODPHP). NHIC supports public health education and promotion by maintaining a calendar of National Health Observances. In addition, NHIC helps connect health professionals and consumers to the organizations that can best answer their questions by providing up-to-date contact information for the most reliable resources.

National Institute on Aging
www.nia.nih.gov

NIA, one of the 27 Institutes and Centers of NIH, leads a broad scientific effort to understand the nature of aging and to extend the healthy, active years of life. NIA is the primary Federal agency supporting and conducting Alzheimer's disease research.

PUBLICATIONS

End-of-Life: Helping with Comfort and Care

This publication provides guidance and help in navigating and understanding the unfamiliar territory of death, based on research by the NIA and the NIH. It includes suggestions on finding appropriate healthcare providers and a listing of national organizations related to end-of-life care.

National Institute on Aging. 2012. 68 p. Print format, available from the National Institute on Aging Information Center, PO Box 8057, Gaithersburg, MD 20898-8057. 800-222-2225.
Website: www.nia.nih.gov/healthinformation

Free print copy and free online access at https://www.nia.nih.gov/health/publication/end-life-helping-comfort-and-care/introduction

How to Care for Aging Parents, 2nd Edition

By Virginia Morris. Workman Publishing, New York, NY 2004.
www.careforagingparents.com

This book covers a wide range of information on medical, financial, housing, emotional, and practical issues. It includes an index of useful organizations and services. The chapter on "Doctor Do's and Don'ts" gives advice on being an informed and outspoken patient and finding/assessing a good doctor or specialist. I recommend it not only for caregivers of aging parents but also for caregivers of aging spouses.

Below are further resources I gleaned from friends and acquaintances that look helpful.

ON FINDING DOCTORS

Best Doctors

http://www.bestdoctors.com/what-we-do/health systems

This resource collects your case records, images, and tests and offers consultation. It is increasingly covered by insurance programs. The phone is 617-426-3666.

The *Huffington Post* published "10 Apps to Help you get the Health Care You Need."

http://www.huffingtonpost.com/2014/02/24/find-a-doctor-apps-medical-health_n_4826391.html

US News and World Report publishes a listing of the country's best hospitals: http://health.usnews.com/best-hospitals

A current medical student sent, through his mother, this *Huffington Post* article titled "Is Your Doctor A Republican? The Answer May Affect Your Treatment": http://www.huffingtonpost.com/entry/doctors-political-affiliation-care_us_57f267a1e4b024a52d2fc0ba?

This student recommends teaching hospitals for complicated illnesses. Also he advised that the Alpha Omega Alpha Medical Honor Society will tell you if a doctor was very outstanding in his or her class.

ON FINDING COUNSELING

Hospice in Princeton has sent me several useful booklets: "Finding Your Way After the Death of a Spouse"; "Getting Through the Holidays When You've Lost a Loved One"; and "On the First Anniversary of Your Loss." These booklets are published by Abbey Press Publications. Visit: www.carenotes.com or call 1-800-325-2511 for a catalog.

To search for hospice care and resources in your community, type "hospice" and your location into an internet search engine to see services available near to you.

Many churches, synagogues, and other faith and self-help organizations sponsor grief groups whose members share their experiences of loss and find comfort in each other's advice. Often they are involved in activities like staffing soup kitchens, thereby at once helping others and diverting themselves from grief. Check local resources, or type "grief groups" and your location into an internet search engine to find such groups near to you.

A MEDITATION ON GRIEF

In 2011, author Krista Tippett interviewed Zen abbott Joan Halifax, who provided a ten-minute guided meditation called "Encountering Grief." It can be streamed or downloaded here: http://www.onbeing.org/blog/encountering-grief-guided-meditation/4983

RECOMMENDED READINGS (GUIDES AND ADVICE)

The following reading lists are incomplete, intended primarily as suggestions. At my local public library, for example, I found few pertinent books listed under "mourning" (though many with puns on "morning"). "Grief" was a more useful subject heading.

Many people facing death, their own or that of a loved one, have recommended Atul Gawande's book to me. Harold Kushner's book has been for years a staple of grieving sessions. Of the other books in this eclectic list, their titles offer a fairly clear guide to their content.

Bonanno, George A. *The Other Side of Sadness: What the New Science of Bereavement Tells Us About Life After Loss.* New York: Basic Books, 2009.

Gawande, Atul. *Being Mortal: Medicine and What Matters in the End.* New York: Metropolitan Books, 2014.

Ginsburg, Genevieve Davis. *Widow to Widow: Thoughtful, Practical Ideas for Rebuilding Your Life.* Boston: Da Capo Press, 1995.

Konigsberg, Ruth Davis. *The Truth about Grief: The Myth of Its Five Stages and the New Science of Loss.* New York: Simon & Schuster, 2011.

Kübler-Ross, Elisabeth and David Kessler. *On Grief and Grieving: Finding the Meaning of Grief Through the Five Stages of Loss.* New York: Scribner, 2005.

Kushner, Harold. *When Bad Things Happen to Good People.* New York: Schocken Books, 2001 (twentieth anniversary reprint).

LaGrand, Louis E. *Healing Grief, Finding Peace: 101 Ways to Cope with the Death of Your Loved One.* Naperville, IL: Sourcebooks, 2011.

McCormack, Jerusha Hull. *Grieving: A Beginner's Guide*. Brewster, MA: Paraclete Press, 2006.

Meekhof, Kristin and James Windell. *A Widow's Guide to Healing: Gentle Support and Advice for the First 5 Years*. Naperville, IL: Sourcebooks, 2015.

Morris, Virginia. *Talking About Death Won't Kill You*. New York: Workman Publishing, 2001.

O'Hara, Kathleen. *A Grief Like No Other: Surviving the Violent Death of Someone You Love*. New York: Marlowe and Co., 2006.

Schaefer, Gerald J., with Tom Bekkers. *The Widower's Tool Box: Repairing Your Life After Losing Your Spouse*. Far Hills, NJ: New Horizon Press, 2010.

Tippett, Krista. *Becoming Wise: An Inquiry into the Mystery and Art of Living*. New York: Penguin Press, 2016.

Viorst, Judith. *Necessary Losses: The Loves, Illusions, Dependencies, and Impossible Expectations That All of Us Have to Give Up in Order to Grow*. New York: Simon & Schuster, 1986; Free Press edition, 1998.

Walter, Tony. *On Bereavement: The Culture of Grief*. Philadelphia: Open University Press, 1999.

RECOMMENDED READINGS (MEMOIRS AND FICTION)

These books have all been recommended to me by friends and acquaintances. I comment on many of them in the course of this memoir, but I have not read every word in each of them. I can say, though, that the memoirs, like Gallagher's poems, deal directly with death and loss, of a spouse, a child, or a parent. Paul Kalanithi's book is unique because he writes not as a survivor, but as a man facing his own death. The novellas by Tillie Olsen and Leo Tolstoy treat approaching death. The novels by Wendell Berry, Leah Hager Cohen, Ellen Douglas, and Jesmyn Ward deal more obliquely with sadness and sometimes reconciliation.

Your librarians might help you survey these books and choose among them, as well as find other books that best suit your experiences, tastes, and needs.

Alexander, Elizabeth. *The Light of the World: A Memoir*. New York: Grand Central Publishing, 2015.

Barnes, Julian. *Levels of Life*. New York: Vintage Books, 2013.

Berry, Wendell. *Jayber Crow*. Washington, DC: Counterpoint, 2000.

Cohen, Leah Hager. *The Grief of Others*. New York: Riverhead Books, 2011.

Douglas, Ellen. *Can't Quit You, Baby*. New York: Penguin Books, 1989.

Didion, Joan. *Blue Nights*. New York: Vintage Books, 2012.

-----. *The Year of Magical Thinking*. New York: Vintage Books, 2007.

Gallagher, Tess. *Moon Crossing Bridge*. Saint Paul: Graywolf Press, 1992.

Kalanithi, Paul. *When Breath Becomes Air*. New York: Random House, 2016.

Lewis, C. S. *A Grief Observed*. San Francisco: Harper, 2001.

Macdonald, Helen. *H Is for Hawk*. New York: Grove Press, 2015.

Oates, Joyce Carol. *A Widow's Story: A Memoir*. New York: HarperCollins, 2011.

Olsen, Tillie and Leo Tolstoy. *The Riddle of Life and Death* [Olsen's "Tell Me a Riddle" and Tolstoy's "The Death of Ivan Ilych"]. New York: The Feminist Press, 2007.

O'Rourke, Meghan. *The Long Goodbye: A Memoir*. New York: Riverhead, 2011.

Ozaki, Y. T. *Japanese Fairy Tales* ("The Mirror of Matsuyama"). New York: A. L. Burt Company, 1908. (The story can be read here: http://etc.usf.edu/lit2go/72/japanese-fairy-tales/4844/the-mirror-of-matsuyama/)

Rosenblatt, Roger. *Kayak Morning: Reflections on Love, Grief, and Small Boats*. New York: Ecco, 2012.

Trillin, Calvin. *About Alice*. New York: Random House, 2006.

Ward, Jesmyn. *Salvage the Bones*. New York: Bloomsbury, 2011.

Panthea Reid

ABOUT THE AUTHOR

Panthea Reid has been an NEH Fellow, a Fulbright lecturer, an Honorary Fellow of Birkbeck College, University of London, and President of the South Central MLA. She holds a PhD from the University of North Carolina at Chapel Hill. A member of Phi Beta Kappa, she is Emerita Professor of English at Louisiana State University.

Reid is the author of *Art and Affection: A Life of Virginia Woolf* (Oxford, 1996), called "a sensitive and meticulous biography" by *Library Journal* and which earned a starred review from *Publishers Weekly*. Dubbed a "biographic bombshell," Reid's biography *Tillie Olsen: One Woman, Many Riddles* (Rutgers, 2009) earned another starred review in *Publishers Weekly* and was called a "richly textured history" by *Forward* and "a marvelously evocative book" by *The Advocate*.

After the death of her husband, Jonathan Swift scholar John Irwin Fischer, in 2015, Panthea wrote *Body and Soul*, a memoir about their life together and reflections on his sudden death as well as sound advice and resources for those dealing with grief and loss. During this time, Panthea finished for John his last work, which also appears to be the last work of Jonathan Swift to reach publication. Swift's *Word-Book*, edited by Arch Elias and John Fischer, was accepted for publication by University of Delaware Press right at the time she finished *Body and Soul*.

Made in the USA
Middletown, DE
09 May 2017